BILLIE
WHITELAW
...WHO HE?

MOUTH:
(contd)

... yes ... all the time the buzzing ... so-called! ... all that together ... imagine! ... whole body like gone ... just the mouth ... lips ... cheeks ... jaws ... never ... what? ... tongue? ... yes ... lips ... cheeks ... jaws ... tongue ... never still a second ... mouth on fire ... stream of words ... in her ear ... practically in her ear ... not catching the half ... not the quarter ... no idea what she's saying ... imagine! ... no idea what she's saying! ... and can't stop ... no stopping it ... she who but a moment before ... a moment! ... she couldn't make a sound ... no sound of any kind ... now can't stop ... imagine! ... can't stop the stream ... and the whole brain begging ... something begging in the brain ... begging the mouth to stop ... pause a moment ... if only for a moment ... and no response ... as if it hadn't heard ... or couldn't ... couldn't pause a second ... like maddened ... all that together ... straining to hear ... piece it together ... and the brain ... raving away on its own ... trying to make sense of it ... or make it stop ... or in the past ... dragging up the past ... flashes from all over ... walks mostly ... walking all her days ... day after day ... a few steps then stop dead ... stare into space ... then on a few more ... stop and stare again ... so ... drifting around ... day after day ... then that time she cried ... the one time she could remember ... since she was a baby ... must have cried as a baby ... perhaps not ... not essential to life ... just the birth cry to get her going ... breathing ... then no more till this ... old hag already ... where was it? ... Croker's Acres ... one evening on the way home ... home! ... a little mound in Croker's Acres ... dusk ... sitting staring at her hand ... there in her lap ... palm upward ... suddenly saw it wet ... the palm ... tears presumably ... hers presumably ... no one else for miles ... no sound ... just the tears ... sat and watched them dry ... all over in a second ... or grabbing at the straw ... the brain ... flickering away on its own ... quick grab and on ... nothing there ... on to the next ... bad as the voice ... worse ... as little sense ... all that together ... can't - ... what? ... the buzzing? ... yes ... all the time the buzzing ... dull roar like falls ... and the beam ... flickering on and off ... starting to move around ... like moonbeam but not ... all part of the same ... keep an eye on that too ... corner of the eye ... all that together ... can't go

MOUTH:
(contd)

on ... God is love ... she'll be purged ... back in
the field ... morning sun ... April ... sink face
down in the grass ... nothing but the larks ... so
on ... grabbing at the straw ... straining to hear
... the odd word ... make some sense of it ...
whole body like gone ... just the mouth ... like
maddened ... and can't stop ... no stopping it ...
~~something she~~ - ... something she had to ... what?
... who? ... what? ... no ... ~~no~~ ... SHE! ...
(pause and movement 3) ... something she had to
- ... what? ... the buzzing? ... yes ... all the
time the buzzing ... dull roar ... in the skull ...
and the beam ... ferreting around ... painless ...
so far ... ha! ... so far ... than thinking ...
~~another thought~~ ... oh long after ... sudden flash
... perhaps something she had to ... had to ... tell
... could that be it? ... something she had to tell ...
tiny little thing ... before its time ... no love ...
spared that ... speechless all her days ... practically speechless ... how she survived! ... that time
in court ... what had she to say for herself ...
guilty or not guilty ... stand up, woman ... speak
up, woman ... stood there staring into space ...
mouth half open as usual ... waiting to be led away
... glad of the hand on her arm ... now this ...
something she had to tell ... could that be it? ...
something that would tell ... how it was ... how
she - ... what? ... had been? ... yes ... something that would tell how it had been ... how she had
lived ... lived on and on ... guilty or not ... to be
sixty ... something she - ... what? ... seventy?
... ~~good~~ God! ... on and on to be seventy ... something she didn't know herself ... wouldn't know if
she heard ... then forgiven ... God is love ...
tender mercies ... new every morning ... back in
the field ... April morning ... face in the grass ...
nothing but the larks ... pick it up there ... get on
with it from there ... another few - ... what? ...
not that? ... nothing to do with that? ... nothing
she could tell? ... all right ... nothing she could
tell ... try something else ... think of something
else ... oh long after! ... sudden flash ... not that
either ... all right ... something else again ... so
on ... hit on it in the end ... think everything keep
on long enough ... then back in the - ... what? ...
not that either? ... nothing to do with that? nothing
she could think? ... all right ... nothing she could
tell ... nothing she could think ... nothing she - ...
what? ... who? ... what? ... no ... no! ... SHE!
... (pause and movement 4) ... tiny little thing ...

SHE

interrupting
Buzzing

God Fornicates
Hack

Questions

Tell Court

About Tell
TELL

The forgiveness

PAST

·

BILLIE
WHITELAW
...WHO HE?

by
Billie Whitelaw
AN AUTOBIOGRAPHY

St. Martin's Press 𝄞 *New York*

For
Robert and Matthew
with love

Samuel Beckett's correspondence to the author is
reproduced by permission of the Samuel Beckett Estate.

Pages from the manuscript of *Not I* by Samuel Beckett
reproduced by permission of the Samuel Beckett Estate and
Faber and Faber Ltd.

Part of the lyrics of 'Run Rabbit Run'
copyright © 1939 by Noel Gay Music Co Ltd &
Campbell Connelly & Co Ltd, 8–9 Frith Street, London w1v 5tz.
Used by permission. All rights reserved.

Library of Congress Cataloging-in-Publication Data

Whitelaw, Billie.
Billie Whitelaw : who he? : an autobiography / by Billie Whitelaw.
        p.   cm.
        ISBN 0-312-13929-2
1. Whitelaw, Billie.   2. Actors—Great Britain—Biography.
                        I. Title.
        PN2598.W463A3   1996
    792'.028'092—dc20   [B]   95-47396   CIP

First published in Great Britain by Hodder and Stoughton

First U.S. Edition: April 1996

10   9   8   7   6   5   4   3   2   1

w2: Who he, I said filing away, and what it?
SAMUEL BECKETT: *Play*

Contents

Illustrations

With Michael Gambon in *Tales from Hollywood* (*Donald Cooper*)
In Peter Nichols's *Passion Play* for the RSC (*Donald Cooper*)
In *The Greeks* for the RSC (Donald Cooper)
With Albert Finney in *Charlie Bubbles*
In *The Krays*, 1990, with Gary Kemp (*Rank*)
In *Leo the Last*, with Marcello Mastroianni (*United Artists*)
With Gregory Peck in *The Omen* (*Twentieth Century Fox*)
On location in Paris with Matthew
With Matthew and Bobby Moore at Upton Park (*Michael Fresco*)
Matthew and his girl-friend, Nicola
Robert (*Wolf Rilla*)
In our cottage in Suffolk (*D. Jones, Evening Standard*)
Progress to the Park – my first West End show as a leading lady, 1961

PROLOGUE

PROLOGUE

1

Anxious to Please

My first memory is sitting cross-legged at the bottom of the garden at 52, Bourne Road, Coventry with the girl next door, digging up dirt with a couple of teaspoons and eating it. I liked the taste. I can still feel that grittiness in my mouth. I was two years old and wanted to know what dirt tasted like. I didn't eat the worms, but my mother told me off all the same. I never did it again.

It was 1934. We lived on an estate belonging to the GEC, where my father worked as a foreman electrician; there was me, my mother, my father, both Liverpudlians, my elder sister Bobs (whose real name is Constance), and my Uncle Leon, who wasn't really my uncle but a pal of my father's. They had met in the trenches during the First World War and he had come to live with us long before I was born.

My father was a vain man. I often caught him looking at his fingernails to make sure they were clean, or if he passed a mirror, stealing a glance, then smoothing his hair. He had a lovely thick head of black hair.

My mother suspected he was a bit of a womaniser. She also thought he was a mean man. On the few occasions when she went with him to the local pub, he bought rounds for everybody. My mother would ask for a port and lemon, but, when they came home, my father would promptly take the cost of the drink out of her housekeeping.

My mother and father didn't get on, but they loved me. I always felt I had two fathers – my real father and Uncle Leon, who was as fond of me as I was of him.

I liked being fathered by two men. I always seem to have had two men in my life. Two fathers, then husband and lover, later husband and son.

I remember the warm feelings Daddy and Uncle Leon gave me. Uncle Leon and I used to make pobs – a nourishing dish made with

3

bread and milk and sugar and, if we were lucky, a raw egg beaten into it. It was nice sitting cross-legged with Uncle Leon, eating pobs together.

When I think of my father I remember the smell of his breath which at weekends was usually beery, and the smell of the steaming porridge which we both ate. He'd sit me on his knee in the garden and sing the old Flanagan and Allen song, 'Underneath the Arches', to me. A lovely memory – my father smelling of beer and singing, with our little dog Smudge sitting at our feet. I always felt very close to my father.

I often thought my mother and sister were on one side of the family, my father and I on the other, with Uncle Leon the neutral element. I was too young to take sides, but when my parents rowed, I banged on the wall and screamed at them, hoping they would stop. I can't remember a time when they didn't quarrel and fight. They were quite serious rows, usually about money. My father probably did have affairs, and I think one of them was quite serious. He liked to call my mother a 'long-nosed bugger'. Then they would throw things at each other. Once, my mother flung the dinner at him and it hit the wall. On another occasion, when my mother and sister were doing the ironing during the height of a row, the iron went where it was not meant to go. I seem to remember my sister's arm was burned.

I've always had a feeling that Mum married my father because she became pregnant with my sister. They left Liverpool in the early Twenties and went to live in a place called The Mumbles in Wales. That's where Bobs was born. Whether the move was to have the baby or in order to find work I never knew.

As for me, I was obviously a belated accident. I think my father was very disappointed I was not a boy. When I was six weeks old my mother took me back to Liverpool, to be seen by the rest of the family. My father was given instructions to have me registered as 'Diana'. He may have had a few jars on the way to the Town Hall, because he wrote 'Billie' on the birth certificate. Years later, when I'd be about five, he strode in with a budgerigar in a cage, saying to it: 'If you lay a bloody egg, I'll break your blasted neck.'

I think my father was desperate for some male company. I can only assume the budgerigar was female, because three weeks later, the bird had flown. The family came to the conclusion my father objected to having another female foisted on him.

Though Daddy apparently adored my mother, if they had been a couple of today I feel sure they would have divorced. My mother just didn't feel the same for him as he felt for her. But in those days people in my class couldn't afford to split up. You made your bed and had to lie in it.

My mother was a hopeless housekeeper. She rarely paid bills, and invariably had to rob Peter to pay Paul. I grew up being afraid when the doorbell went, ready to duck down in case it was someone demanding money: the rent collector or the milkman or the gas man. Even now, I still sometimes pretend I'm 'not in'. I don't have a bell at our cottage.

No meal was ever ready on time. Mum spent most of the time day-dreaming or, as she called it, meditating. I can see her now, in our Bradford wartime home, wearing a faded maroon dressing-gown, hardly the most elegant of garments, standing with her elbow on the mantelpiece and staring out of the window towards the Pennines and Ilkley Moor. She would stand there, in front of the kitchen range, which was in the sitting-room, holding a cigarette at an angle, quite a bit out to her left side, but with enormous delicacy, like a great lady. In the other hand she held the flap of her dressing-gown up to her hip, as if picking up the folds of a beautiful evening dress. She would stand like that for hours, day-dreaming. Meanwhile, the cushions would be raised too high on the settee, because Mum used to stuff old papers and bits of clothing underneath them, anything she couldn't ram into a drawer and out of sight. This was her idea of tidying up before Daddy came home. If you couldn't see the mess, it wasn't there. When I brought friends back from school, this would embarrass me, as it was obvious to most people that there were things tucked underneath the cushions.

On the sideboard Mum kept a lot of little boxes. Later in life, whenever I came home to visit, one of the first things I would do would be to poke through them all, sorting out the old familiar bits and pieces, all smelling of Mum's cigarettes.

I loved the fact that these boxes hadn't been emptied since my childhood. To me they were stuffed with treasures: yellowing news cuttings, pins, marbles, a game of Fives. For decades afterwards, those oddments gave me a feeling of security, a feeling of home. I still have them.

Mum was a very good-looking woman. She had worked as a milliner before her marriage and she played the violin, certainly well enough to entertain troops during the First World War. She had also sung 'Alice Blue Gown' to them, but had lost her voice, because, she said, she smoked too much. But she still sang 'Alice Blue Gown' to us in the kitchen, holding her hands in front of her like an opera singer, with palms turned upward and one hand inside the other. That was part of my earliest musical education, together with Tommy Dorsey playing 'One O'Clock Jump' and the Andrews Sisters singing 'Sunny Side of the Street'.

Mum felt she'd been cut out for better things. When she 'meditated', she thought about her illustrious lost past: she was a descendant of a very old Lancastrian family, Le Norreys, aristocrats of French origin who lived in Speke Hall, a Tudor mansion outside Liverpool. The Norreys had married into the Buccleuch family, descendants of Charles II and Nell Gwyn. My mother talked incessantly about her legendary background. 'It's all in the annals of history,' she would explain to all who would care to listen. She would regard herself as a throw-back to the glorious times of Speke Hall, a bit like Edith Sitwell and the Plantaganets. I think Mum hoped she would marry 'above her station' and be taken back closer to where she felt she rightly belonged.

I was never quite sure whether the stories of Speke Hall and the Norreys family were true or not. The middle name of the male children from my great-grandmother's line has always been Norreys. My father, however, thought it all a lot of old rubbish.

Yet as I grew up, listening to Mum's endless stories of our great days at Speke Hall, and all the historical names, I began to conjure up visions of living in this house once I'd grown up, and having a little French maid of my own. We seriously considered having a go at getting Speke Hall back, since Mum was convinced we had a legitimate claim to it. It began to seem monstrous to me that we were living on bread and dripping, while in fact we were rightful owners of one of England's Great Houses.

As I grew up, I forgot about Speke Hall. But half a century later – I'd meanwhile had a son and named him Matthew Norreys, just in case! – I was acting in Beckett's *Rockaby* and *Footfalls* on 42nd Street in New York. In a theatre next door, David Warrilow and Alvin Epstein were performing a different Beckett bill. One of the props they used was a huge old tome called *The History of Old English Houses*. Throughout the play this book lay open on a particular page. One day I visited the set and took a closer look at that page. It showed a picture of the Tudor mansion, with text describing the Norreys family of Speke Hall – exactly as my mother had told me all those years ago . . .

My father didn't speak about the past at all. He was a Liverpool man, who had spent the war in the trenches, slept in the mud and became slightly deaf, though it's possible he inherited a hearing problem. All the Whitelaws were hard of hearing. We always had to shout in order for my father to hear. I came to hate raising my voice. Even now I am always begging everybody to turn the radio or the TV down. 'Take the top off,' I ask my husband Robert when he's listening to a Mahler symphony and he protests: 'But there are 120 people playing *fortissimo!*' and I say: 'Well, turn it down a bit.' I can't stand loud noise, but I love bird-song. Living in the country, as I do now, I lie back in bed in the morning, or wander into the garden in my dressing-gown with a mug of tea, listening to all the voices in the dawn chorus. Birds can't sing loud enough for me.

My father had a pension because of his hearing difficulties. The doctor had to give him periodic tests; the pension authorities needed to know if his hearing was getting worse. They'd drop things behind him to catch him out, and he thought, they must think I'm an idiot, I can still feel the vibrations. How clever of Dad, I used to think.

I remember Dad sitting me on his knee, probably after a row with my mother, and saying to me: 'Bill, you're the only woman I've ever really loved.'

At the time, I found that very nice, but I also felt that perhaps he shouldn't have said it . . . It was a bit disloyal, I thought.

When I was about three, still living in Coventry, we moved to a rented house in Siddeley Avenue, near to the Rootes and Armstrong-Siddeley factories. There, we had a family living opposite us, with seven daughters. Every daughter was named after a flower – Pansy, Rose, Violet, etc. They always seemed to have runny noses and uncombed hair. My mother commented: 'I've never seen a bunch of girls in my life that looked less like flowers.'

The house in Siddeley Avenue had two rooms downstairs and a kitchen. One of the downstairs rooms was turned into a bedroom for my maternal grandfather, a seafaring man who slept there some-times. He used to sit by the fire, smoking and chewing thick twist, which he'd spit out into the grate. It wasn't phlegm, just a sort of brown saliva that made a sizzling sound as it hit the fire.

Just as I like to associate my father with beer and porridge, and my Uncle Leon with pobs, when I think of my grandfather I recall a lovely feeling of being carried downstairs by Mum after a bath. It would be freezing cold in the house and I'd still be wet but all wrapped up in a towel, and a bit afraid that Mum might trip and drop me. Then she would safely deposit me with my grandfather in front of the open fire to dry. I loved that.

Eventually my grandfather went into a home. Neither Mum nor

her sister Anne would go to see him, not even when he was dying. I felt a bit censorious of my mother about that. I later learned that Mum actually hated her father. It seems he wasn't a nice man at all. He beat his wife, my maternal grandmother, who had been incredibly beautiful and elegant – a Real Lady – and a Norreys, of course. Apparently my grandfather used to come home and lay her out cold. Mum told me he had once taken some flowers out of a vase and chucked the water over my grandmother's face in order to bring her round. She died of cancer in Liverpool before I was born.

At this time I lived in the shadow of my sister, who was ten years older, a beautiful and intelligent teenager. When she went out with my father, people used to think she was his girlfriend. She'd been to Stoke National Primary School, where she was a great success, winning the coveted Southern and Craner Award. When I was five, I went to the same primary school. I hated being taken away from my parents. My first day there was dreadful.

I was only reconciled to school because it was a mixed school and I fell in love with a boy called Walter. We played 'chase' in the playground, and I leaned up against the school door, trying to look like Deanna Durbin, singing 'My own, let me call you my own', and hoping Walter would think me attractive. So there I was, six years old, draping myself around this door, thinking, I bet I look attractive, and hoping that Walter would hear me, and stop and listen . . .

When I look back at Walter, who must have been all of seven years old at the time, I don't see a little boy at all. I see a man much much older than me, someone really mature *and knowing* . . .

I remember running around the playground showing off, tucking my skirt up into my knickers, doing handstands up against the wall. I did my handstands at the drop of a hat. As soon as I got outside the school gates, I'd cartwheel all the way down the street and round the corner, till I got home. Neighbours would tell my mother: 'Just seen your Billie coming home from school – on her hands as usual.'

I was always anxious to please. As a child I was thought to be a dumb little curly-top, who had to be patted on the head and not taken seriously. I looked with such envy at my sister. She was clever, attractive and bright – and a woman! Bobs had won scholarships. I was hardly 'university material', though words like that were never used at home.

There was never any money in the house, that was the root of all our problems. My cousin Ray used to nick sweets. I stole bits and pieces from fruit sellers' stalls – an apple or an orange. We were of course always stealing apples out of the trees; that was called scrumping, and was fair game. I never stole anything from Woolworth's. That was considered proper stealing.

We had meat once a week, the Sunday joint. This was made to spin out till Tuesday; it was served cold on a Monday and made into shepherd's pie the next day. The men would always get their share first.

In Siddeley Avenue before the war, tea would always be bread and jam or bread and dripping which I loved – the fat from the meat and the juices from the bottom of the roasting tin.

I'd take my bread and dripping or my jam butty to my Uncle Leon's bedroom and sit on the floor, listening to *Children's Hour* on his radio. It was half in English and half in Welsh. It didn't seem to matter that I didn't understand the Welsh part. I would listen to the radio, in the same way as later I watched films. It didn't matter much what was on. What was important was the feeling of being there.

The wireless played an enormous part in all our lives. My Uncle Arthur, my father's brother who lived in Liverpool with the rest of the Whitelaws, was very deaf. Yet he had a large home-made radio. He was a fanatical radio ham, picking up other people's voices and sending out messages on this contraption – a strange hobby for a man who was hard of hearing.

I grew up in a tradition in which husbands and wives did not get on, where violent rows were the norm, where women could only feel happy and relaxed when the men were out of the way.

Auntie Anne, my mother's sister, seemed to me to have the same relationship with her husband as Mum did with Daddy. Neither seemed to have much time for any male member of the family. They both loathed their brother, my Uncle Roscoe, a sailor who had been a semi-amateur variety performer and entertained in various ports. Eventually he jumped ship in New Zealand. Much later Mum and Auntie Anne wrote to Uncle Roscoe, saying: 'Our mother wants you, she's dying, please come and see her.' Uncle Roscoe never replied. Perhaps he never got the letter.

'Oh, mothers and their bloody sons,' was one of Mum's favourite sayings. According to her, all mothers doted on their sons. She looked down on them for this, and considered them silly creatures. Curiously, neither my mother nor my sister ever had sons. My mother had two daughters. So did Bobs. John, my step-brother, had two daughters. Robert, my second husband, had two girls – till he met me.

Yet when my son was born, the only boy in the family, my mother instantly loved him, and did so till the end of her days. I suspect little Matthew was the only male she ever loved unconditionally. She died when Matthew was thirteen. What a pity she never knew him as a man. It might have changed some of her ideas about the male sex.

Before the war, we always went to Liverpool for our holidays. I liked spending my holidays in Liverpool. I had a little friend there called Betty, who had Down's Syndrome. I used to try and teach Betty lessons. It didn't seem to me that there was anything exceptionally wrong with her, I just thought she was a bit slow. But Betty must have been twice my age.

Though my mother and father's family were still living in Liverpool, we always stayed with the Crofts, four maiden aunts who were not really my aunts any more than Uncle Leon was my uncle.

The Crofts lived together in a house on an estate in Allerton. They were fond of me. Auntie Bessie Croft was my mother's oldest friend. They'd known each other since they were seventeen – wartime chums who liked to enjoy themselves. Later they worked together at the Kardomah, a popular chain of teashops like Lyons, with coffee rather than tea the speciality.

The four maiden aunts dressed in Edwardian fashion. They wore long black clothes, black stockings and black velvet hats. They had very large feet and wore 'sensible' shoes, rather like a grown-up little girl's shoes, with a strap across the instep and a button. Auntie Lou and Auntie Phil, who slept together in the same bed, had bits of beard sticking out of their chins and moustachios. They parted their hair down the middle, plaited it and coiled it around their ears like earphones.

These two liked to tease Bessie, who was not as extreme as the others and wore makeup, for her flightiness. They had a very dominating mother who looked like something left over from the Boer war, and kept an enormous framed photo of her hanging in the sitting-room. Years later, when I acted in the film of Beryl Bainbridge's *The Dressmaker*, we had a similar photo on the set. It was supposed to be the mother of the two sisters, played by Joan Plowright and myself. The feeling of *déjà vu* I had when I first saw this picture sent shivers down my spine.

When their mother died, the four Croft girls made a pact that they would always stay together. I don't think Auntie Bessie approved of this, but she was probably kept on a very short rein. Being a child, I was not supposed to know that my Uncle Leon, who often came on holiday with us, was sweet on Auntie Bessie. (Why Uncle Leon didn't just go up there and grab her I shall never know. I daresay it wasn't done in those days.) Later I was to learn that Auntie Bessie had secretly given birth to two illegitimate children, fathered by some eminent Liverpool businessman.

I sometimes fantasised that I was one of them. I enjoyed playing make-believe games, and, like most kids, often wondered if I was adopted.

Mum tried to get Bessie away from the other Crofts, so that she could marry Uncle Leon, but it didn't work out.

Each aunt had a specific function in the house, and was indispensable. The youngest of the Crofts, Auntie Bessie and Auntie Margaret (who worked in the office of the Liverpool Police and was fun to be with) were the Earners. Auntie Lou and Auntie Phil were Cook and Housekeeper respectively. I found Aunties Lou and Phil a bit sinister; I never liked it when Auntie Phil bathed me.

My father's sister, Auntie Olive, whose seafaring husband had jumped ship and left her with a young daughter to bring up, was a very warm person. She had a mouth full of enormous teeth. In fact, all the Whitelaws had huge teeth. My mother claimed that she only married my father because of his marvellous teeth. They were, she said, the reason she loved him, although I don't believe Mum ever loved my father at all. At most, she became infatuated with him when they met. Ironically, after they married, my father had a road accident. He was slung on his face and dragged a couple of hundred yards along the street. It knocked out every tooth in his head.

My mother was always telling me: 'Don't pull your mouth like that, you'll end up looking like your father.' I couldn't see anything wrong with that. To me Dad was a very good-looking man, even after he had false teeth.

We always spent these pre-war holidays in exactly the same way, visiting the Whitelaws, my father's family who lived in Aigbeth, while we were staying with the Crofts.

Next door to the Crofts lived the Percivals. Their son Robert was handsome, noisy and very active, about ten years older than me. I always felt Robert Percival and my sister Bobs were meant to be sweethearts, and that he'd end up as my brother-in-law, but when Bobs did marry it was to Cliff Baron, a rather shy young man she'd met when serving in the WAAFs. They had two daughters, Anne and Linda. At her wedding, my sister wore black – the most attractive and useful suitable garment she could get with her available wartime clothing coupons. The close-fitting jacket dipped at the back, emphasising her tiny waist. To her younger sister, Bobs looked like Ava Gardner.

From my Liverpool days I remember Robert and Bobs rigging up a home-made telephone, made out of bits of string and a couple of tin cans. One tin can was in his bedroom and the other in our bedroom, and if you pulled on the string and spoke down your own tin can, you could be heard at the end of the other can.

Bob Percival hoped to join the Navy, but one night he had to go to bed early, telling his mother: 'I've got a bit of a headache, I don't feel very well.' Next morning he woke up and thought he had lost his voice. His mother tore up the stairs. All Bob could see was her mouth opening and shutting. He couldn't hear himself shouting. Overnight he'd gone stone deaf. He had meningitis. The reason I tell this story now is that decades later my son contracted this dreadful disease.

For a long time Bob was at death's door and in dreadful pain. To stop him from throwing himself about, he had to be strapped to the bed. When he was finally permitted to get up, Bob had to learn to walk all over again. That didn't stop him from doing what he wanted to do with his life – to go to Paris to study art and French. Incredibly enough, that's what he did, although he could only lip-read. Bob became a fine painter, but couldn't make a living at it. So he worked at Lewis's in Liverpool as a commercial artist, drawing two-piece suits and things of that sort for newspaper advertisements.

Bob Percival and I didn't see each other again for a long time. We were to meet again in the early Sixties, when my first marriage broke up. I was playing Desdemona to Laurence Olivier's Othello for the National Theatre, which was then at the Old Vic. He came down from Liverpool to stay with an old mate of his, the writer Neville Smith – who a few years later wrote the script for *Gumshoe*, the film in which Albert Finney played a sort of Humphrey Bogart and I played the Lauren Bacall part.

One day Neville rang me. 'I don't think you know this,' he said, 'but Bob Percival is staying with me. He hasn't got enough money to buy himself a single tube of paint.'

We were just going off on tour. I knew I'd be away for a month, and asked Bob to stay at my flat in Datchet, by the river. Then I rushed down to Windsor and bought four eight-by-eight pieces of hardboard, which I sliced down the middle. Then I drove to the local art shop in Eton with a big cardboard box. I told them: 'Fill that up with everything an artist needs to paint from scratch: brushes, paints, turps. Just fill up the box.'

I got two crates of wine, put them in the spare bedroom, and asked Neville to send Bob round. 'The key's under the mat,' I told him, and went off on tour. Bob was able to start painting.

He became absolutely obsessed with Laurence Olivier and with Jocelyn Herbert's marvellous sets for the production. He made painting after painting of *Othello*. I still have some of these paintings. One hangs in my son Matthew's studio flat in Camden Town. Bob painted picture after picture of Olivier, and also of the Old Vic Theatre, showing lights reflecting on rainy pavements.

John Dexter, the director, who had allowed Bob to watch the production from the wings, had decided that during the stabbing of Cassio, all the lights should be put out, so that all you could hear were invisible shouts, yells and screams. Bob couldn't hear anything, of course; it drove him crazy. I got him a copy of the play, marked the bits which were played in darkness, and told him what was going on. When the lights came on again he would know what had been happening.

I managed to have quite long telephone conversations with Bob Percival. He had learned to talk through a third person, usually his wife Sheila. He'd say: 'Tell Billie this, tell Billie that.' Bob became the most extraordinary lip-reader I've ever encountered.

Years later he went to Canada, where he spent a lot of time with the Eskimos and painted snow. My sister thought he did this because it suggested silence, with everybody in the same boat.

Bob went to Canada alone, but later sent for his wife Sheila and their family. Still totally deaf, he became well known as a painter. He even managed to get his own programme on Canadian TV. But bad luck had not left him: in Toronto he was standing in the car park of a supermarket, and failed to hear a truck that had got out of control. The truck pinned him against a wall and crushed him from his stomach downwards. The doctors thought at first they'd have to amputate both legs. In the end they amputated one leg and worked desperately to save the other. Afterwards it only just held together with bolts and nuts and bits of wire. I sent Bob a telegram: 'Beethoven was deaf and Sarah Bernhardt had one leg, and if they can make it so can you.'

The telegram made him laugh.

Even that was not to be the end of his troubles. The false leg gave him endless problems. The stump became ulcerated. He told me that if he had known what was going to happen he would have left the bloody leg where it was. They had chopped it off because of the pain. Yet he could still feel pain. 'I know my leg stops there,' he would say, 'but I still feel the pain in what's left of my leg.'

When he was able, he responded to an invitation from Camden Square in London, where I was living with my second husband by this time. There was a problem because we had ten steps leading up to the house. Bob said: 'I'm going to turn up at Camden Square with a bloody parrot on my shoulder, and when I get to the bottom of those steps I'm going to throw my crutches down.' And he did just that. Somehow he managed to get up those steps without his crutches. I opened the double doors for him and watched him climb. I was very moved.

After that Bob got Crohn's Disease. You can't have your stomach squashed like a beetle without consequences. Bob told me he often had to submit to internal examinations, which felt like having the wrong end of a whisky bottle stuck up your backside.

But misfortune had not yet finished with Bob. His daughter married a healthy young man, but after a car crash, he became a total vegetable. Bob and his wife Sheila took it in turn to look after him, so that their young daughter could have some sort of life.

I've told the story of Robert Percival at some length because I feel the richer for having known him.

I was just seven when war broke out. We were still living in Coventry, which became the most bombed city in Britain. It shattered my family life for ever, something I didn't realise until I came to write this book. After the age of seven I was never again to live a normal family life.

I was evacuated to a little village called Barford in Warwickshire. I didn't want to go. We were surrounded by factories in Coventry (Rootes, Armstrong-Siddeley, etc.) and although not eight years old, I knew that there was a good chance that all my family could be killed. I didn't want my family to die without me.

I was evacuated with my school, Stoke National. We were put on a bus and my mother came down to see me off. Poor Mum was in great distress. I had a label with my name on it round my neck, and a gas mask over my shoulder. I had to take a rolled-up blanket with me, and Mum had stuck an orange and an apple into each end.

We arrived in this unknown village and were taken to a school where we were shepherded into a big classroom. No one explained anything; none of us dared to speak. I was petrified. We were taken out two by two. Where were they all disappearing to? I thought I'd never see any of them again. When my turn came I was teamed with a girl called Betty, whom I didn't like and who didn't like me. I had always been really horrid at school to this little girl, hiding her hat and gloves behind the lavatory door so that she'd get into trouble at home. I don't think I was a very nice little girl. I thought it must be God's revenge that I came to be paired off with Betty in this strange village.

Betty and I were taken into another classroom and a woman called out: 'Right, Mrs Court, and here are your two . . .' Mrs Court came up and led 'her' two little girls away, one of them being me. Everybody laughed and applauded, as though we were a prize in a raffle.

Mrs Court took us to her tiny cottage. I have memories of being plonked into the kitchen sink, and being washed with cold water that ran from a well tap.

Our schooling continued in the little village school on half days. I was aware that some people in the village didn't want us there at all. Mrs Court had been given a list of duties connected with evacuees which she was determined to carry out. They included doing exercises in a doorway. For me it was a strange new world. Betty and I shared a bed. I wet it every night and hoped Mrs Court would think it was Betty.

Mrs Court had told us that Hitler ran the garage down the road. If I didn't behave myself he would get me. I was sure bed-wetters were on top of his list. Whenever I had to pass that garage, I'd put my head down and run like hell, hoping he wouldn't see me.

Sometimes we were given Red Cross Food Parcels. Mrs Court assumed we had to eat the vitamin pills and evaporated milk all at once, and I began to dread their arrival. I was invariably sick.

Betty soon went back to Coventry. She probably got fed up with my bed-wetting. So did Mrs Court. I was unhappy and longed for home. On the radio Vera Lynn sang:

> Goodnight children everywhere,
> Your Mummy thinks of you tonight,
> Lay your head upon your pillow,
> Don't be a kid or a weeping willow.

Every time I heard this song I howled. I sat in front of the radio, with tears streaming down my face, thinking, I must look so pathetic

– if my family could see me now, they'd *have* to take me home. So I cried harder. It wasn't difficult. (So many children cried when they heard Vera Lynn singing this song, the BBC eventually had to ban it.)

Mum came to see me at Mrs Court's whenever she could. She told me that my father was doing war work at his factory, whilst Bobs, who was seventeen, was working at Rootes. I would watch Mum get off the country bus at a stop near a little hump bridge. Each time, I begged and begged her to take me home. One day, during a visit, she told me: 'All right, Billkins, next time I come, I'll take you back with me.'

Next time Mum came, I sat there waiting, with my clothes laid out and everything in place. But when she got off the bus I saw at once that she hadn't brought a suitcase with her. My heart sank. I felt a pain in my solar plexus. My mother hadn't brought a suitcase: I would have to stay.

I told myself I'd run away, and one day I actually did run off. I can't remember the exact circumstances, but somehow I managed to get back to Coventry by bus. I begged Mum not to send me back again. I think Bobs was sent to Barford to collect my clothes . . .

Shortly after that, all hell broke loose. Coventry was Coventrated, as the Germans called it. (Now Coventry is 'twinned' with Dresden, a city that we devastated.) I remember the ack-ack guns roaring until they ran out of ammunition, the scream of planes and bombs. Then the Germans started machine-gunning the streets. My father's only concession to the bombs whistling down on us was to lean his head a little to one side in case the centre light, a typical Thirties lamp, which was always full of dead flies, fell down.

The Blitz had started, and there I was, in the middle of it. I had a friend in the street, Colin Watkins, who became a headmaster. (Fifty years later he still sends me hand-painted Christmas cards!) The Watkinses, who were our neighbours, had an Anderson shelter, a corrugated iron contraption, laid over a hole in the garden, into which you could clamber during a raid. Sometimes I was allowed in there, as we didn't have a shelter of our own, but we usually stayed in bed anyway.

By now our road was an absolute mess. An aerial torpedo had landed on the other side of the street. Had it landed on our side, I wouldn't be sitting here writing this. Every house was damaged. The street became a crazy adventure playground.

Only recently Colin wrote to me about those wartime days. He remembered eating slices of Kraft cheese with me. 'We never had those at home and I loved it when your mother gave us some on a piece of sliced bread. We didn't have pre-sliced bread at that time. Do you remember the day we were playing "shops" in our air-raid shelter, and a German fighter bomber swooped low over the street? We later learned that it had been strafing workers leaving the Standard factory.' I certainly remembered. Late one night during a raid, Colin came round to our house because a delayed-action bomb had dropped outside his own. Mum was standing at the front gate, smoking. 'Come in and stay here,' she said. 'I'm going back to bed.'

The other day, working on the film *Deadly Advice*, I heard Edward Woodward telling young Jane Horrocks how exciting the war had been, how everyone had been helping everybody else, how there had been this universal feeling of camaraderie. 'I don't know about your war, Edward,' I butted in, 'but it doesn't sound like the one I went through. I found all of it horrible and frightening.'

Can both versions be true?

The bombs didn't affect me as much as being away from home. Mum wanted to send me back to the little village, which meant safety, but I cried and pleaded: 'Don't send me back there, Mum, please.' So I was allowed to stay in Coventry.

As soon as it got dark, we were supposed to traipse off to the shelters. (Apart from the Watkins' dug-out, there was the choice of a big public shelter up the road, or a smaller one in our own street.) We were not very good at observing this rule. On the rare occasion we did go, it was usually to the street shelter. With a direct hit, it would have offered us no protection whatsoever. The sirens would go, and the air-raid wardens would come running down the street, shouting. They needed to know who was where, so that they would know whom they were digging out if the need arose. Often they'd get cross with the Whitelaws, and start banging on our door, shouting: 'Come on out, everybody, everybody out.' We would invariably still be in bed.

One afternoon Mum and Bobs and I were at the pictures, as the air-raid sirens sounded. Mum wanted desperately to get us home, but this wasn't allowed. We could hear almighty explosions nearby. The warden bundled us down the stairs of one of the big city-centre shelters, where people crowded in, clutching parcels of food and drink. It soon became packed; I remember the smell of sweat and beer. I curled up in a corner. Mum was saying: 'Never again, we're never ever going to the pictures again.'

Much later, I saw one of Henry Moore's drawings, *Child in an Air*

17

Raid Shelter, and I thought Good Lord, that's me. The face even looked like me.

We had to spend the whole night down there. There was somebody who'd had a few beers, entertaining us with some songs, while the rest of us just nodded off. At dawn we came out, bleary-eyed, and made a run for home. Sometimes the bombers came back in the morning . . .

Most nights we felt just as safe sleeping underneath the stairs. To keep our spirits up, my sister, who was eighteen by now, and I would make up songs. Instead of:

Run rabbit, run rabbit, run, run, run,

we'd sing:

Run Adolf, run, run, run . . .

What added to my own anxiety was that I always wanted to spend pennies and the loo was outside – in the dark!

There's one other wartime experience I remember. I was sitting on a train. Across from me sat a group of soldiers. They must have been young but didn't seem young to me. Mum whispered: 'They've just come back from Dunkirk.' The soldiers looked dirty and terribly weary, but kept up their spirits, singing and playing 'the spoons'. One of the men sat me on his knee while he played and I sang:

> *There'll be blue-birds over*
> *The white cliffs of Dover*
> *Tomorrow, just you wait and see.*

By now I was eight. Proper schooling had become a thing of the past. Our school was hit. I walked to the school building, where I had left some knitting. I picked my way over what seemed like a mountain of debris, collecting bits of shrapnel as if they were shells at the seaside. Later we kids would compare the best bits and do swaps.

There was a six-week period during the war when we were without gas, electricity or water. Although water came out of the tap, we were not allowed to drink it, because of the possibility of typhoid fever. 'Corpses in the pipes,' I heard someone say.

One of my jobs at this time was to go down into a bomb crater, with linoleum and a bucket, to try and get some water. Or we'd queue up at a pump some distance away. We were allowed only one bucket of water. We also had tubs in the garden, to catch the

rainwater. Afterwards you had to scoop the flies off. Often, when making a cup of tea, we had to skim the dead flies off the top.

Water was too precious to pour down the lavatory. Human waste went into the garden. If it was necessary, Mum sometimes allowed one bucket of water to be poured down the loo to flush it at the end of the day.

There was another side to the bombing of Coventry. When I became aware of it, I realised for the first time that people were not all good or brave.

During the worst of the bombing, things had become such a mess that the Coventry authorities abandoned some rationing. To my child's eye, it seemed that suddenly people were coming in from everywhere, driving up in cars, swarming over the shops. They'd heard rumours that there was no longer any rationing in Coventry. I found this disgusting – people invading our ruined city, which had no water, no gas, no electricity, no ration books – all making a beeline for the shops. It was the first time I felt disillusioned with grown-ups.

It was not the only thing that shocked me. A few times I watched enemy aircraft coming down in flames. People would get excited. They'd shout things like: 'Hurray, hurray, one more chalked up.' But there are men in that plane, I thought, being burned to death. No one seemed to care. And yet I was morbidly curious, too. I wanted to look inside the burning aircraft, at the dying men, to see what they were doing . . .

Meanwhile the local ack-ack guns broke all our windows. Sometimes, it seemed to me, they did more damage to the houses than to the bombers. Eventually my mother panicked. Another label was put around my neck.

I remember sitting outside the Rootes factory on my suitcase, while my sister went inside to tell her boss that she had to take her little sister to Liverpool. While I sat there, I looked up into the sky and saw my first dog-fight: a German aircraft and a Spitfire battling it out in the sky, diving down at an angle of ninety degrees and then swerving up to get out of the way, with machine-guns rattling away.

I was sent to Liverpool, from the frying-pan into the fire. I didn't stay with the Whitelaws, as I had expected, but with Auntie Iris, another unrelated aunt – an old school-friend of Mum's. She and her husband, a master of the local Masonic Lodge, lived in a leafy suburb. They were, it seemed to me, *posh*. They had a proper three-piece suite, and *two* sitting-rooms. They had ornaments, and the furniture was always polished. They had a weekly cleaning woman. Their house was spotless. They had no children of my age, just a grown-up married son by Auntie Iris's first husband. They took me in as an evacuee, but I started to feel ashamed of my background. I thought I didn't fit in. That feeling has never really left me. Even when I came to live in a big house in London, NW1, with my second husband, and was well off, I had a nagging feeling at the back of my mind that I couldn't ask people back. My place wasn't really good enough . . .

Auntie Iris and Uncle Alf were very kind. They made a bed underneath the stairs for me, so that I would be more protected from the bombs. But instead of bombs coming down, we sat and watched land mines gently descending by parachute – quite a pretty sight, actually.

Christmas was coming. I knew I looked shabby; I also sensed that not nearly enough was being contributed for my keep to make me look respectable. I'd overhear whispered conversations: 'They should really get Billie a new winter coat,' etc. . . .

Everybody thought I was happy in Liverpool. I wasn't unhappy, I just felt embarrassed. I guessed that no Christmas presents had arrived from Coventry. Perhaps Mum couldn't send any. Coventry was a bomb-site. Clothes were rationed. There was no money. Although I would never admit it, deep in my gut I felt that someone could have sent me *something* from home.

Christmas arrived. Not even a Christmas card. I understood my parents' problems, but the knot in my gut became a little harder. I sensed a lot of last-minute hurrying and scurrying on the part of Auntie Iris and Uncle Alf.

It was Christmas Eve. I woke up in the middle of the night. They had put a big balloon at the end of my bed. I saw a horrible face staring at me, a face with ears on it. I was so frightened I pulled the sheet up over my face. Oh please, I thought, let it be morning soon – there's something horrible at the bottom of my bed . . .

Daylight came: Uncle Alf and Auntie Iris had managed to fill a pillow-case with all sorts of things. Most of them seemed babyish to me. There was a tin with coal in it and a funny little horse, about two inches high on a little stand. When you pressed it, the horse's head went down, the tail swished and his knees buckled. I was not supposed to know that Uncle Alf and Auntie Iris had done all this for me. And I couldn't understand what I was supposed to do with a tin with coal in it. I was told later it was supposed to bring me luck.

I felt resentful and humiliated at having to play-act Christmassy oohs and aahs of delight. All I wanted to do was cry. I would have felt better if they'd said: 'Look, Billie, it's wartime and difficult to send anything from Coventry.' But nobody said anything.

That's when I realised that sometimes one has to sing for one's supper. You have to try and present the face that people want to see. I still tend to do this. But I don't do it as well as when I was little.

In Liverpool, I was away from home. I felt my childhood had ended. To get to my new school I had to follow a railway line. I preferred a short-cut, daringly stumbling across the rails. A policeman put a stop to that.

Pretending to be playing, I would deliberately break my gas mask, swinging it by its straps, as I came in through the door, so that it shot down the corridor, and smashed against the wall. An air-raid warden finally had to explain patiently that this wasn't a good way to treat one's gas mask. 'You might need it one day,' he added ominously.

It didn't make any difference to my behaviour. By this time the whole family was split up. I continued to live in Liverpool with Auntie Iris and Uncle Alf. My father, whose firm had been evacuated, was staying in digs in Bradford. My sister, Mum and Uncle Leon were still in Coventry.

Meanwhile, the air raids continued both in Liverpool and Coventry. I have a memory of standing in the garden, listening to the roar of the flames, watching the sky as it glowed like a sunset gone mad. Only recently a film director was telling me: 'When you think of the war, it's all in black and white, isn't it?'

'Like hell it's in black and white,' I said. 'It's bright orange and reds. It's the roar of flames and the smell of burning.'

When Liverpool started to be bombed regularly, Auntie Iris got worried. Soon I was put on another train on my own, to Bradford this time, with another label stuck round my neck. It was cold and dark at Foster Square Station. I couldn't see Daddy anywhere. Eventually a lady and gentleman came up to me and explained that Daddy couldn't come. I was to go home with them for a few days.

Next morning I went for a walk to see where I was. The first little shop I came to was a baker's. I couldn't believe my eyes. In Coventry and Liverpool it had been difficult to get even bread. Yet here, I suddenly found myself outside a shop without a long queue. And the window was full of bread and cream cakes.

Cream cakes!

It seemed to me I had landed in fairy-land. The contrast was quite shocking. After a while, Daddy arrived and took me back to his digs, and showed me where I was going to live. I shared a back room with him.

Daddy's landlady had a son of about my age called Jack. We used to hang out of the window, Jack and I, calling people names as they walked along the street. Sometimes Jack peed out of the window. There was only an outside lavatory and a chamber-pot, which was often full. We were terrified of spilling it. One day Jack was on his way to school when a bus came round the corner. He stepped out into the road and was killed. He was only eight. That was the first time I experienced a death of someone I was close to. More was to come.

Daddy started to look for a house in Bradford where the whole family could live together. Uncle Leon would have to stay behind because of his job, which made me feel sad.

Neither Mum nor Bobs was looking forward to this move. Had my sister's deepest longings – of becoming an actress – been realised, she would by now have been studying at RADA in London. Just before the war, when Bobs was sixteen, she had been given an audition there, and was accepted. They were willing to pay her fees but not her keep. It was out of the question for my parents to find the money. Mum often spoke about this, and how upset she was at not being able to let Bobs fulfil her ambitions. She consoled herself with the fact that the war had broken out a year later, so Bobs couldn't have gone to RADA anyway.

Unable to have a theatrical career herself, Mum seemed determined that at least one of her daughters would succeed where she had failed. Such ambitions as I might have had were still dormant. I certainly wasn't aware of wanting to be an actress. And when I did go into the theatre it certainly wasn't because I'd seen Peggy Ashcroft play Juliet. I'd been to the theatre only once, to a pantomime in Coventry before the war. I think it was *Puss in Boots*. I was only five, but I still have the clearest memory of Sandy Powell singing:

> *If Father Christmas lost his whiskers*
> *Coming down the flue,*
> *What would the poor kids do,*

Toodle-oodle-oo.
He would run like Donald Duck
With all his toys for you,
If Father Christmas lost his whiskers
Coming down the flue.

I've heard that song only once, fifty-seven years ago, but I still remember every syllable, every inflection of Sandy Powell's voice. The lights on the stage were dazzlingly bright. Sandy (who was probably forty) appeared to me as a lovely granddaddy figure.

Though this was the only time I visited the theatre as a child, I loved to play dressing-up games with my friends Colin and Bernice in Coventry, which we took very seriously. Mum would let us use old clothes, tablecloths, curtains, etc. We would improvise a plot. I would usually end up in tears. Somehow my 'roles' were always sad. If anyone had to die or be injured, it was invariably me.

'Why can't you play *happy* "Let's Pretend" games?' Mum would ask, when I was in tears again.

With my friends in Bradford, it was the 'falling down the mountain' story that really got to me. We'd collect and pile up all the cushions and pillows in the house and I'd end up falling down this mountain. I thought it was realistic and terribly sad. I'd also get a cuff around my head with a brown paper carrier bag for making such a mess . . .

In 1941, the Whitelaws settled down in a council house – 3, Ruskin Avenue, Bradford. I see Mum and me sitting on an upturned drawer at the side of a big old iron kitchen range, waiting for the furniture van to arrive. Bobs had to stay in Coventry a bit longer; her legs had been badly cut by glass during an air raid. Shortly after arriving in Bradford, she joined the WAAF.

Poor Mum knew nobody in Bradford. She missed Bobs and became depressed. She and Daddy had dreadful rows. She hated the house. Paradoxically, Bradford seemed to me a haven of peace after the horrors of Coventry and Liverpool. The Luftwaffe left us alone and there were cream cakes in the shops. The big local story concerned The Night The Bomb Dropped. It must have dropped two miles away – near Heaton Woods. No one was hurt. But it was Bradford's bomb . . .

A few months after we arrived, my father complained of pains in his legs. He was sent to Bradford Royal Infirmary for some tests.

When I think of this time, I can see Dad's back, as he walks away from the house, so carefully dressed, a blue and grey scarf round his neck. I remember his vain, slightly self-conscious walk. I didn't know then I would never see him like this again.

I was not allowed to visit him in hospital; they said I was too young. On visiting days, when I waved to him through a window, I had a hollow feeling in my stomach. The doctors and nurses told my father he had a bad case of bronchitis. In fact he had lung cancer. When they sent him back from the Infirmary, he arrived home on a stretcher, carried by two ambulance men.

All the neighbours were watching from behind net curtains. Daddy looked so thin, his teeth much too big for his mouth. We had eight steps going up to the front door. The ambulance men had trouble manoeuvring the stretcher up those steps. A couple of times they almost dropped him as he tried to hold on to the sides of the stretcher. He was wearing pyjamas. I was standing on the fourth step and couldn't take my eyes off him. He was trying hard not to cry. He wouldn't look at me; he just stared straight ahead. I didn't know the word then, of course, but I had total empathy with him on that long climb up to the front door. He had been robbed of his most precious possession – his dignity. I was nine years old, but I understood.

For a while, he rested on the settee in our sitting-room. Then he had to stay in the front main bedroom, which he was never to leave again.

Mum slept with him in that room, either in the double bed or in a chair. They still managed to row . . . there was life in the relationship yet.

I slept in the next room. The walls in a council house are thin. I could hear everything. 'This can't be bronchitis,' he'd groan. 'It can't be.'

Listening to this, I knew for certain that it wasn't bronchitis, though I had been told nothing. I wondered then, and still wonder, why people treat children like idiots. During those awful days, I felt older and wiser than I do now. Everything was sharp and clear to me: *my mother didn't want me to know Daddy was dying* . . .

Very well, I'd pretend. I pretended with all of them.

'It will be spring soon,' I'd tell Daddy at his bedside. 'We'll go for nice long walks when it gets warmer.'

I knew damn well there would be no more spring walks with Daddy.

Death makes me very angry . . .

Now I noticed that the mirrors had been taken out of Daddy's room. He looked dreadful. I longed to share my anxieties and tears with my mother or sister, but I couldn't. I wasn't supposed to know that anything was amiss.

How I envied Bobs and Mum when I saw them together, both of them close to tears. I had to turn the other way, play my role of Happy Little Billikins. Most children are anxious to oblige. I was. And I was getting quite practised at playing my assigned part. Yet I felt bitter. A child certainly can feel bitter.

Daddy started to beg me to find him a mirror, any mirror. So I would walk about downstairs, count up to a hundred, then come back to tell him I couldn't find one. And I knew he never believed me. I thought it was dreadful that an intelligent man should not be allowed to deal with his own death. Yet – would I have handled it better?

My father had great faith in Advocaat, a sort of egg-nog with brandy. He thought that if he could only get hold of some Advocaat he'd get better. In wartime, alcohol was scarce; I went to every pub in the area, right up the Haworth Road. I could be very stubborn when the occasion demanded it – something that was to stand me in good stead thirty years later. It was like something out of a nine-teenth-century novel. I banged on pub side doors or walked into public bars, pleading, 'My Daddy is dying. Advocaat will make him better. Have you got any?' I got a bottle.

At night I could hear my father scratching at his blankets and moaning to himself, and I'd put my head under the covers and say over and over again: 'Please God, let Daddy be dead by the morning.' I wanted him to die because I loved him.

I was rarely at school during this time. Mum needed me to run errands.

There came a time when I was no longer allowed to go in to see Daddy. He looked terrible; Mum thought he would frighten me. My sister was now home on compassionate leave from the Air Force. Through whispered conversations I gathered that Daddy was start-ing to behave strangely. Once he reared up, and tried to grab Bobs . . . Was it to give her a hug? To ask for help?

More time passed. One day, Mum asked me if I would like to spend the weekend with a neighbour.

'Oh yes,' I replied enthusiastically, thinking: *this is it then*. I would rather have stayed with my mother and sister. I wanted to be there when Daddy died. I would have liked to share my tears. Apart from that, I felt no emotion at all.

So I was packed off. It was spring. I remember I had nits in my hair. I waited. I thought, perhaps the doctor will come and give him an injection. I knew doctors sometimes did that. Yes, I thought, that would be for the best.

On that Sunday afternoon, Mum came over to see me.

Here it comes, I thought.

Poor Mum – she looked so embarrassed, she had no idea which way to start. I wanted to tell her: 'You don't have to say anything, Mum, I know. I've known for ages.'

So we just sat there. After a while she said: 'Billie, I'm afraid Daddy's dead.'

'Yes, Mum,' I said. 'I know.'

Mum looked at me blankly for a few seconds, as if I hadn't understood. Then she left the room. I didn't cry. That was that.

My sister came to the neighbour to collect me. Both Mum and Bobs must have thought I hadn't quite understood, because I didn't cry. I had bottled up my tears for so long I *couldn't* cry. That Daddy was dead was not news to me.

Bobs did her best to make me understand as we walked home.

'Don't you understand?' We stood in front of our house; she pointed up to the bedroom window. 'Daddy's dead! He died up there! He's dead!!'

All I could say was: 'I know.'

We never did share our tears – alas.

Back at school, I felt strangely excited. There had been a girl called Audrey in my class. I remembered that when Audrey's father had died, she had cried all through Prayers and Assembly. The headmistress had mentioned how sad it was that Audrey's daddy had died. At the time I thought, gosh, how strange and different Audrey looks suddenly. So when I went back to school, with a note from Mum saying my daddy had died, I kept thinking, I wonder if I look different now, I wonder if I look the way Audrey looked, even though I wasn't crying at all. I thought, I *must* look different now. The other girls are probably thinking, what must Billie be feeling?

What I actually felt then was that I was the centre of attraction. And I still had nits. Oh, the shame of it.

Strangely enough, I found it easy to cry over make-believe games. Yet when my father died, whom I had loved, I couldn't shed a single tear.

After my father died, it always seemed to be dark. At home, Mum was utterly exhausted. We went to Scarborough for a week, and stayed in a boarding-house with Victorian wooden mantelpieces that contained a mirror and tiny pillars. Everything seemed to be dark and gloomy here too.

After that, my mother's family came down to visit us in Bradford. We four young cousins slept in the same double bed – my bed, the bed where my daddy had died.

I was often afraid that my father would come out of the old wardrobe. Lying there, I'd think, Daddy, if you're in the wardrobe, please don't come out. I imagined he might be in the wardrobe because some of his clothes were still there.

My mother got a widow's pension of two pounds, ten shillings. I got an orphan's pension – seven shillings and sixpence (38p). It was impossible to live on this, so Mum had to go to work – in a place called Sharpe's, a long way to walk, packing birthday cards and Christmas cards. Strange war work, but that's what she did.

I began to feel responsible for Mum. My sister was back in the WAAF in the North of Scotland, working as a radar mechanic. Uncle Leon was still in Coventry. So now there was just Mum and me.

Mum left for work before I went to school, and didn't come back until quite late. Whatever state I left the place in when I went out in the morning – that's how I found it when I came back. The curtains never seemed to be drawn back. It was dark when I left, dark when I returned home, so there was no point.

Yet when I look back to my early childhood, before the war years, it's always summer, bright and warm . . .

I was now ten, and attending Thornton Grammar School. Whatever shopping needed to be done, I would do on the way home. I wanted to have a hot meal ready for Mum when she came in. That, to me, meant rounds and rounds of hot toast and dripping.

There wasn't much else I could give her. On our pantry slab, I'd be able to find a number of chipped cups and bowls with dripping – some with mould on top, packets of Bird's Eye custard, half-empty packets of flour, a few Oxo cubes, a bottle of HP sauce and some odds and ends, such as little jars of half-eaten fish paste, not really fit to eat. Mum never threw anything out. Those pots were like a sacred fixture.

'Oh dear,' Mum would tell the neighbours, 'when I come home Bill always has a great pile of toast waiting for me. I don't really want it!' (Years later she told me she didn't have the heart to leave it.)

During the winter, I'd use sugar and bits of bacon rind to get the fire going in the kitchen range. Those rations should have been used for eating, but I wanted warmth more than food. Eventually I got sick of using my edibles to light a fire, and of coming home with freezing blue hands and feet, after having to take three buses to and from school, often with long waits at the bus stops.

I decided to get a gas poker. I wasn't going to argue with Mum about this. I went off to the Gas Board to ask for one. With my seven and sixpenny orphan's pension, I felt quite responsible. I managed to get the Gas Board to come round and was surprised that they did this on a child's say-so, but I did get my gas poker, blithely asking the gasmen to add the cost to the gas bill.

Meanwhile, the washing piled up in the bath. It stayed there for so long, it became greenish and smelled of mildew. I felt so sorry for Mum that I ended up doing the housework – the *minimum* I should add – rather than have her confront a mountain of it when she came home. I hated doing housework; I still do. I was never a goody-two-shoes. But it was better to help than drown in a mess.

When Mum worked at weekends, I cooked the little Sunday joint in the old 'New World' gas cooker, and boiled two veg. I also got the job of making butter go further. I'd dole out milk and margarine and slosh them around with the butter ration, mixing it all up to make a sort of cream.

For all my mother's hopelessness at housekeeping, she always kept *herself* spotlessly clean, and made sure I did the same. I never went around looking dirty. Twice a day she would make me wash what she called my nooks and crannies, and when I went to the outside toilet (which had lots of newspapers hanging on a string – it was my job to cut up newspaper and hang it up in the loo), she always saw to it that I washed my hands and bottom. Mum was very strict about that.

It's the cold winters I remember from those days. I became a dab hand at getting dressed and undressed underneath the bedclothes. It was so cold up there in the unheated bedroom, I just couldn't bear to strip off. Having washed and scrubbed myself in the freezing downstairs bathroom, I'd rush upstairs, get into bed fully dressed, take my clothes off and keep them next to me all night, *under* the sheets. Next morning when I heard Mum call out: 'Bill, time to get up,' I'd put the same clothes on – underneath the bedclothes.

Though Mum wasn't much of a housekeeper, she was a good mother to me. She just wasn't cut out for the sort of life that had been thrust on her. I remember watching her trying to clear out the copper boiler in the kitchen, which had mildewed washing in it. As she tried to clear this thing out, all five feet one of her, she was saying to herself: 'No one's going to break my spirit, Bill, nothing's going to break my spirit.' I made a decision then. Maybe it's a cliché, but I was a child and didn't know about clichés. I looked at her and thought, this is not right. I'm getting out of this, and I'm taking you with me.

And I did it. It's one of the few things I feel proud of in my life: I bought Mum a house long before I bought one for myself.

I wasn't stupid at school. Despite the domestic chaos and my father's death, I managed to pass what would later be called the eleven-plus examination. I was ten and passed with a red tick, with meant with honours.

My mother wanted me to go to the same school that Bobs had gone to, Stoke Park. We went back on a visit to Coventry, which had been reduced to rubble, and stayed with the Gallaghers, my mother's sister and her family, and my cousins Ray and Pat. And there was Uncle Jack Gallagher, who believed in 'the strap'.

The three of us youngsters slept under the stairs and sometimes crept out at night to have a midnight feast. My Auntie Anne kept lovely sliced beetroot soaked in vinegar in her pantry. We kids bet each other who'd have the guts to nip out to the kitchen and get hold of the beetroot. We'd dive back onto the mattress and get beetroot all over the sheets, and next day out came the strap.

The bombing started again and seemed worse than before. Mum and I fled back to Bradford.

There now came a period in Mum's life that I didn't like. I'm much older now than my mother was then. I don't blame her for anything, good luck to her, if it gave her some happiness at the time. Mum started going out with a friend of hers. It seemed to me, a ten-year-old, that both these women wore skirts that were too short, and that they wore too much makeup.

My mother didn't look like my mother any more. I thought she looked tarty, and I didn't like it. Mum was just forty-two at this time, but I hated her looking like this. Her friend started to wear her lipstick drawn over the rim of her upper lip, like Bette Davis, and then Mum began doing the same thing. I couldn't bear it. Poor Mum just wanted a bit of fun and company, and who can blame her? When she came back to the house at night, she'd sometimes bring a friend but would have to leave him at the door, because I was still up and waiting. I had every intention of staying up. I became stroppy and refused to go back to bed till we were on our own.

I know what's going on out there, I thought. They're playing Romeo and Juliet. I didn't like that. I thought it was a bit dirty, although I wasn't at all sure what Romeo and Juliet did – other than kiss to the count of ten – or more if you were good at it!

By now I was well aware of my own sexuality. I had been for a long time, starting with leaning up against that wall at school trying to flirt with Walter, hoping to look sexy, and singing Deanna Durbin songs. What exactly it was I thought I wanted from Walter, or anyone else, I had no idea. All I knew then was that I wanted to be looked at. And I was anxious to please.

At this time I was frightened to be left alone at night. I wrote long letters to my Uncle Leon, who was living in digs in Coventry. I still slept in Daddy's bed but didn't like going up to it in the dark. There was no light on the stairs.

One very windy night, I heard a rapping or banging noise coming from Daddy's bedroom. None of Hitler's bombs had made me feel as terrified as when I heard that noise, because when my father had wanted something, he would bang on the floor with a stick. I remember thinking, he's come back! Much as I loved my father I didn't want him to materialise. We had put a clothes-horse with all the washing on it in front of the range, and I hid between the drying clothes, waiting for Mum to come home. When she did come, the banging was still going on. I was faint with fear. We crept up the stairs and into the bedroom. The window was open; the wind, blowing at a freakish angle, kept getting under a loose piece of carpet, banging it down on the floor . . .

I hated being left alone at night and swore I'd never leave a child of mine to be frightened by ghosts and weird night sounds. And I never have.

Thornton Grammar School was just outside Bradford, near where the Brontës had lived. The junior school was adjacent to a church; we'd play hide-and-seek between the gravestones.

Most of the time I had a feeling of not really belonging. I remember thinking, you'd better start to learn how to be alone. That's how it's going to be for you.

This was true not only of my childhood, but of my first marriage. I often felt I was living inside an ice-cube, or standing behind a thick pane of glass.

Lots of good things happened to me as a child, but it's no good pretending I had a happy childhood. I've heard people say: 'She's only a child, she'll get over it, children don't mind.' Well, children do mind, and they don't get over it. I minded like hell my father having cancer and dying horribly. I minded the air raids, and the fear they instilled in me. I minded being sent away from home. I minded the curtains being drawn, and living in a darkness lit up by just one sad electric bulb. I minded having no money, and having to fight to keep myself warm and clean. I minded the struggle to light a fire, and being surrounded by dirty dishes.

As for the facts of life, as sex was called then, they were handed on to me by my mother. There was no such thing as sex education in our school. As my breasts started to grow, my mother would remind me: 'There's safety in numbers, you know.' Which meant having two or three boys around at the same time. Going around in a gang was the best way of preserving one's virginity.

One day, Mum sent me off to the chemist with a note to get some sanitary towels. She showed me the note and said: 'Now, Bill, do you know what these are for?'

And I said, 'Yes, Mum.'

And she said, 'Oh well, that's all right then.' That was the end of my sex education.

Or not quite, because when I got married for the first time, Mum drew me aside and said: 'Now remember, Bill, a slice off a cut loaf is never missed.'

After forty years I'm still trying to work out what she meant.

I never got over my father's death. The older I got, the more I missed him – long after my mother had remarried, and I was myself a married woman.

At this time, whenever I heard a popular song called 'You Are My Sunshine', a banal lyric with a boring tune, I became gripped by a sadness I didn't understand. It wasn't till my mother happened to mention some thirty years later that after Daddy died, and my sister had to go back to the Air Force, she always cried whenever she heard it on the wireless. The tune reminded her of Bobs going away. After that explanation, I no longer felt sad when I heard it. They could play 'You Are My Sunshine' till the cows came home.

Yet the painful way my father died stayed with me all my life. On my wedding night I was disturbed by a vivid dream. My father had come back for me. I took no particular interest in psychiatry or psychology at the time, nor had I read any Freud, so I had no explanation for the dream. Just as I embarked on my marriage, my father appeared to me, wearing his blue and grey striped woollen scarf. He stood at the side of the bed, then walked away from me. The image was exactly the same as when I saw him walk away and into hospital ten years earlier.

There was only Mum and me at home now. I was barely eleven, but I felt I had to look after her. One day, when Mum was out, I became ill. I remember Mum tucking me up on the settee before going out to work. I got myself a drink but still felt terrible. A huge blister was spreading over my tummy. I got panicky and went up to the window, to make faces to attract the attention of the neighbours. There was, of course, no telephone and someone had to go to a phone box. Eventually the doctor, a woman, came round. She was furious with me. 'How dare you call me out,' she yelled at me. 'It's only food poisoning.'

Meanwhile, disorder continued at home, with Mum still robbing Peter to pay Paul. Rent arrears piled up; there were so many other calls on the money. I was sent off with the rent book. I queued up to pay, hoping that nobody would see all the blanks in the rent book, the weeks we hadn't paid. 'Go and tell your mother not to leave it so long in future,' the rent collector said, and I wished to God he'd keep his voice down.

Mum probably never knew how embarrassed I felt. Nor did she suspect how I hated it when she sent me round to the neighbours to see if they had any fags 'to spare'. Mum was a heavy smoker. She needed her cigarettes till the day she died in 1979. They became her only real pleasure. She couldn't and wouldn't stop.

In wartime, cigarettes were at a premium. They were 'in short supply', one of the many things 'you couldn't get'. They played a large part in people's lives. Outside the pubs the signs were up: 'No Beer – Sorry'. The sweet shops boasted: 'No Sweets or Chocolate'. Things weren't as bad in Bradford as they were in Coventry. Even so, Mum constantly sent me round to scrounge cigarettes.

My family never emptied ashtrays. When all the cigarettes were finished, one collected all the butt-ends, 'nickers' as we called them, because you nicked them. It was my job to collect all the nickers from all the ashtrays and dig out the remains of tobacco. That would make another cigarette. Then the end of *that* cigarette would be added to the next collection of nickers. When it was impossible to make the nicker go further, it was smoked right down to the bitter end by means of a pin. I used this forty-odd years later, in the film *The Dressmaker*, which was set in wartime Liverpool.

*   *   *

Life in Bradford improved when Mum met the man we called Jumbo. His real name was Tommy Moore. When he moved in with us, Mum tried to kid me they were married. I knew damn well they weren't. The wedding was much later.

I called the man who was to become my stepfather Jumbo because he had a fleshy face and big ears. He reminded me of an elephant. He and Mum had met at the Hare and Hounds, a pub nearby, that a group of Mum's friends went to all the time. The pub was used like a club; it was a bit classier than some of the other pubs in the area. Mum liked that.

Jumbo seemed to be quite well off. He drove an Austin Seven, which he had difficulty in squeezing into. He was divorced from his wife and had a son, John, eight months younger than me, who stayed with his dad at weekends. Jumbo liked to take us out to posh places, even to restaurants like the Box Tree in Ilkley. Taking us to places like that, he said, was part of our education.

It was a better deal than anything I had been used to. Jumbo, I felt, was from a better background than our own. His father had been a wool merchant, with offices at the back of St Paul's in London. I assumed that he was one of the directors of the firm. Then, when the father died, Jumbo and his sister Agnes (whom I still feel very close to) thought they were going to be rich. As it was, the father had left nothing. He'd lived a pretty fast life and told his children very little about the state of his business. Jumbo worked for some time as a sales manager, but not long after that his job collapsed. The cupboard was bare.

Mum and Jumbo loved each other, but Mum probably felt sometimes that she was back where she had started – at least financially.

When I knew that Mum's relationship with Jumbo was serious, I was greatly relieved. My sister was still in the Forces. Had Mum not remarried I don't think I would ever have left home.

Now Jumbo was on the scene. He and his son John had come to live with us, and I suspect Bobs felt somewhat disconcerted to find a new family at home. As for me, I was happy to welcome Jumbo into our lives. I also embraced John as my brother. To this day, it never occurs to me to introduce him as my step-brother.

My new brother had to make a dreadful decision: he had to face his mother, and tell her he no longer wanted to live with her. He wanted to live with his dad, his dad's new wife, and his new sister. I admired John for his courage. I saw the problem entirely through his eyes. Poor John, I thought. His school was literally next door to where his mother lived; every school day he would have to come quite close to her. How hard that must have been for them both.

Jumbo himself had what he called 'an artistic temperament'. In other words, he was the victim of his moods. John and I sometimes watched him getting out of his little car to see what expression was on his face. If he looked worried and bad-tempered, as though he couldn't quite cope, we kept out of his way. But there was also another side to him. He loved to play the fool; he'd be our clown and chase us round the house with a mop, throwing sopping wet dish-cloths at us. Then suddenly all this jollity would collapse, he'd be bad-tempered and gloomy again, and shout: 'Go on, get out and play, get out of the house.'

But he adored my mother and looked after her from the beginning to the very end. (They died within a few months of each other.) Jumbo loved Mum, even though in some ways she could not have been an easy woman to live with.

Jumbo made a complete contrast to my father. For the rest of their lives together, Jumbo fuss-budgeted around my mother, bringing her cups of tea, little sandwiches, trays of goodies. Years later, when I came home on visits, Jumbo always made sure there was a hot water bottle in my bed. He'd wake me up with a cup of tea and ask if I wanted toast. What a contrast to Daddy! My father could never have done with any of that. He would sit at the table at one minute to one o'clock, and if there wasn't a meal in front of him at one o'clock all hell would break loose.

My mother's character never changed, of course. Nor did her way with the housework. The washing still piled up in the bathtub, though it probably wasn't left quite as long as before. Mum also wouldn't have won any prizes as a chef, but I only have to think of the meals she cooked to experience a lovely warm feeling of 'home'. She could roast a heavenly joint, with superb Yorkshire pudding and a marvellous gravy. Her roast potatoes were wonderful, cut in half length-wise and cooked about as long as the meat, always ending up slightly burnt. She could make beautiful pastry and mince pies at Christmas, succulent apple tarts and apple crumble. She often told me she could make good pastry because she had *cool hands*. I can still see Jumbo – or Gampy as we were to call him a generation later – tucking into great slices of apple pie and Treacle Pudding and Spotted Dick. It's those tastes and smells that make me think of Bradford as *home*: the North of England, rather than the Midlands and Coventry where I was born.

I know I can never go back to the North; there is no place there for me. But I do feel part of it. Not surprising, as my family on both sides are North Country. Years after Mum had left Ruskin Avenue, I went back to walk the streets and 'snickets' (little paths) and back fields of Bradford. A couple of the neighbours were in their gardens. They hadn't seen me for twenty years. There was no: 'Oh what a lovely surprise, Billie! How lovely to see you, do come in and have a cup of tea!' It was just: 'Hello, Bill. Are you coming back, then?' It was as if I'd never been away. When I walked across the cricket field, where we played as children, a man turned round and simply asked: 'Hello, Bill, have you come slumming?' I liked that.

The first evening I met my second husband, Robert, I told him I wanted to take him to show him the moors of Yorkshire. Perhaps I wanted to tell him where I belonged. And when I'm dead, I would like my ashes scattered round the Cow and Calf Rock on Ilkley Moor.

2

Child Actress

By now I had all sorts of odd ideas about what I wanted to do with my life when I grew up. I thought I wanted to be a nurse or possibly a vet. I wanted to work with Albert Schweitzer in Lambaréné. I didn't have day-dreams about becoming an actress. People like me didn't become actresses. That was for people like Edith Evans and Sybil Thorndike and Peggy Ashcroft, who existed completely outside my own culture. As John Osborne writes in his autobiography: 'My background drilled into me the discipline of low expectations . . .'

I would have liked to become a music-hall soubrette. Early on, I went to dancing class, but never followed through. Even now, I like to imagine myself as a sort of latter day Marie Lloyd. Writing 'actress' into my passport has always embarrassed me.

As an adolescent I also thought I'd like to be a nun. I discovered a spiritual side to me, at about the same time that I became aware of another side that was a bit whoreish. I felt guilty about that, I felt I had to fight it. I was a bit too fond of the boys. There was always some boy I fancied; I liked to think of myself as romantically in love.

When I started to go to Saturday-night dances at the Textile Hall in Bradford, there was always someone I hoped would notice me, ask me for the last waltz and take me home to kiss me outside the gate. Mum would yell at me to come in. That made me feel cross and guilty. As I got older I became more and more oppressed by guilt feelings, which were to stay with me for the rest of my life.

I could easily have become a nun or a prostitute, or both. As an actress I have been able to use these two sides of me, the part that is curious, that seeks and wants, and the side that is spiritual.

I never grew up with a solid concept of God. That worried me when I found that most of the children who lived in Ruskin Avenue were Catholics. I had not even been christened and everyone knew it. Mum never got around to it. I felt guilty because I didn't go to church, and – according to my local Roman Catholic friends – was certain to go straight to hell and damnation.

We said prayers at school and I said my bedtime prayer: 'Gentle Jesus . . .' I imagine Mum made me do that. God also made another appearance earlier on, when I heard my poor father moaning and groaning on the other side of the paper-thin wall, and I prayed: 'Please God, let Daddy be dead by the morning.'

I didn't know whom I was addressing in my prayers. It seemed to have something to do with Nature, with power, and inner strength, a force we can draw on when we are in trouble.

When Jumbo entered our lives, he took his son John and me to a very High Anglican church called St Chad's, where there was incense and singing. It seemed very much like a Roman Catholic service. Sometimes I was too lazy to go, but when I did, I always felt better for it.

A time came when I went to St Chad's in the mornings, and to the Methodist Church and Sunday School later on in the day. The Methodists seemed a much jollier lot. They had a youth club and we'd sing songs you could dance to, like:

> I've got the joy, joy, joy
> Down in my heart, down in my heart, down in my heart,
> I've got the joy, joy, joy
> Down in my heart.
> Glory to His name, Oh praise the Lord.

What I liked about the High Anglican church was their sense of theatre, with all the incense and gorgeous coloured robes. After a while, though, I began to wonder if there was possibly something not quite right about priests wearing rich robes of gold one week, and beautiful purple silks the next, and even more magnificent raiments for different parts of the religious calendar. The child that I still was wondered why the churches were so rich, when the meek, who were supposed to inherit the earth, seemed to have very little to show for their meekness.

Much later, after he'd had a sort of nervous breakdown, Jumbo became a Roman Catholic. My own religious experience became more and more like a bag of liquorice allsorts. I went to the Methodist Sunday School because it was fun. (I was asked to play Cinderella in the pantomime, and sang at Sunday School concerts.) Jumbo, meanwhile, introduced me to a totally different kind of Christianity.

As for Mum, she wouldn't participate in any of this. She had no time for Jumbo's Anglican or Catholic leanings. Coming from a Liverpool Baptist background, she felt more at home with the Band Of Hope, singing:

> I am saved I am,
> I am saved I am, I'm S.A.V.E.D.

In Liverpool, you were either anti-Catholic or anti-Protestant. Mum's family were *Orange*, i.e. anti-Catholic, whereas Jumbo drifted more and more towards Catholicism.

Living in the middle of this, I was never able to settle down to any consistent religious activity. Both my weddings took place in registry offices. My second husband is a non-practising half-Jew. Anyway, I have little time for organised religion. Churches the world over seem to me almost as corrupt as the world of politics. Yet I feel admiration for people who devote their lives to helping the under-privileged. And I admire the courage of worker-priests in places like Latin America.

Notwithstanding upheavals at home, I stumbled into a career. By the age of eleven, I had become a radio actor. Before I was twelve, I could read 'my name above the title'.

All this began quite haphazardly. I had developed a stutter. Whenever I was tired, nervous or over-excited, I stuttered.

At the factory where she worked, my mother spoke to a friend who was keen on amateur theatricals. She thought such activity might help my affliction.

Mum needed no persuasion when it was suggested in 1943 that I try to join the Bradford Civic Playhouse. (Her own theatrical ambitions had never got beyond playing the violin a bit, and singing 'Alice Blue Gown'.) And such hopes as she had for Bobs were thwarted by lack of money and by the war.

The Playhouse was run by the playwright and novelist J. B. Priestley and a formidably stout woman called Esmé Church, who wore thick stockings and sensible shoes. Mum hoped these people might not only cure my stutter, but, while they were at it, my Yorkshire accent. At that time, this was thought to be quite a hindrance, should you ever want to work in the theatre.

When I met Esmé Church, she told me to go away and look at Puck in *A Midsummer Night's Dream*. I learned the speech: 'If we shadows have offended, think but this and all is mended.'

She listened to me reciting this. Then she asked gruffly: 'Have you read the play?'

'No,' I replied.

'I thought not. Go home and read it.'

To this day I never read plays unless I have to perform in them. Reading a play I associate with work, and work I associate with fear. In consequence the question of reading plays for enjoyment never arose. Yet when I was about fifteen I came across some Greek tragedies. I liked reading those, possibly because it seemed to me not remotely likely that I would ever be asked to act in them.

For that matter, I still hardly read at all. It's a family joke that whenever I'm asked to read something, I've 'got the wrong glasses on'. Yet somehow I passed my eleven-plus with honours, and though I always sign contracts without looking at them, no one's ever cheated me.

Esmé enrolled me in her evening class of grown-ups. Then later I joined the Saturday morning class for children. There were three or four other kids training alongside me. One of the older boys, whom I remember wearing short trousers, was called Bill Gaskill.

Bill never charged around like the rest of us. He was a serious type, who seemed to be content to remain on the periphery, simply observing. He was certainly never a show-off. I think Bill was still uncertain about what he would do. We didn't meet again until I was a member of Olivier's embryonic National Theatre in 1963, when Bill had become one of our leading directors. He tried so hard to make me give a good performance in the title role of a 'neglected' play called *The Dutch Courtesan*. (The piece had not been produced for two hundred years. I thought it should have stayed neglected.)

One of our 'instructors' at the Civic Playhouse was a 'man' – he must have been all of nineteen years old – called Bernard Heptonstall.

I was most impressed by his tact. When we did floor exercises involving the raising of legs, Mr Heptonstall always asked the girls to face the other way. Mr Heptonstall (or Bernard Hepton, as he later called himself when he became an actor, with whom I was to work frequently) lived at the back of my step-grandmother's house in Bradford with his parents and twin brothers. The twins were part of our gang, and for a while we all knocked around together. Not Bernard, of course; he was the mature, grown-up, elder brother.

In class I did hardly more than skip about, yet I must have shown some sort of aptitude. When Norman Ginsbury came up to the Civic

Playhouse for a try-out of his play *The Firstcomers*, about a group of people who went to America on the *Mayflower*, a child was required. Along with three other kids, I auditioned and landed the part. Esmé Church directed.

(Later I did one other play at the Bradford Civic, *An Italian Straw Hat*. In this production, a number of children, of whom I was one and Bill Gaskill another, had to perform Greek dancing. I still have a mental picture of Bill and myself doing this.)

As a result of my 'début' in the Ginsbury play, I was offered a radio audition with the BBC North Region *Children's Hour*, which at that time was semi-professional. Mildred Dyson, a regular broadcaster who had appeared in *The Firstcomers* with me, got me the audition, which was held at the BBC Studios in Manchester.

I was supposed to wear my best clothes. Having just started at Thornton Grammar School, my best clothes were my school uniform. Mum sat in the gallery of Studio One and watched, absolutely thrilled.

The producer Nan MacDonald asked me to read for a boy's part, little Juan, a gypsy violinist in a series called *St Jonathan's in the Country*. I got the part and earned my first ten shillings and sixpence.

Within a couple of weeks I was embarked on a 'career' in radio. Whenever little boys' parts came along, the BBC in Manchester invariably called on me.

The war was still on, so we needed a pass to get into the BBC. I was eleven and shouldn't have had a pass at all. You weren't supposed to broadcast till you were twelve.

Mum was particularly pleased when I was selected to play a boy called Bunkle in a long-running series by that name.

Bunkle had been dramatised by Bertha Lonsdale from the Bunkle books. Bunkle was a sort of rough and ready Just William, a little adventurer who got into all sorts of scrapes. Bunkle made me 'famous'. That's how I fell into acting.

This broadcasting business didn't turn out to be plain sailing. For a start, it upset Esmé Church, who claimed that playing this rough lad would ruin my voice. She demanded I give up such work before I lost my voice altogether. It became apparent that she wanted to take me under her wing as a serious student of acting. Yet here I was, wasting my talent – on the wireless!

True enough, I never did learn to use my voice properly. It soon became croaky. I wrecked my pharynx, and have always had trouble with my throat.

Yet I was probably well cast for radio. Audiences have to *imagine* what is happening, and I have always 'thought in pictures'. When people talked to me, I looked over their shoulder and saw a picture of what they were talking about. I enjoyed acting in a radio version of *Wuthering Heights* – in which I played Heathcliff as a boy. I loved *Wuthering Heights*: living on the Haworth Road, I could identify with the hero and heroine.

The money I earned playing Bunkle and other boys for the next five years went into a Post Office Savings Account. It certainly helped the family finances to be a working girl.

Yet far from finding my sudden fame going to my head, I felt embarrassed by it. Once again, I had come up against the fact that I was in some way 'different'. I didn't really belong. People were pointing a finger at me and even teased me. That may have been the start of a life-long feeling of being an outsider.

Round about this time, Esmé Church called my mother in one day to ask her impatiently: 'Mrs Whitelaw, what do you intend to do about your daughter?'

Mum didn't quite know how to answer this, but Esmé's peremptory question has passed into family legend. She was sowing the seeds for a fully-fledged drama school of her own, which was eventually to turn out people of the quality of Tom Bell, Edward Petherbridge and Robert Stephens. She had me down to go straight from school to this establishment, and was even prepared to give me a drama school scholarship. But her one condition was that I stopped broadcasting. I would have been happy to do that – but Mum certainly wasn't. What seemed to me an endless argument ensued between Mum and Esmé Church, who insisted that if I was to join her school, I would have to stop work.

Mum had met my stepfather Jumbo by this time, and Esmé told them plainly that unless I did so, she would wash her hands of me. I didn't stop broadcasting, so she washed her hands of me.

I would much rather have stopped radio work (which often made me sick with worry) and gone to a proper drama school. Had I done this, I might not still be carrying a permanent school satchel on my back. I might not have felt for the rest of my life a permanent amateur.

So I think a wrong decision may have been made on my behalf. At home, arguments continued, and similar rows were going on at Thornton Grammar School, where I was told that if I didn't stop broadcasting I would be slung out. I also had to go and report my problem to the Head of Education.

So, far from my broadcasting being exciting and glamorous, I felt it to be the cause of permanent conflict. I often wonder whether that's why acting has always been associated for me with disruption and nervousness.

In the end I carried on with both school *and* radio work. I had no ideas about an acting career, of becoming another Sarah Bernhardt – even if I'd heard of her. Acting only interested me as a way of earning money.

I never went to the theatre as a child – except, as I have said, once – to a panto. (I still don't go – unless it's through the stage door.) Theatre-going was not part of my cultural background.

There never seemed to be time for it, or money. Mum was working; she had neither the leisure, nor the means, to take me to the theatre. Nor, later, did I have the sort of boyfriends who would want to take me to the theatre. 'Going out' meant a hop or the pictures.

For that matter, no music was ever heard or played at home. What my brother John and I enjoyed was *Jack Jackson's Record Roundup* programme. On Saturday nights we looked forward to his signature tune, 'Caravan'.

Yet the first time I heard Tchaikovsky's First Piano Concerto on the wireless I was quite bowled over by it. I went out, bought the record, and got very enthusiastic. Poised on the edge of the settee, I made Mum listen to it. She sat there, with a dutiful smile on her face, one hand inside the other, palm upturned, while she listened. Then she said: 'Oh yes, that's very nice, Bill,' and got up to go. I protested: 'No, wait – that nice tune is coming back again,' and the poor woman had to sit there until the whole piece was finished. The nice tune never did come back, but she said again: 'Yes, Bill, that's very nice.' From Tchaikovsky I progressed to the Grieg and the Rachmaninov Second Piano Concertos.

One evening Jumbo, who loved classical music, went to great expense to take me to the Eastbrook Hall to listen to a concert conducted by John Barbirolli. At the end of conducting the *Rosenkavalier* waltzes, he stepped down off the rostrum, and – to thunderous applause – fell flat on his face. (Many years later I was able to tell him this story. He was much amused. A lovely man.)

What gave me the greatest pleasure in those days was neither the theatre, nor music, but 'the pictures'. I would go either to the Bradford flea-pit, the Coliseum, which was a bit too rough for me, or to the cinema across the road. But it was the third of the cinemas, the Elite, Duckworth Lane, that gave me my cultural education. If an A-certificate (intended for adults over sixteen) film was on, a gang of us would stand outside the Elite and stop grown-ups:

'Please, sir, will you take me in? Please, lady, will you take me in?'

Children under sixteen were allowed into the cinema for an 'A' film but only if accompanied by an adult – *any* adult. Nobody then imagined that this could involve any sort of danger. It was something every child did if it wanted to see an 'A' picture. I was never molested. Today, one's blood would run cold at the thought of a pubescent girl asking strangers to take her into a darkened cinema.

I liked Rita Hayworth and Betty Grable musicals. I fell in love with Gary Cooper – with his cowboy outfit and hat to one side, and that unique Gary Cooper expression on his face. I wondered how I was going to spend the rest of my life if I was never going to meet this wonderful man. Whereas Gary Cooper was romantic love, I *lusted* after John Garfield, whom I saw as a boxer in *Body and Soul* and as Lana Turner's lover in *The Postman Always Rings Twice*. I was quite interested in Humphrey Bogart and Alan Ladd, but not in the demented Gary Cooper sense. I was also impressed with two black dancers called the Nicholas Brothers.

It was actors, not actresses, who always made an emotional impact on me. I admired actresses like Bette Davis and Joan Crawford, but could not identify with them.

Much later, seeing Marlon Brando for the first time in *On The Waterfront* had a most crashing effect on me. I was twenty-one at the time. It was the first time I had seen someone behaving rather than acting. I could believe in everything he did and every word he spoke.

I never liked the Three Stooges, and only started to like the Marx Brothers in my fifties. As a child, I'd thought all that running about with bent knees and false moustaches was silly.

When I think back on British films of this period I see Jack Hulbert and his dear wife Cicely Courtneidge, who to me were really a variety act. Most British films I saw at this time seemed to have nothing to do with life at all, either real or fantasised.

When I got a little older, I liked going to the pictures even more, because in the back two rows there were double seats, and if I had a boyfriend, we would do a bit of snogging. I enjoyed that.

When I was about eight, my mother wanted to give me a big treat. She took me to see Disney's *Fantasia*. I thought it was going to be another lovely frightening film like *Snow White and the Seven Dwarfs*. I sat there waiting for the film to start. I waited and waited. Finally I asked: 'When's this film going to start, Mum?' And she turned to me and said, 'It already has started, Bill.' What a disappointment – there was no story.

I now began to lead a kind of double-life: at home, everything continued as before, yet every week, I could read my name in the *Radio Times*. I was no longer like the other kids at school. Part of me found it exciting when another script plopped through the letterbox and I could earn another ten and sixpence. Yet I objected to having to put up with being teased about my acting in class.

During my first few weeks of radio work, Mum accompanied me on the train to Manchester. After that I went on my own. I would leave Bradford at the crack of dawn, and change trains at Huddersfield. Sometimes, going back, I'd miss the connection to Bradford, and didn't get home until very late.

We would start a read-through at ten o'clock. I always arrived early. When one day I saw that the BBC Northern Orchestra was also using Studio One, a long studio with a balcony, I'd wait and nose around all the musical instruments that were stored there, and plonk and clatter away on them. One day I was caught red-handed by the conductor of the BBC Northern Orchestra, Charles Groves. He was rightly outraged by the sight of an eleven-year-old playing about with his orchestra's precious instruments. After that, he left 'Do Not Touch' notices hanging about the place. This didn't prevent me from sneakily plonking the glockenspiel or banging on the timpani whenever I had time to kill. When Charles Groves caught me at it the second time, he got very cross indeed.

Forty years later, Robert and I were coming home to our house in Camden Square one night. Suddenly I heard a voice call out: 'Goodnight, Billie.' I turned round and there was a white-haired man – Charles Groves, by this time a 'Sir' and in charge of the opera at the Coliseum. He lived a few doors away from us with his wife, Hilary, whom I'd known as a child, because she was a sound mixer in Studio One. She twiddled the knobs as she sat next to our producer, Nan MacDonald.

Most of the radio work I did during those years I've forgotten, but when I was a few years older, I remember working with people like Ken Platt, Freddie Sales, Wilfred Pickles and Jimmy James, all household names at the time.

The work was so chaotic I often felt two steps ahead of a nervous breakdown. We recorded the shows in a theatre in front of an audience. Several recordings were done on the same day and, waiting for our turn, I'd sometimes see people like Al Read and two very slim young comedians called Morecambe and Wise finishing their recordings.

The scripts were never ready in time; they were frantically written on the day. The shirt-sleeved scriptwriters worked at white heat in a smoke-filled cubby-hole, like characters in a 'B' movie, while we were already on the air. When the red light went on, pages of script would be passed from hand to hand. Jimmy James, a visual comic, had difficulty holding a script, and the pages would slip from his fingers, so we would try to ram the pages back into his hands while we were still recording.

Meanwhile I was kept busy playing little boys. Nan MacDonald, known as Auntie Nan, gave her cast a lot of freedom. We were often allowed to improvise. The ability to 'vamp' helped no end in my Radio Variety days.

I was also very close to a trio of other BBC aunties: Auntie Vi Carson, who became famous as Ena Sharples in *Coronation Street*, Auntie Doris Gamble, and Auntie Muriel Levy. One of the other youngsters who worked with me at that time was Tony Warren, who later invented *Coronation Street*. The character played by Auntie Vi was based on his granny.

Meanwhile, at home and at school, rows about my work continued. I was sometimes doing as many as two radio shows a week. Not only Esmé Church objected. Mr Beaton, my headmaster, also complained that I was missing too much schooling, and that when I *was* there I was clearly tired. My mother was given an ultimatum: either I stopped all radio work or I would be asked to leave.

It was decided that I should leave before I was thrown out. I was duly transferred to Grange High School for Girls, which I loathed. Grange High School for Boys was next door. I hated the way the boys were always hanging over the gate, whistling at the girls. I was used to mixed classes at Thornton Grammar, but at this new school the boys clustered around the Girls' School, waiting for us to come out, and making silly remarks.

By the time I was sixteen, I had become a radio veteran and had a couple of hundred radio plays under my belt. During this period I was getting to know people who lived 'on the other side of the street'. They were better off than my own family, and lived in houses on Heaton Avenue; like Auntie Iris, they had cars and new-fangled things like refrigerators. I felt ill-at-ease with them.

One day I got back from school and, while having my tea, I heard myself playing Bunkle. It was probably the first time I had done a *recording*. John laughed his head off. As for me, the toast stuck in my throat. I thought I was too awful for words. I wept buckets, and didn't want to act ever again. (I've felt that way many times since.)

It still hadn't really registered with me that I had 'embarked on a career', that, from playing little boys, I might go on to bigger things. I knew of famous radio actresses, like Marjorie Westbury and Gladys Young, and loved listening to *Paul Temple* and *Saturday Night Theatre*, but all that, I felt, had nothing whatever to do with me.

Sometimes legendary people would come up north to do the odd radio show in Manchester. I remember Carl Bernard walking in, so good-looking, so much like a real actor, with his camel-hair coat and trilby hat on the side of his head. To me, that was a Proper Actor. Real Actors wore camel-hair coats and trilbies. Real Actresses looked glamorous and wore lipstick.

I started meeting some remarkable people and have precious snap-shot images to look back on: arriving early for work and seeing Gracie Fields, dressed all in black, perched on top of a grand piano, with her legs crossed. She looked far more glamorous and well-dressed than I'd expected. I suppose I had believed in her 'mill-girl' image. I also remember the cricketer Sir Learie Constantine, a most gracious man, who joined us in a children's panel game. He would only give me his autograph if I, a twelve-year-old, gave mine in return.

(This reminds me that a few years later I had every intention of marrying a black man, if only to shock my mother and stepfather out of what I then thought of as their right-wing complacency.)

I continued to live two quite separate existences. What I thought of as *real* life I enjoyed most when it snowed. I see myself in Bradford, carrying a sledge up a hill and flying down, through snow and ice. Or walking home from school, daring myself to take a short-cut over deserted back fields past a lunatic asylum, feeling a sense of drama in my own bravery. As I walked, the clouds often seemed so dark and low I thought that they would touch the top of my head. It was thrilling and frightening; it was the world of *Wuthering Heights*.

Walking past the asylum, I thought I might bump into one of the inmates. That self-inflicted sense of fear and foreboding was far more dramatic and exciting to me than any amount of acting.

Jumbo, aided and abetted by Mum, was still determined to further my 'theatrical career'. He started to cultivate Richard Burnett, of Harry Hanson's Court Players in Bradford, going to the lengths of offering the theatre his collapsible top hat when one was needed as a prop. His efforts bore fruit, and when Leeds wanted a child for a production of *Pink String and Sealing Wax* at the Princes Theatre, Bradford, I got the part.

All the actors in this play seemed incredibly glamorous to me. I was quite unable to work as they did. At this time, and for years afterwards, I never actually *learned* a script. By the time I'd worked out how to play my part, I knew the lines. If I didn't know *how* to play it, I couldn't even begin to learn it. It's only when I started working with Beckett that I had to go through the hard slog of *learning lines* meticulously.

Because of my false start, I've never been able to regard myself as anything but a hard-working amateur. Offered a part, I never think of how other actresses would do it, or have done it. All I can do is to draw on my own early experience of life, my childhood, my remembrance of loss, of fear, of death. That's all acting has ever been for me – the digging up of personal feelings, of experiences I'd rather *not* have had. My childhood has not only made me the person I am, but the actress I was to become, whatever that may be. Perhaps that is why I got on so well with Samuel Beckett: I always understood the *feelings* he wanted to convey, even when I didn't understand the words.

At every school I went to, I felt an Outsider. At Barford I was a refugee from the bombs, at Daisy Hill Primary in Bradford I was teased because I had a stupid boy's name. I was re-christened Billie Shitelaw. At Thornton Grammar I was the girl who did all those radio plays. Anonymous I was not.

In order to belong somewhere, I joined the Girl Guides. I became Patrol Leader of the Snowdrops. I didn't have a uniform. Having no idea what Girl Guides wore, I hurried to the Girl Guide shop, and fitted myself out with all the gear: lanyards, badges, whistles, things sewn on sleeves. I turned up at the first meeting, and found everybody else wearing plain blue dresses. I must have looked like a fairy on a Christmas tree. The Girl Guide Captain took me on one side: 'You've got to take all that off, Billie, you're not entitled to wear any of that.' I had more stuff on me than she had. I thought you just went into a shop and bought them. I didn't know you had to earn those badges. In the end, though, I earned quite a few of them.

At Grange High School I had to hide my identity. Part of the deal made for me was that I would do no more than four radio programmes a term. (This didn't work out. I did far more; the ten and sixpences were too useful.) The school's other condition in accepting me was that Mum and Jumbo would agree for me to be called by my middle name – *Honor* Whitelaw. The headmistress didn't want it to be known that I was 'the Billie Whitelaw on *Children's Hour*'. This didn't work out either, because whenever the teacher called out 'Honor Whitelaw' I sat on my hands, and refused to answer. I came to be full of resentment and rebellion. When I sat for a French exam I put 'Billie Honor Whitelaw' at the top of the paper, plus the date. Then I put my pen down.

There may have been a bit more to this than schoolgirl rebellion. Part of me has always wanted to be anonymous. Another part resented having to pretend to be somebody or something I was not.

School and radio work continued side by side. Wilfred Pickles, whom I had met at the BBC, told my mother that I must find an agent in London. I was made to write to Al Parker, the famous theatrical agent. Eight times I had to write this letter, not only because I couldn't spell (I still can't), but because every time I took up the pen to write I started to shake.

Nothing happened, of course. I was then told I must have some good photographs taken. I had to look my best. We went out and spent every last bean we had on a beautiful long grey gabardine coat and a hat with a feather in it. Even though I had curly hair I went out to have it permed. Then I bought a royal blue dress with lace all round, a lace piece at the top and little lace frills. That is how I went to London to have my photograph taken by Angus McBean, the famous theatrical photographer.

On the way, as I walked down Sowden Road, I ran into Harold, the boy who lived across the street, a plasterer. I'd always found it marvellously exciting to see Harold come home after work, splattered all over in plaster and muck. He's been building, I'd think, working on mill chimneys which reach up into the sky – an early touch of the Hilda Wangels, I daresay: later I was to play Ibsen's *The Master Builder* on radio with Leo McKern. In my mind's eye I saw Harold building great monuments, and that's what crossed my mind as he came by. That to me was romance.

I got on a bus, with my hat with a feather, which kept on sticking into the eyes of people going to work. They must have shaken their heads at this stupid girl, dressed up to the nines with a feather in her hat, getting on a bus to Foster Square Railway Station.

Of all the other new people I met at this time, the most important to me were Joan Littlewood and Ewan MacColl, whom I knew as Jimmie. That was his real name – Jimmie Miller. Later, I learned that he had changed his name because he feared he was going to be called up. He was a revolutionary pacifist, I think, and didn't want to be traced. Joan and Jimmie were freelancing at the BBC in Manchester to earn some money.

Joan drew me like a magnet. She was different from anyone I had known before. Politics and art were indivisible to her. Being eleven at the time we met, I had never given thought to such matters. I just took to her and Jimmie at once. To me they were just a couple of actors, like me, working for the BBC Northern Region *Children's Hour* to earn a crust. One day, shortly after the war ended, Joan told me they had formed a group who got together at a place called Ormesby outside Middlesbrough, for holidays and weekends. Would I like to join them? They worked in the servants' quarters of a big mansion house. Nobody had heard of these strange strolling players at the time. They called themselves Theatre Workshop.

We slept in a communal dormitory and rehearsed in a barn. Rosalie Williams did movement classes based on the work of Rudolf von Laban, a legendary name, then totally unknown to me. When they put records on the gramophone, and moved about to the music, I suddenly thought I knew what I wanted to be: a dancer. I moved quite well. I had been up on my points when I went to ballet class. But this was a different sort of dancing – 'free movement', which I understood right away. I listened to people banging on drums and banged drums with them. I got up and danced in the middle of the group, believing that I was 'expressing myself'.

I loved these exercises, whirling around to the music, pretending to be an animal or a human being in a given situation, then lying down and relaxing while someone came and kicked us around the floor like rag dolls.

This was the life for me! I'd found my element!

Being the only child in this crazy set-up, I wasn't allowed to stay up late. So I would lie alone in the big dormitory, listening to the sound of stamping feet, the surging, rhythmic music that came to me through the trees. Even now, whenever I hear Kodály's *Háry János*, it brings back that time of discovery, a feeling of at last *belonging*.

I liked the absence of commercial thinking at Theatre Workshop, any thought of 'Let's do this, we'll make a quick buck'. Yet paradoxically, when I had started acting it was indeed to make a quick buck, to earn a bit of money.

We all ate together at Theatre Workshop. Before a meal we would say grace in the form of a variation on the Whippenpoof Song:

> We are poor little lambs who've lost our way
> Baa baa baa.
> We are little black sheep who've gone astray
> Baa baa baa.
> Lousy ham actors all are we,
> Doomed from here to eternity.
> Lord have mercy on such as we,
> Baa baa baa.

Then we'd all sit down and eat our soup, and I would be moved to tears.

Everyone took it in turns to wash up and clean and do all the domestic work. There were no posh jobs you could work up to; there was no hierarchy, or at least I imagined then that there wasn't. For all their democratic inclinations, Joan and Jimmie were very much in charge.

Theatre Workshops didn't do conventional plays. They worked on 'projects' like *Johnny Noble* and *Uranium 235*. Instinctively I responded to their approach – allowing a play or a role to grow from a little seed, to let things happen organically. That also stood me in good stead in my work with Samuel Beckett.

I realised that Joan Littlewood wasn't just another actress. Although I always think of her as a second mother, it's strange to recall that when we first met she was roughly half the age I am now.

I see an energetic woman with big eyes and a full mouth, a concentrated gaze. She didn't seem to give a tuppenny damn about saying the right thing. What was to me the most awe-inspiring characteristic of all was that Joan was in no way bogged down with a desire to please. I so wanted to be like her. She didn't seem to care what she looked like either, always in easy clothes: a red or yellow woolly beret, flat shoes. She didn't pose, although, decades later, I have come to realise that Joan did pose, but in her own particular way.

Joan's sticking two fingers up at the Establishment, and ploughing her own furrow, had a lasting influence on me. Years later I would still find myself saying and doing things in order to shock, *à la* Joan Littlewood.

We met infrequently over the years that followed. Joan went off

to Africa, I was working hard as an actress. One night, at a club owned by the jazz singer Annie Ross (who had married a member of the cast of *Progress to the Park*), I saw Joan sitting at a table. I went across to her, squatted on my haunches, and we talked for quite a long time. Her parting shot was: 'Go and dance barefoot in the sand, or go back to Yorkshire.'

Years later, after the death of her great love Gerry Raffles, I saw her on TV accepting some sort of theatrical award. I was hoping she'd hand it back with a biting comment, but she accepted it and kissed the stage. I wanted to shout: 'No, no,' at the screen.

I didn't want Joan to be like the rest of us.

The Theatre Workshop company included people like Howard Goorney and John Bury (whom I seem to remember being in naval uniform, and who became Peter Hall's designer) and Harry H. Corbett – not the puppeteer but the actor. The Harry Corbett I first got to know was certainly not the Harry Corbett everyone knew from TV's *Steptoe and Son*. This very good-looking, earnest actor and director was, I thought, destined to become a classical actor – hardly a light comedian. He was a typical Theatre Workshop member, energetically denouncing the commercial theatre. Many years later, *Progress to the Park*, which Harry directed, was to be my first theatrical success as a leading lady in the West End. I also played opposite Harry in the first TV version of Tolstoy's *Resurrection*. Soon his career took a far more commercial turn than mine. Although we worked well together, our paths never crossed again.

One day, as I squatted on the grass with Jimmie Miller, who was wearing a purple gnome's hat, he picked up a book and asked me to read with him. I was very nervous, still afraid to be confronted with the printed word. I thought I might stutter. Jimmie wanted me to read *Romeo and Juliet* with him. He had it in mind to get me to play Juliet. To him, I was at thirteen nearer to the character Shakespeare had envisaged than the 'old' actresses who conventionally played the part. I was so terrified I was almost sick. Thank God it never happened. I never played Juliet.

I went on a memorable trip with Theatre Workshop to Staithes near Whitby. During the day I would leap about with the others. In the evening Jimmie would teach me folk songs. At that point of my life – I was nearly fifteen – I wanted to join Jimmie, I wanted to sing more than I wanted to act. To watch him striding up and down, the power of his voice filling the dining-hall – the memory still makes my hair stand on end. If only I'd had 'the Gaelic' . . .

What my first husband may have seen in me later was an image

I perhaps projected at this time – that of a half-grown, naive actress, belting out the proletarian folk songs Ewan MacColl had taught her.

It was put to Mum that I leave school and join the company on a permanent basis. For the first time in my life I was fired with excitement. I should have done it. Theatre Workshop certainly had enough people who could have completed my education. I desperately wanted to go, but, as I was under age, I had to continue going to school, where I learned nothing.

I didn't understand Theatre Workshop's politics. I just knew their way of life made sense to me. To Jumbo, they were the proverbial red rag to a bull. Both he and Mum strongly disapproved of everything Theatre Workshop stood for. She thought of them as a thoroughly undisciplined lot – a bunch of Communists. At one point Jumbo wanted to sue Joan and Jimmie for 'abducting a child'.

Joan told me that everyone has some artistic ability within them, it just had to be drawn out. I agreed with that and still do. I had no grandiose ideas of becoming a successful actress, no fantasies of driving about in an expensive white stretch limousine, wearing a mink coat, showing off an expensive bouffant hair-do. (I have done all those things since. And always felt totally out of place and stupid.)

Years later, when I was an ASM at Keighley, Howard Goorney, obviously backed by Joan, came round to ask me to join Theatre Workshop for a tour of Finland, Poland and Czechoslovakia. I would have loved nothing better.

'Come on, you're a big girl now,' he told me. 'You're working! Come and join us.'

But I felt I couldn't so openly disobey Mum and my stepfather. Joan said later she wanted me to join them, but only after I'd shown the guts to defy my parents. I never did have the guts. Not until I was cast in the Theatre Workshop production of Alun Owen's *Progress to the Park*, in 1961.

There is a footnote to all this. Had I gone to Prague with Theatre Workshop, I would have met a man called Robert Muller, a twenty-three-year-old journalist from London, at the time on a visit to the city. I almost met this man again in the early Fifties, but am keeping that story. Ten years later, Robert and I both spent month after month rehearsing Armchair Theatre TV plays in the same building at Teddington, he as a writer with director Philip Saville, me in the next-door studio, working with Ted Kotcheff in Alun Owen plays (*Lena, O My Lena, No Trams to Lime Street*). We never met. Then Robert Muller became a dreaded drama critic, and I did all I could to avoid meeting him. I also rejected a TV play he had written,

My first pin-up picture, taken for front-of-house in Peter Hall's repertory company in Oxford. Maggie Smith was a student.

With my father, in 1933 in the back garden at 52 Bourne Road, Coventry. I remember his lovely, beery breath to this day!

My beautiful maternal grandmother – every inch a Norreys. My grandfather frequently hit her.

Mum, long before my sister and I were born, minus her violin, doing a concert for the troops in Liverpool, during the First World War.

Me, aged six. Shortly afterwards war broke out and I was evacuated to the country. Family life ended.

(*Right*) My sister Bobs, the beauty of the family – friends compared her to Ava Gardner – in her WAAF's wartime uniform.

(*Right below*) My stepfather, Mum's second husband, first called 'Jumbo', then 'Gampy' by the next generation. Seen here with Mum on a visit to my Girl Guide's camp.

Uncle Roscoe, seaman and amateur entertainer. He jumped ship in New Zealand and went on the halls, professionally.

Radio star, aged fourteen, in Manchester, wearing one of Mum's old jackets. I earned 10/6 (fifty pence) for playing boys in *Children's Hour* plays.

Sick with stage fright every time – I appeared in over two-hundred *Children's Hour* plays. Here, I'm with an even younger colleague, wearing my best emerald green dress and red shoes.

The start of my career. Working hard as assistant stage manager and playing innumerable maids at the Tivoli, New Brighton. The name of the play, I've forgotten.

Sophistication. An exhausted seventeen-year-old trying to look glamorous. This must have been about 1950.

My first series – *Time Out for Peggy*. I was in my mid-twenties, mostly playing dizzy blondes and busty typists. Mum visits me on the set. Proud of each other!

(*Opposite above*) At Brands Hatch with my stepbrother, John Moore, then a young racing driver, now a business man. We frequently see him, his wife Anne, and their two daughters.

(*Opposite below*) Flavour of the Year. The first of the ABC-TV Armchair Theatre plays I did with Alun Owen and Ted Kotcheff. The play. *No Trams to Lime Street* is famous, the tape is wiped.

Bolshy actress – Alun Owen's *Progress to the Park* was first presented at Theatre Workshop, Stratford East, then transferred to Shaftesbury Avenue. (One night I chopped my hair off. Lord knows why!).

apparently with me in mind. I thought *Pleasure Where She Finds It* was pornography. Rosemary Leach played the part – brilliantly.

Meanwhile, despite my career as a 'radio star', and emotional awakening through Theatre Workshop, I was still a schoolgirl. Thanks to a contribution from my sister, and the money I earned on the radio, I was now able to go to a private school, the City High School for Girls in Bradford.

Here, suddenly, I became a genius. In the maths class, hardly my best subject, my hand shot up every time a question was asked, until the maths master began to look straight past me. I realised I'd do better to sit on my hands. My hand never shot up again. I thought, if I'm the brightest person in this maths class, the others must be a pretty dud lot. Many years later I experienced a very similar feeling of absurdity, when I went to a photographic exhibition at the National Theatre, and saw a photograph of myself, which someone had captioned: 'Billie Whitelaw, actress and intellectual'.

Jumbo, a very devout man, and subsequently a Roman Catholic convert, knew I hadn't been christened. He set about putting this to rights. While I was about it, I was to be confirmed as well. At the age of seventeen, I was received into the Anglican Church.

Before I was permitted to walk down the aisle, clutching a candle, I had to receive instruction. Mum remained firmly anti-Catholic. While we all tramped off to the Anglican church, she just got on with preparing the joint and two veg. (In the evening I'd be off to the Methodist church for some fun.)

I received instruction, and sat in the presbytery with a good man who made me cry and probably for quite the wrong reasons. I felt an aura of sexual vulnerability in this man's presence. He certainly wasn't making advances, but I was an adolescent and becoming sexually very aware. The priest would take my hand and hold on to it. I'd start to cry and sob. I suppose it was easier to sob on his shoulder. Though he never touched me, I felt deeply uncomfortable, I couldn't quite understand why. Being alone in a darkened atmosphere with a man holding my hand, aroused something in the pubescent teenager that I could not then have put into words. When this is all over, I thought, I don't want to come back in here.

After it was agreed that I would be christened and confirmed at the same time, I found I didn't have the required white dress. I had to make do with a short-sleeved summer dress covered in white-blue spots without centres. It looked like a dress with elongated Polo mints all over it. I felt a fool walking down the aisle, with the Bishop of Bradford looking on benignly.

I was christened and anointed with oil. I thought, well that's all right then. Perhaps I won't have to go straight to hell now.

While my sister has always had a horror of death, I've never been afraid of it. Even when I had been evacuated, the thought of death hadn't worried me. But I didn't want my family to be killed by bombs, whilst I was the only one left alive. What I was frightened of was not death, but being left totally alone.

After my confirmation, I could go to Holy Communion, which I did. I also went to Midnight Mass, which I loved – the same girl who, at her private school, had the cheek to demand from her head-mistress that we hold a mock election, and who stood for the godless Communist Party; the same girl who, at a quarter to five, before every *Children's Hour* broadcast, would lock herself into the lavatory just outside Studio One, and get down on her knees, put her arms round the lavatory pan, and say: 'Please God, please God, if you get me through this next hour, I'll never be horrid again. Just get me through the next hour, God, and I'll never be a bad girl again.'

Even as a child, I often felt ashamed to be a member of the human race. Perhaps once I'm twenty-one, I thought, once I'm a grown-up, everything will be different. I'll understand the human race at last and it'll all be OK. But when I was fifteen, as I undressed in the dark one night, the curtains didn't pull properly; I looked across to Ilkley Moor and saw lights flickering on the horizon, like a string of pearls. In a flash I suddenly realised that nothing at all would change on my twenty-first birthday. Nothing would *ever* change. This was it – better try and get on with it, bob with the wind . . .

My jaundiced view of the human race has never changed. Most people seem to me corrupt, many are over-ambitious, a lot of them are cruel. And I play a part in all this.

Only two things have given me real joy in life: my son (after twenty-seven years I still haven't got over the miracle of giving birth) and Nature itself – thousands of miracles I can observe every day in our garden in the heart of the Stour Valley.

Before I was fifteen, I started to go to the Saturday night hop at the local church hall, hoping some good-looking boy would think I was glamorous. I was aware of sex, but dumb, quite unaware of the signals I must have given out. Today some Judge would probably say I was asking for trouble. I usually went out with the girl who lived opposite, Maureen Dirkin. We worked out a jive routine which I can still do. Going to Saturday night hops I found both exciting and dangerous. There were now various boys I liked, and on a Saturday night I'd hope the best-looking one would take me home.

There was a whole gang of us at this time. We'd go out cycling and hitch-hiking and have detailed sexual discussions about how far we allowed boys to go. A fumble above the belt at the pictures was all right; below the belt was absolutely out of bounds. Sitting in the back row at the pictures, I sometimes had to slap a boy's hand and say: 'No, below the belt is not allowed.'

Any girl who claimed to breach those iron rules was deemed to be racy, yet one would love to listen to her boastful confessions. How well I recognised that scene in *The Dressmaker*, which Beryl Bainbridge had written for Jane Horrocks and the randy GI. 'That's rude,' she tells him in the back row.

Beryl and I first met when we were about thirteen, acting together for *Children's Hour*. We found we had a very similar background. I never thought Beryl would become one of our leading novelists. I don't know why I should say that, but she seemed to be just like the rest of us – a bit nearer to my type than some of the other kids acting at that time, someone I felt I had more in common with. We seemed to share similar romantic problems and messes.

Although years later we lived in the same part of Camden in London, we met rarely. But then it hardly ever occurs to me to ring someone up and say: 'Come round for a drink,' though I quite enjoy gathering people up at the end of a working day and taking them home. I just don't like taking the initiative socially. I do remember Beryl coming out to Datchet, and our talking for hours, long and earnestly, about our love problems. I have a feeling we could both still do that – half a century after we first met.

My brother John was not interested in any of this. He had his own group of car-mad friends. The garden was always full of 'spare parts', while they tried to build the next 'world-beater'. Later John did very well on the racing track. Cars have always been his work and hobby.

When I was not quite seventeen, I asked the priest at St Chad's Church if we could have a youth club. I also started organising potholing trips. Before long we'd all stamp down the aisle in St Chad's in our climbing boots and potholing gear. Some church members complained about this band of scruffy ragamuffins storming into a house of God. I thought Jesus Christ could have no objection to a bunch of healthy, active young people taking Holy

Communion, before going off hiking and climbing, to look at the wonderful world God had created.

Meanwhile I had become Head Girl at school, and took every opportunity to make great rallying speeches for our 'Communist Party'. I'd also sit by the window at 3, Ruskin Avenue in my school uniform, and moon about the boy from the house opposite, who must have been eighteen, and on whom I had a real crush. I thought he'd never take an interest in me, a mere schoolgirl.

Mum and Jumbo were still determined to get me 'into the theatre' the moment I left school. Just as well perhaps, as without them I would never have progressed beyond the underwear counter at Busby's, the family-owned department store in Bradford. That's where I worked whenever there was no job going in the theatre.

The Busbys were always very nice to me. Jumbo had worked there for some time as a buyer. From Eric Busby, who owned an art gallery, I bought a painting by Peter Brook (the painter, not the director), who later became fashionable. When I bought this painting he was unknown; I was one of the first people to buy his work. (Curiously enough, when I worked with James Mason in *The Water Babies*, he told me he collected Brook's paintings.) I paid twenty-five pounds for mine, which still hangs in the most important place in the living-room at our cottage.

If someone were to ask me where I come from, I would point to that painting. It shows a cul-de-sac in Bradford, a bit of a slum. Right at the back, you can see an outline of the moors. Strangely enough, I've never actually lived in a house like that. The housing estate I lived on was not a slum at all. Kids never ran around without knickers or with snotty noses there. Men never wore their trousers tied up with bits of string, though I remember my father, during the brutal winters, wrapping newspapers round his trouser legs and tying them up with string to keep him dry when he walked to work. Yet I only have to look at that painting to get a feeling of home.

At Busby's I worked in lingerie and hosiery. I enjoyed selling dressing-gowns and nightdresses. Whenever I saw customers going in the wrong direction I'd put them right. If I saw them putting something on that they looked an absolute dog in, I'd tell them: 'No, that isn't right, Madam,' and scour the rails to make sure they would find something suitable. Anxious to please, I'd rush off to other departments and ask: 'Can I have this, can I have that?'

The manageress of the lingerie department at Busby's later tried to persuade me not to go on with an unstable theatrical career, but to stay at Busby's and work with her. I think I might have risen in the department store world. I liked the people that worked there. In my heart of hearts, though, I probably knew I was only 'play-acting'.

I went back to school for a couple of months, and then worked in Harry Hanson's company in Leeds, in a play called *Easy Money*. I now learned the most important lesson of my career. There was a character actor called Frank in the company. I don't even remember his second name. He was probably about thirty-eight, but I was sixteen, and he seemed to me older than God. One night, during the performance, I carelessly missed an entrance. At the end of the show this actor called the company together, and asked them to stay on stage. Then, in front of everybody, he tore into me. He was absolutely right to do so. On that rep stage in Leeds he taught me what it meant to be a professional.

The next night I was so terrified that I charged on stage about two pages early. 'Oh dear, I'm sorry,' I cried out, turned round and ran off again. I think by now the other actors were in despair about me. But for the rest of my life I was never again late for anything.

After Leeds, I did a special week in rep at Dewsbury for R.S. Stevenson, a man of the theatre who also ran a laundry on the side, or perhaps he had a laundry, and ran a theatre on the side. Then I was at last offered my first proper job in rep.

In late 1949, I became assistant stage manager with the Saxon Players at the Tivoli, New Brighton. Mum and Jumbo saw me off. I left with a trunk. I knew I would never go home again. Mum knew it, too. From now on, I'd only be visiting. I'll never forget Mum's face. She desperately tried to keep her tears back. My stomach was turning. I kept thinking, this is it, I'm leaving home. For good.

As an audition piece, I'd done *St Joan*, but the job of ASM kept my feet firmly on the ground. I was still doing radio. Late every Saturday night, I would take the ferry across the Mersey, then bolt to Lime Street Station to get on the train to Manchester for a radio show. On Sunday night I'd rush back to the Tivoli, to start rehearsing next morning. I wouldn't have missed any of it for the world. My work in New Brighton gave me a total understanding of the nuts and bolts of the theatre. I learned to take the curtain up and down, cut up jellies for the electrics (the coloured sheets for the lighting), cue the lights, find props, sew costumes, make cushions, do anything that needed to be done to get the show on its feet. (History repeated itself with my son. The first job Matthew did when he left home at eighteen was to work backstage with a theatre company in California.)

In weekly rep, despite actors' tantrums and temperaments, the technical side had to go like clockwork. Every play seemed to have the same set: a room with french windows upstage and a backdrop, supposedly leading to a garden – the famous 'anyone for tennis?' windows. In the centre, there would always be the behind-the-settee table.

I was very keen. I wanted to do well. Even though I was the lowest of the low, I developed into a bit of a bossy-boots.

In New Brighton I spent my first Christmas away from home. I was now seventeen and totally on my own. I was glad I could go to Midnight Mass.

The usual disasters came my way both as an ASM and small-part actress – banging into outraged actors in full view of an audience, or closing a door with the doorknob coming away in my hand, so that neither I nor anybody else could get offstage. I got the biggest laugh I've had in my entire career for walking about on a stage in New Brighton with a doorknob in my hand.

I stayed six months at the Tivoli. It was next door to an amusement arcade, into which I sometimes wandered to watch all-in wrestling.

I was always the last to leave the theatre. Towards the end of our season, while clearing up, I was able to watch 'rehearsals' for the summer show that was following us in, very like the 'revue' in which poor Archie Rice appeared. This helped me a lot when, forty-three years later, I played Mrs Archie Rice in a television version of *The Entertainer* with Michael Gambon. The scenes filmed at the Hackney Empire, with 'tasteful' artistic nude tableaux alternating with a blue comedian, took me right back to my old Tivoli days.

This particular Tivoli comedian was very bad-tempered and usually the worse for drink. He wore a red nose, shoes four sizes too big and always swore when he came off. He hated the audience and called them all the names under the sun. And this rubbish was taking over from us! I became very emotional over this dreadful decline. Theatre Workshop had been Fun, but the Tivoli had been Art.

At the Tivoli, I also had my first experience of the Casting Couch. It was with the manager. I hope he's not still alive to read this. It was fairly obvious that I was still a virgin. This was 1949. Nobody had ever heard of sexual harassment. After the first company read-through, this man sidled up to me and said: 'Before you go to anyone else, come to me.' I didn't understand what he was talking about. I thought he meant I ought to talk to him if ever I had work problems and needed advice.

I soon realised that wasn't what he had in mind at all. After all, he was The Manager. He was very important and ran around in a white sports car. One night, he got me drunk on gin, then took me back to my digs in his car. He came in with me; it was a fiasco. My landlady came down because she must have heard me call out. I couldn't take the alcohol he'd plied me with; I was sick all over the carpet. The landlady was very understanding, but after that the manager often made life very difficult for me. One night he said to me in a nasty tone of voice: 'Don't you shave under your arms? You've got hair under your arms.' I was deeply hurt. I did not have hair under my arms, I always shaved. It was just a shadow.

Meanwhile, there were other problems to contend with. I had to rush about in places like Birkenhead and Seacombe, and all round the Wirral, often in the pouring rain, with the Mersey washing over the top of the pier, trying to con people out of furniture and silver – props for the show.

I was not only the last person to leave the theatre, I was also the first to start in the morning. Sometimes I had to go weeks without a bath. One day I saw my back in a mirror. Because I hadn't had a bath for so long, it looked as though I was wearing a sleeveless sweater.

My job in New Brighton was about as low as you can get in the theatre, but I didn't know that then. I didn't feel sorry for myself. I got on with it. I made four pounds a week, good money, and later it was upped to four pounds, ten shillings. I had to pay for my digs out of that.

Later, at the Theatre Royal, Leicester, where I had become a 'proper' acting member of the company, being a bossy-boots came to my rescue. In *Peg o' My Heart* I played the maid who enters, carrying a beautiful dog. I had to hand the animal to a well-known local actress called Thelma Rogers. We had taken care to have three beautifully groomed dogs lined up. They were always brushed by their proud owners before one of them went on.

One night, however, as it came nearer and nearer to my entrance, it became clear that this time not one damned dog had turned up. I had to make my entrance with a dog, so come hell or high water I'd have to find one.

The theatre was next to a fish market. Still in costume, and over-riding the stage manager, I rushed out of the theatre and into the market. My thinking went as follows: since the theatre was next door to a fish market, there had to be some scavenging animals lurking about somewhere. I rushed through the entire market (which was closed), looking through all the stinking rubbish bins. What I finally came up with was an old cat. It was a scavenger. I grabbed it. It scratched and squawked in my arms but I rushed back to the theatre and got on to the stage just in time – though the animal I carried fell somewhat short of being a beautifully tended dog. Breathlessly, I plonked the dreadful moggie on milady's satin dress, and spoke my line, which with artistic licence I'd altered to: 'Your cat, milady.'

The actress threw up her arms in horror. The terrified cat fled out through what was supposed to be a blazing fire-grate, and appeared to be incinerated. Everybody got a round of laughter and applause. I was told off, but it was recognised that I had meant well.

At the end of the Forties, the J. Arthur Rank Organisation often sent their stars to do weekly rep between films. People like Derek Bond and Barbara Murray turned up in places like New Brighton to play leading roles. Among the visiting actors was one I shall always remember. Nor will I ever forget the first time I saw him. It was eleven o'clock at night. I was cleaning up the props, ready to take them back to the shop in the morning, when a crumpled face came leering round the corner. The man was muttering to himself. Good God, I asked myself, who's this? Some tramp who had strayed into the theatre from the pier? It turned out to be an actor called Wilfred Lawson.

Needless to say, I had never heard of Wilfred Lawson. He played the lead in a famous rep piece called *Ambrose Applejohn's Adventure*. I was riveted by him. He seemed to need to hold on to the mantelpiece in order to stay upright. He'd groan and mutter his way through every performance, whispering his lines, then suddenly, for no apparent reason, break into a great shout, while clinging to that mantelpiece. I often wondered whether Wilfred Lawson was in some sort of pain. Was he drunk? Was he suffering? Was this perhaps great acting? I didn't know. What I did know was that anybody who ever watched Wilfred Lawson, or indeed worked with him, could never forget him. On the one hand, I was always ready to leap to the rescue in case he fell down. On the other, I realised this was the first time I had come in contact with a great artist.

For another reason I also remember Ralph Lynn, one of the great stars of the famous pre-war Aldwych farces. I thought Ralph Lynn was older than my grandfather. But he was spry and very friendly. Watching him work, I thought how remarkable – this old man can show a young juvenile how to leap over the back of a settee, roll over on the seat and fall on the floor!

One day he said to me: 'My dear girl, I'm playing Huddersfield next week. Do come over and we'll have tea at my hotel.' I went to Huddersfield, but instead of having tea downstairs, he'd had it set out in his room. As I picked up my cup, he suddenly reached out blindly and started chasing me round the furniture, muttering: 'Oh Billie, oh Billie, isn't this terrible, isn't this dreadful?'

I had no idea what he meant. Wasn't what terrible? What was the matter with the old gentleman? Finally I rushed out of the room. I never saw Ralph Lynn again. Actually I now recall him with great affection! I thought he was a nice old man who had taken leave of his senses.

About this time, I met a rugby player I shall call David. I was seventeen, coming up eighteen. David was a few years older, about six foot four inches tall, big and beefy and handsome, what would now be called a *hunk*. He played rugby for the Leicester Tigers and called me his 'Pocket Venus'. What he did for a living I can't remember. When we got engaged, David insisted I gave up the theatre. His parents didn't think it was right for a future daughter-in-law to be an actress, which in those days was considered to be just one step above being a prostitute. So I left my tatty rep digs, and went to live with David's family.

They had the sort of house I had once looked at with envy, like the ones on the other side of Height's Lane in Bradford. David's mother was obviously a very good housewife. The furniture was always beautifully polished. Rightly, she felt that she had to prepare me to look after her son properly. She began to train me in the arts of housewifery. My previous training had been self-taught at the age of ten, after my father had died, and Mum was out at work. I cooked the weekend joint and did the shopping. I certainly wasn't house-trained in the sense David's mother understood the word.

I started to resent this after a while. After all, I'd 'given up my career' for this engagement. The first thing David's family did was to find me a *proper job* in the bra and corsetry department of Marshall and Snelgrove in Leicester. I thought, OK, Bill, blow with the wind. I even felt a sense of relief. I no longer had to clutch that lavatory bowl before a performance, or worry about my voice. I found it embarrassing, however, to be recognised by theatre-goers, while measuring them up for their 'stays'.

At work and at home I was now being groomed in the niceties

of dainty tea-cup living. Meanwhile, in the back of his car, David introduced me to the joys of sex.

After a while I began to feel uneasy about my new life. I started to dramatise my existence. I wrote Mum heartbreaking letters, bleating that what I was experiencing had nothing to do with 'the real me'. Everything in my new life made me feel like an alien. A 'bottom drawer' had been started: what the hell was a 'bottom drawer'? Pairs of sheets, folded tablecloths and sets of table napkins were being collected, and carefully stored away.

One day I pushed all my immediate possessions into a brown paper carrier bag and got on the first train to Bradford.

I did go back to meet David – at a hotel, but only to return his engagement ring. With tears in my eyes, I told him that my parents had been absolutely horrid, *insisting* that I break the engagement. In their view, we were not really suited.

I wasn't born a Gemini for nothing. I wept over the letters I'd written to Mum, wanting her help in breaking off my engagement. Now I wrote tear-stained letters to David, saying that my parents had refused to let me get on with my own life.

For a member of my profession, I think my behaviour was not untypical. Most of us tend to believe our own fantasies are the truth. (In any other job we would simply be called 'mad'.) In that sense, if in no other, I was a typical actress from the very start.

David came to see me a couple of times, trying to persuade me to go back to him. I could now play a renunciation scene. If you read this, 'David' – what a lucky escape you had! Had we got married, there would have been a big provincial wedding, and I would have learned to give a tea-party, but you could not have put up with me for more than six months.

After breaking off my engagement, I worked for Busby's again. If I was out of work on a Saturday, they would let me start work on the next Monday. One Christmas I was helping out in the toy department. It was a hectic time. Working among the toys, I suddenly felt faint. I remember thinking, oh dear, I think I'm going to faint. How interesting. My fainting was genuine, but I stood outside myself and watched, feeling both foolish and intrigued. I also hoped my feet were in a graceful position.

I never went back to Leicester, but in 1950 got myself a job as ASM in Keighley. The star was a very good-looking young lady with incredible dark eyes. Years later, I was watching my favourite TV news programme. Suddenly, there she was, not as an actress, but as one of their leading reporters. Then she began another career, and became a novelist of considerable stature, justly famous for her first book, *The L-Shaped Room*. Lynne Reid Banks and her husband Chaim Stephenson, the sculptor, are still good friends of ours. Chaim's sculpture, *Job*, will always have a prominent place in our home, wherever that may happen to be.

While I was working at Keighley, Nan MacDonald rang to tell me to go up to London at once. The BBC were holding auditions for a TV production of *The Secret Garden* and were looking for seventeen-year-olds.

I did the audition, landed a part in *The Secret Garden* and started work at the BBC in London with Dorothea Brooking. My fee was eleven guineas a week for the eight-part series. (My subsistence allowance was more than the actual fee.) That's how I came to London from the North. I never went back.

I played a little housemaid who becomes the companion of the heroine. Thirty-seven years later, in another (American) production of *The Secret Garden*, with fondly remembered old colleagues (now knights) Derek Jacobi and Michael Hordern, I played the house-keeper, Mrs Baylock. My most vivid memory of the earlier pro-duction is of a houseboy handing me the fox that I had to carry to the house in my arms. The animal emptied its bowels all over me. There was nothing to do but carry on.

In those days everything on TV was live. They worked with enor-mous cameras. If they wanted a close-up, the camera went right up to your face. I did one whole scene with a camera on my foot. It needed a lot of concentration to keep the smile on my face. In rep I learned to become a professional; on TV I learned to grin and bear it.

From now on I was rarely out of work. I was cast in a documentary series written by Ted Willis, called *Patterns of Marriage*, directed by Caryl Doncaster, which was considered 'daring' for its day and got a vast amount of publicity. As a change from TV, I was offered a part at the tiny Gateway Theatre in Notting Hill Gate – what would now be called 'The Fringe'.

By now I had my own room in Chepstow Villas, a kind of large rooming house, with a woman living on the ground floor, working a sort of switchboard and taking in the milk. Guests had to be out by eleven o'clock. There was another actress living there, who looked very glamorous with well-groomed hair. My own hair still looked – as Mum put it – like straw on a muck cart.

Soon I was cast in my first West End play, *Where There's a Will*, put on by Jack Payne, the dance-band leader, who'd become an impresario. I was working with people like Edward Woodward and Bill Owen now. The thought of working in the West End terrified me. Each night after rehearsing, on the walk home from the tube station to the flat, I hoped I could break a leg and be released from my contract.

During rehearsal Chloe Gibson, the director, told me to wear an elastic roll around my bust, which was painful and uncomfortable. I couldn't imagine why I needed to do this. Forty years later, working with Bill Owen, he told me that my breasts had been strapped down on Mrs Jack Payne's strict instructions. (Evidently Mr Payne had an eye for the girls. Mrs Payne thought my breasts were prominent enough to distract her husband.)

As things worked out, when the play did come into town I was no longer in it. Whether Mrs Payne was responsible for relieving me of my terror of a West End appearance I shall never know.

Just before this time I had got caught up with a group of people in Notting Hill Gate. Here, in 1950–51, life was a bit like a pale imitation of the Left Bank. We'd drink cappuccinos and cheap cider, and smoke and philosophise far into the night. I was mixing with ballet dancers, painters and students. If anyone had nowhere to sleep, they could always come and sleep on my floor. I loved it.

My career was opening up. I was being asked to dinners and parties by the kind of people whom I'd always thought of as being a cut above me. The first time I went to a cocktail party I was confused. Why was everybody talking *at* everybody? Why didn't anyone talk *to* anybody? I came away not knowing one single person any better than when I'd walked in.

Maybe that's why I started to behave badly in public. Drink can go to my head very quickly, particularly if I'm nervous, or if my adrenalin is running fast. I have never been at ease at cocktail parties or formal dinner parties. I'll often upset people and afterwards be ashamed of my behaviour. Half-way through the second course I will look around me, wondering aloud how many thousands of people have died of starvation while we've been toying with the caviar starters. I've been most unfair to such people. They've probably contributed far more to charity than I have. (Over the years I think my behaviour has improved, but I never go to parties unless I'm pushed.)

The play I did at the Gateway had two actors in it called Peter. One of these Peters, whose second name was Vaughan, went as far as asking me out to lunch, which meant a drink and a sandwich at the pub next door. At this time I'd never slept with a man. Such sexual experience as had come my way had been with my fiancé David in the back of the car, as was the custom in those days.

And now there was Peter Vaughan, a big fellow, who ended up in my room that afternoon and, to my astonishment, got me into bed. I had not intended this to happen, nor indeed wanted it to happen. I was sexually naive. I think Peter found this exciting. But I wished he had waited until I got to know him. My father hadn't been dead all that long. I was still in my teens and, although not aware of it at the time, still grieving for my father. Peter was nearly thirty, 'an older man'. I now felt that I was his. I belonged to him. That's how I drifted into the relationship called marriage.

In 1952 it had become the 'in' thing theatrically to be working class and to have come down from the North of England. Peter presented a public-bar-pint-of-ale image, though this had little to do with the real Peter Vaughan, whose father was a bank manager. His people lived a highly respectable middle-class existence in a little Shropshire town called Wem.

Things developed rapidly. Peter went up to Hull, where he was doing a week in rep, and told me to follow him. I was too inexperienced to realise that we were not suited. Peter was too vigorous for me. He didn't know, and nor did I then, and at that time I could not have put it into words, that my sexuality was not to be found between my legs, but between my ears. I have never understood 'fucking' as a demonstration of love. Yet we were to be married.

Peter sent me home to get Mum's permission. I was still under age. As with David, I hoped Mum would refuse – at least for a while. She didn't.

Peter seemed to arrive on the next train. As I remember it, Mum and Gampy just stood there, looking feckless. I stared down at Mum as she stood over the consent form. She signed. Later she told me: 'You'd have gone back to London anyway, Bill, and started living together. So I thought I'd better sign the form.'

We went back to London on the next train. Very quickly after this, we were married. My mother called it a 'hole-in-the-corner affair'. She wasn't far wrong. We got married at Kensington Registry Office. Peter wouldn't have any sort of reception. His parents refused to come. So there was just Mum and Uncle Leon from my side of the family, and Peter's friends Bob and Toni Wilson, who later became helpful friends of mine. The whole thing seemed such a non-event to me that I didn't think to take a taxi. Mum and I got the tube from Gloucester Road to High Street Kensington. I wore a not very new green suit, clearly a bad omen, since you're not supposed to wear green at a wedding. Afterwards Peter marched us round to the local pub. Peter at that time had contempt for the 'gin and tonic and little things on sticks' brigade. After a drink, he said: 'Right, that's it,' and took me off to Kensington Church Street for spaghetti and chips. I felt badly about leaving Mum and Uncle Leon on their own, without even a bowl of soup. That was it – my wedding day. I was a married woman, but I was never to be a proper wife to Peter.

Peter and I were both working at this time. I think he was performing in *Worm's Eye View* at a local rep, while I was doing a lot of television. We had moved into a room in Courtfield Road. On the night before the wedding he'd moved out, so that Mum could stay with me. She was not supposed to know that bride and bridegroom had already been living under the same roof. It was at this point that she made her mysterious pronouncement: 'Now, remember, Bill, a slice off a cut loaf is never missed.'

On Christmas Eve, a couple of months after our wedding – we were going to a party at Bob and Toni Wilson – Peter looked at me and said: 'Will you please go out and see if you can get some clothes to make yourself look a bit older.' Evidently Peter didn't want to turn up at his best man's party, accompanied by a child. I had about half an hour before the shops closed. I rushed out and bought a middle-aged dress. It was emerald green and had a cross-over front, which simply produced a vast cleavage. I then put up my hair in a sort of top-knot, with all the rest hanging down. It made me look like a cross between Alice in Wonderland and Lolita.

My new husband could demonstrate concern, but it was not really in his nature to be gentle or tender. Yet for much of the time we got on reasonably well. We would have been much better off as brother and sister or as good mates. It was probably right for me to be taken in hand by an older man at this time. I was a complete scatter-brain. I blew where the wind took me. I behaved irresponsibly and got into all sorts of messes. I was always giving money away. In the end we were neither of us particularly faithful to each other. I rationalised my own infidelities by telling myself I needed tenderness. When I was away, working, I would frequently start a relationship with another actor. In the Fifties this was known in our world as LDC

(Location Doesn't Count). I found it comforting to sob on someone's shoulder, to do the reverse of a man's 'my wife doesn't understand me' routine. I wanted to be cuddled.

I was rarely out of work, whereas Peter had yet to be 'discovered'. Poor Pete – stuck with an immature, flighty flibbertigibbet wife, with hair like straw on a muck cart – who would often find me, after two glasses of wine, three sheets to the wind. I could see him beginning to grow more and more resentful.

Peter was a great cricket fan. We often went to local cricket matches. (Another cricket enthusiast was an unsuccessful, not very highly rated, young actor in our group. His name was Sean Connery.) Sometimes we went with Reggie Smith, a BBC Third Programme producer. Reggie was married to the novelist Olivia Manning, who portrayed him as 'Guy' in her Balkan Trilogy, which was later acclaimed as a BBC classic serial called *Fortunes of War*. Reggie knew a lot of the folk songs that Ewan MacColl had taught me. We enjoyed belting them out together. I had a feeling Peter would have liked to be able to join in.

As I got more and more work, Peter's difficulty in dealing with this was starting to show. He became increasingly aggressive, and his anger made me nervous. I knew he had a problem with me, but I didn't know how to handle it, or what it was that brought on his sudden rages. At these times I felt like a schoolgirl being railed at by an angry master. Not understanding his anger, I couldn't put it right. I just stood there, waiting for it to stop. Often my silence enraged him more, and he would verbally lash out. Though at cross-purposes right from the start, Peter and I weren't unhappy all the time. There certainly was an affectionate side to our relationship. He would call me 'Whittle', I would call him 'Sprout'. We simply weren't cut out to be man and wife. Within weeks of being married, I realised we'd made a bad mistake. It didn't really worry me all that much. I just told myself: 'Never mind, there's nothing you can do about it now.'

About eighteen months into our relationship, I joined Peter in Birmingham for my twenty-first birthday. For some reason he wouldn't let me tell anyone it was my birthday – let alone my twenty-first. I had a miserable day.

By this time I was Queen of the Kitchen Sink on television. People had begun to recognise me in the street. One evening in Birmingham, after Peter's show and a few drinks, we were standing in a bus queue. Peter started shouting at me. I found this aggression in public too much and just walked off. When I got back to the digs

Peter went mad. How dare I walk out on him in a bus queue! He threw money at me and told me to get the next train back to London.

At this time, working actors were either doing seasons in rep or going out on tour. It was quite usual to live in other actors' flats while they were away. A friend of Peter's, Oliver Gordon Battcock, took out a company to Newfoundland every year. He let us rent his flat in Redcliffe Square.

One day, when I came back from work, a bald-headed man stood in the kitchen, cooking cauliflower. Peter said: 'Oh, this is my friend Donald Pleasence, he's got marital problems. He's going to stay with us for a few weeks.'

Seven years later Donald was still with us. Whenever we packed our bags, Donald would come along. Eventually he became our next-door neighbour in Datchet, but in the mid-1950s Peter and I lived with Donald in two furnished attic rooms just off the Portobello Road, where on Sundays I'd go down to the market to pick up bits of throwaway greenery for next to nothing.

When I say *furnished*, I mean that I'd taken the tatty curtains off the window and tacked them on to a couple of tea-chests. They were our tables.

We had a galley kitchen, and shared a bathroom two floors down, with eight other people, including a shady 'psychiatrist'.

When a production of Anouilh's *The Lark* with Dorothy Tutin was being mounted, Donald was asked to audition for the part of the Dauphin. He wanted this part very badly. He learned some of the speeches and rehearsed them in front of Peter and me, wanting our comments. I thought how brave he was. I wouldn't have dared open my mouth in front of either of *them*.

Donald got the part. He was on his way.

Peter and I used to say Donald would have to wait until Peter Lorre died before he really came into his own. He certainly enjoyed his success. After one of his working trips to the US, he returned to Datchet with an enormous Cadillac.

He married four times (I knew three of his wives), and had at least one grandchild older than some of his children.

He appeared in countless Hollywood movies, and must have made more money than all of his old mates put together. At least he enjoyed spending it. At the drop of a hat he would take his entire family to stay at the luxurious Colombe d'Or in the South of France, which caused a local *habitué*, Dirk Bogarde, to remark to me: 'The Pleasence family have made it almost impossible to eat at the Colombe d'Or.'

*　　*　　*

Much of the time I felt guilty. I had read somewhere that if the mounds beneath your thumbs were large, it meant you had too much sexual drive. Actually I wasn't interested in sex as such at all. I did have a certain sensuality, which I enjoyed. Spending a relaxing evening over a meal and some wine, with someone stroking my arm, was pleasurable and lovely. What happened after the meal was an extension of this. Meanwhile I'd be looking at the mounds at the bottom of my thumbs, wondering if there was something wrong with me, and willing them to become flat . . .

Peter became increasingly and understandably jealous. At a party in the Earl's Court Road, he thought a man was being too flirtatious with me. He came out with a lovely line: 'I don't care whether you're J. Arthur Rank or Sir Alexander bloody Korda, you leave my wife alone!'

He marched me out into the rain and raged at me all the way home, along Earl's Court, down Redcliffe Road to Redcliffe Square. Windows went up, and when we got in I ran into the spare room, sobbing 'I want Daddy.'

Peter came charging in, looking like one of the demonic characters he plays on TV. 'What's that? You want a divorce?'

I could only repeat: 'No – I want my daddy.'

I couldn't stop crying. I wanted to see my father so much; yet when he had died ten years previously, I couldn't cry at all.

I am not sure whether our marital problems were primarily sexual or professional. Probably it was a mixture of the two. Peter still had outbursts of rage. I still stood there like a naughty schoolgirl.

I began to turn down work, hoping this might make things better between us. Possibly I needed a reason to say 'no' to work offers, because by this time my stutter had come back, mainly when I was nervous, and the thought of work always makes me nervous. Stage fright has stayed around me like an invisible bogeyman.

We were now living on the top floor of a house next to a pub opposite Warren Street tube station. One spring day in 1953 the telephone rang. It was for me – a man from *Picture Post*. He had seen my photograph in the *Daily Express*, and wanted to come round with a photographer to do an interview with me.

By now I had become very nervous about press coverage, afraid it would upset Peter. The man on the phone was just about to give his name and make an appointment for the photographer, when I heard Peter coming up the stairs. I thought, if I tell him it's *Picture Post*, and that they want to photograph and interview me, he'll go berserk. I heard myself saying to this man: 'No, sorry, no, I can't do this,' and hung up on him. The journalist, who (as I later learned) was having his first day in a new job, never did come round with the photographer. Fourteen years later he became the father of my only child, and thirty years later my second husband.

THE BECKETT YEARS
1963–89

3

Play

A great many people helped me to make the jumps from child actress to small part player, from hopeless Young Hopeful to Queen of television's Kitchen Sink. In that kitchen I might have stayed all my professional life, going on to working-class mums, eventually ending up with indistinguishable grumpy grannies' parts.

If I can blame one person for (without knowing it) giving me a kick-start to another sphere altogether, it must be John Dexter.

John and I worked together in 1961 in *England, Our England*, a kind of musical revue at the Princes Theatre, which is now called the Shaftesbury. It was written by Keith Waterhouse and Willis Hall. Dudley Moore wrote the music, on one occasion dictating a song to me down the telephone late at night for inclusion the following day. The show was choreographed by Gillian Lynne, a brilliant dancer who now came into her own and later did the choreography for *Cats*. From there she went onward and upward.

The director was originally a friend of mine, Reggie Smith, but somehow this didn't work out, and John Dexter was brought in to play the ringmaster and crack the piece into final shape. John had the reputation of being a sadistic director, but I always got on with him. 'I don't care whether you agree with what I'm saying or not,' he'd say, 'just do it, and we'll worry about it later. We've got to get the show on its feet.'

I nearly didn't go on at all in *England, Our England*. I was so gripped by panic the night before our out-of-town opening in Brighton that I sat down in my room and started to make two lists, one headed 'Reasons for opening', the other 'Reasons for not opening'. I promised myself that whichever list came out the longer, that's what I would do.

It was a close shave, but 'Reasons for opening' turned out to be the longer list. Had it gone the other way, there would have been no *England, Our England*, no further work for me, and no book.

In Brighton, John brought Laurence Olivier and Joan Plowright backstage, and we met them later in the bar. Not long afterwards I got a telephone call from the National Theatre at the Old Vic, saying Sir Laurence wanted to see me.

I thought it was somebody sending me up – just as I did when I was telephoned by the Variety Club of Great Britain a few years earlier, to be told that I'd won their annual award. And again, when thirty years later my agent asked me to call Downing Street, and a lady at the other end asked me if I'd care to accept the CBE from Her Majesty the Queen.

This wasn't merely mock modesty. I knew I was hardly National Theatre material. I had no knowledge of classical theatre, had not even been to drama school. I had become quite well known on television, and had transferred to the West End with the Theatre Workshop production of Alun Owen's *Progress to the Park*, but all this work came out of my North Country background. All through the middle Fifties and early Sixties I was typecast as a battling working-class lass, usually seduced by the boss's son, in what I called 'trouble up at t'mill' plays – *Love on the Dole*, *Lena, O My Lena*, *No Trams to Lime Street*. Even Galsworthy's *The Skin Game*, O'Neill's *Beyond the Horizon* and *Anna Christie* come into this category. *The Lady of the Camellias*, when it came my way, seemed to me to be basically the story of a prostitute in love.

So I went down to the Old Vic to meet Sir Laurence in his office. The offices of the NT were hardly spectacular – just a clutch of wooden huts in a side street at the back of the Vic.

When I walked into Olivier's hut, I felt like someone who'd been summoned to the headmaster, to be told one had been accepted to a new school. I was scared but also excited when he said something like: 'Darling girl, you really must come and join us.'

Oh dear, I thought, what do I say now? I felt totally out of my depth. This time I was really going to be rumbled. After the interview I rang my mother. I always did that.

'That's nice, Billkins,' she said.

In every generation there seems to be a list of young actors and actresses who are asked to do everything. In the early Sixties I seemed to be on that list. Even so, I don't think Olivier would have thought of me if it had not been for John Dexter, another working-class upstart. I had a feeling at that time that Olivier was afraid of being thought a bit old-fashioned; he needed people who had a non-establishment profile. Kenneth Tynan may also have had something to do with it. The leading critic of his time, who once wrote of me as 'a female version of Albert Finney', had become Olivier's literary manager.

It was quite some company I was asked to join: grouped around Olivier were Michael Redgrave, Diana Wynyard, Edith Evans, Max Adrian and up-and-coming young people like John Stride, Derek Jacobi, Lynn Redgrave, Ian McKellen, Robert Stephens, Frank Finlay and Robert Lang – not to mention ardent youngsters like Michael Gambon and Anthony Hopkins who came on to carry spears and say: 'My liege.'

Those early Sixties at the Old Vic are now thought of as a theatrical golden age. Olivier occupied the so-called Lilian Baylis Room, which had a television set in it and a magnificent roll-top desk which had once belonged to Lilian Baylis. Facing this room was a long mirrored dressing-room, and there at any one time circa 1963 you could see sitting side by side Joan Plowright, Maggie Smith, Rosemary Harris, Geraldine McEwan and now – Billie Whitelaw. There was also a small dressing-room adjoining the big one, where Edith Evans lived. I rather dreaded this *grande dame* of the theatre. After Dame Edith had left, Robert Stephens and Albert Finney moved into it.

The first thing I was set to do in this company was a John Osborne adaptation of a Lope de Vega play. I thought it a very good role, a kind of Spanish Saint Joan, and I said to myself, aha, that's why they've asked me to join the company, to do parts like that. It certainly wasn't to supplant the company's *ingénue*, Louise Purnell. We were miles apart as types. In fact I was probably brought in to replace another down to earth North Country actress, Joan Plowright, who had gone off to have Olivier's baby.

Maggie Smith I had known since we worked together with Peter Hall at the Oxford Playhouse, when we were both about twenty. We'd also spent a holiday together in Majorca. Naturally I felt very nervous on my first day at the Old Vic. I remember passing Maggie on the steps, thinking, thank God, at least there's someone I know here who'll put an arm around me and embrace me. Maggie walked straight past me. My heart sank. Actually I'm very fond of Maggie. We have a mutual respect for each other. She can be a bit of a bitch at times, but she's also capable of acts of great generosity. She's certainly a more generous person than I am.

The play John Osborne had adapted never happened. I shall never know whether it was because John was unhappy with it, or the company. It was supposed to have been directed by George Devine. George was now left with a cast of actors and no play. It was decided to do a Sophocles play, *Philoctetes*, as part of a double bill. That used up most of the actors but left Rosemary Harris, Robert Stephens and myself without parts.

What happened next went like this, but I have to say that I'm taking more than a little poetic licence in reconstructing this event. George Devine had a friend in Paris, a fairly bizarre writer called Samuel Beckett. A play of his had just opened in Germany which had parts for two women and one man. The perfect substitute! George quickly got in touch with Beckett, who agreed to translate *Play* into English. And so some time later I was presented with this short, extraordinary piece. I went home to read it. My first thought was: what the hell am I going to do with this? My second thought: what a pity the Lope de Vega play fell through. I had no idea what *Play meant*. On paper it seemed to be about a man, his wife and his mistress, all of whom were stuck in urns. Somehow I felt the story wasn't all that important. What mattered was the way the story was presented.

At this time I'd hardly heard of Samuel Beckett. All I knew about him was that Brenda Bruce had done a strange play of his, in which she was buried up to her neck in earth. And I hadn't even seen that, only photographs. I read *Play* again. My reaction was now: don't worry if you don't understand it, but do it fast.

Rosemary Harris and Robert Stephens naturally wanted to know more about the characters they played, the meaning of the piece, and why the man had left his wife, and what sort of pre-history the mistress had, etc. I somehow felt this wasn't what mattered. The excitement would come from the musicality of the piece, rather than the story-telling. I wasn't in the least bothered by the lack of characterisation or psychology. (Later, when I was to act in Beckett's *Not I*, I certainly didn't *characterise* Mouth as a seventy-year-old woman who kept saying she was sixty.)

None of the Beckett plays I did later had much to do with normal characterisation or psychology. To me, they have all been hooks on which to hang a specific human condition. They are not plays *about* anything, they represent emotional states of mind. In the case of *Play* it was the mind exploding in chaos and confusion – often expressed with humour. This I could understand only too well. In my own life I have often had rows going on in my head, yet when I've met the person I've wanted to row with, I've said nothing but: 'Oh well.' The rage has gone round and round in my head and repeated itself long after the confrontation. That seemed to me the point of *Play* – three people, all of them caught up in a loop of emotion, going over this emotion over and over again.

What struck me was that whereas most writers would have written a three- or four-act play about this given situation, Beckett wrote a short breathless one-act play, which does not seek to illustrate the subject, but simply presents it.

There is one line in *Play* where the Robert Stephens character says: '– pardon, no sense in this, oh, I know.' I feel that's Beckett responding to those critics and academics who are trying to analyse their own ideas about 'sense'.

I can no longer remember how George Devine fielded all the questions that were asked about *Play*. In any case, after we'd worked on the piece for about a week a new element was introduced. I walked into the rehearsal room one morning and found a man in a raincoat quietly sitting there: the author. His hair looked as though it had been crewcut by some back-street barber. He wore John Lennon-type glasses at the end of his nose. That made me notice his pale, pale blue eyes and his air of intense concentration.

Beckett said nothing. Sitting there in his straight-backed chair, he just listened to us. George would do all the talking at rehearsals: the two men seemed to have a perfect rapport going. Beckett did not talk to the actors directly, he seemed to have absolute faith in George. He also knew that George would listen to what he had to say – when there was something he wished to say.

From the beginning I had a sneaking feeling about where we had to get to with *Play*, which was to go very, very fast, almost incomprehensibly fast. I therefore wasn't particularly interested in an analysis of the play or of the characters. I didn't seem to need explanations, I just wanted to get on with my bit.

After rehearsal, George gave notes; then Beckett would speak to us in turn in our dressing-rooms. He sat down at my dressing-table. This was my first private encounter with a man with whom I would work more than anyone else during the next twenty-five years. For about ten minutes he said absolutely nothing, he just pored over the script. I said nothing either. Had I asked him many questions, I don't think we would ever have been able to enter into the relationship we had. I soon realised Beckett was a most gentle person, a *gentle man* – kind, quiet and private.

Silences never worried Beckett, and they never worried me. I felt myself drawn to this man, his quietness, his concentration. He would read the script, and I have a memory of him saying: 'Billie, will you bring your pencil over here and look at page 2, speech 4, fifth word. Will you make those three dots, two dots.'

Looking through the script of *Play* as I'm writing this, I can see that there is only one speech with dots, and I've crossed one dot out with my pencil. 'The strain . . .' it says, 'to get it moving, momentum coming.' Obediently I've crossed out one dot. If this sounds like Pseuds' Corner, I can't help it. I knew exactly what Beckett wanted. In my script I find I've drawn a little arch over the dot. I can't read or write music, but if I were a musician I'd have put a crotchet here instead of a quaver.

I understood him when he said: 'In the next line will you just cut out "and".' There are five words: 'Kill it and strain again.' I cut out 'and' so that it became: 'Kill it, strain again.' That changed the rhythm of the sentence, it made it more dynamic. In another sentence he would have me cut out every 'I am' and make them all into 'I'm'. He would also cut 'would not' and make it 'wouldn't', or vice versa. Such changes altered the rhythm of a sentence. I was never in any doubt as to what he meant.

Working on *Play* was not unlike conducting music or having a music lesson. As we went on, Robert Stephens and Rosemary Harris felt it was all going much too fast, and that the story was interesting. Wouldn't it be a good idea to let the audience in on that story? I remember telling myself: 'Just keep out of this, Whitelaw.' I said nothing, but had the feeling that the guts of the story would come out in the dynamic rhythms of Beckett's word-music.

I may not have realised it at the time, but these minute changes that Beckett wanted were an important part of our work-in-progress. In my script I find I've marked the actual *stresses* of syllables, to actually relish the syllables, to use them for rhythmic purposes. The first musical note I gave myself in *Play* is where the character says: 'Less confused, less confusing. At the same time I prefer this to . . . the other thing.' And over the dots before 'the other thing' I've written: 'Da, da, da,' which was the beat I tapped out in my head between the words. I tried to think of the words not as carrying specific meanings, but as *drum-beats* – a sort of Morse code, I suppose.

During none of these occasions did Beckett ever say anything personal to me. He would be correct and courteous, but he would never say: 'You were good,' or 'You haven't got that quite right.' Without anything being said, I could tell what he thought by the look on his face. I knew when I was moving towards something he wanted me to do. In fact, during all the years of working with Beckett, the only time he ever praised me directly was a whispered sentence after we'd done the television version of one of his plays, but I'll come to that later.

Out of our way of working came what I call 'the laugh button'. The mistress in *Play* has to sound a particular laugh. One day a maniacal, robot-like automatic laugh came out of my mouth, going right up and down the scale – what I called my laugh button.

While we were rehearsing with George Devine and the usually silent Beckett, all the time whipping up speed, I began to have a feeling that Kenneth Tynan and Laurence Olivier were probably getting wind of something rather strange going on in our rehearsal room. When they finally came unexpectedly to see a rehearsal, they were horrified. I thought to myself, OK, just do what you feel is right, do what Beckett and George want you to do, and get on with it.

After the run, Beckett, George, Olivier and Tynan went into a huddle without the cast. Tynan looked outraged. He said: 'It's going so fast nobody can understand a word of the dialogue. This is poetry and I can't hear any of it. It's beautiful poetry, I want to be able to hear the damn thing.'

Standing at a distance, I thought, Oh God, Ken, you've got it wrong, you've got it quite wrong.

As it was, Olivier agreed with Tynan. He insisted it must all go much slower. There followed a God-Almighty row but it didn't happen in front of the actors. I think Sam kept well out of it. The rows continued in the huts behind the Old Vic. Olivier and Tynan stuck to their guns: they wanted us to go slower, they wanted to hear the dialogue, they wanted to be told the story.

George now threatened to walk out. If *Play* wasn't done the way Beckett and he agreed it should be done, he wasn't going to do it at all. George and Beckett won, and we went on doing it the way they wanted us to do it.

After Tynan and Olivier had decided that we were all quite beyond the pale, we really started to build up speed, with George pointing to each one of us in turn.

As we built up more speed, we had to learn to articulate very, very clearly. I tried to gain a few seconds by not opening my mouth very wide, hoping that I could gain time that way, but I found that to be useless. The only way to speak quickly is to open your mouth *very* wide *and* to articulate very, very clearly.

Sometimes, after rehearsals, we'd all go and sit in the pub next door to the Old Vic. I felt very close to George; I also warmed to the rapport between George and Sam and Jocelyn Herbert, George's lady, who was to design so many Beckett productions. Jocelyn would never interfere directorially. She was simply encouraging, warm and kind. I've come to love her dearly. She always gave me the impression that what I was doing was good, and she could do this without actually saying very much at all.

At rehearsals Sam continued to say very little. What he had to say he said concisely: 'You can't go too fast for me,' was one note via George. 'Don't act out the story,' was another. Later, when we worked together on other plays, he would reiterate over and over again: 'No, no, that's too much colour, too much colour,' clearly a euphemism for 'Please don't act'.

The three urns that we were standing in were brown and slimy green. The make-up Jocelyn had devised was a mixture of oatmeal, surgical glue and jelly. The stage management mixed it like a pudding, a crazy breakfast in a bowl. We all made up in the same room and would take it in turn to spread great dollops of this stuff on to our faces. As the breakfast dried on our skins, we would then cover it with makeup – a pancake of white, sludgy brown and slimy green. We took care never to clog up the eyes; Beckett insisted that he wanted to see our eyes. Even in the later plays we did together he always said: 'Whatever else you do, I want to see your eyes.'

The extraordinary bonus about this makeup (and I don't know if Jocelyn knew this was going to happen) was that, as we began to speak our lines, bits of this makeup started to flake off our faces. *It looked as though we were disintegrating in front of the audience* – a quite startling effect in the theatre.

A vital element of the production of *Play*, quite original and typically Beckett, was that the characters were not allowed to speak until a light flashed on to them, prodding the characters into life. *Play* was not so much a trio as a quartet for three voices and a light. The light is probably the most important member of this quartet. You only spoke when the light was on you. When it went off, you shut up. I called the light 'the cow-poke'.

Tony Ferris, the stage manager who operated the lights, had a much worse job than any of us actors. Inevitably, during the run, the light would occasionally land on a face that didn't know its lines and Tony would have to sling his light around until one of us was able to kick off again.

Before making up, we would sit in our dressing-room with Tony Ferris, and do the play once or twice before going on. After that we would get dressed and made up for the play, going down on to the stage, muttering to ourselves like crazed mice.

In this production, and I think this was Beckett's original idea, the entire text of *Play* is repeated at the end, but as in a nightmare, the

second time round when the lines are repeated they are not necessarily spoken in the same order . . .

Looking back on this production after thirty years, I'm no longer
quite certain whether at the Vic we really did it differently the second
time round, or whether we said: 'Look, this is just impossible; we
can just about get through it twice, but *not* in a different order.'
Maybe we managed to do so, but possibly the first time the 'correct'
repetition was done was when Martin Esslin recorded the play for
BBC Radio.

Beckett didn't come backstage after the first night to talk to the
actors. As I was to learn later, he never attended his first nights. But
at least we knew the play had been done the way he wanted it, and
it turned out to be quite an astonishing evening.

I had no idea at this time that doing *Play*, and working with
Beckett, was to be a watershed in my life. It would certainly be quite
wrong for me to claim that appearing in *Play* changed my life. To
me, it was just another production in our repertory; a difficult play,
exciting and stimulating to do, but as soon as the curtain had come
down I was busy on something else.

It would also be idiotic to claim that working with Beckett turned
me overnight into a single-minded Beckett convert. I didn't even
bother to read anything else he had written, but then I'm afraid it's
a flaw in my character that I only tend to read plays that I've been
asked to act in.

Play had a certain success, it caused much curiosity and comment,
but I don't remember ever sitting down to read the notices. If reviews
are around, I'll certainly pick them up to read them, but I never rush
out to get the papers after the first night, and it didn't occur to me
to do so after *Play*. I feel that if the reviews are bad I don't want to
know them, and if they're good someone is bound to tell me.

Certainly neither Tynan nor Olivier came round afterwards to say:
'You were right all the time.'

Play opened on April 7th, 1964 and stayed in the repertory for
several months. I needed to keep up a regime of mouth and tongue
exercises to keep my face muscles supple.

Often during performances of *Play* we all got the shakes. I needed
somewhere for the tension to go. Usually on stage you're moving
your arms and legs about – that gets rid of some of the tension. In
Play, confined as we were to our jars, there was nowhere to move.
Jocelyn had put a metal rod inside each urn and connected all the
urns together to give us something to grip. I always knew when one
of us had 'gone'. Suddenly the urns would start to shake and I'd

think, Hello, Bob's off. Probably it wasn't him at all, but me. Anyway, whoever it was, the movement had a knock-on effect and would ripple right the way through the urns so that by the end of it we'd all be shaking. It was a relief when the curtain came down and we could get out and stretch. Yet I always looked forward to the next performance of *Play*; I found it both frightening and exciting.

With *Play* I gained a new confidence. It was the first time that I felt totally in harmony with the director, designer and writer. Far from feeling inadequate because I hadn't been properly trained, here this almost became a plus for me. We were working with a totally new set of rules, and this set I liked. I was not afraid of breaking these rules, because *nobody* knew what they were.

For the first time I felt part of the creative process, I knew I had something to offer. The nearest I'd ever come to that feeling before was leaping about at Ormesby Hall with Ewan MacColl and Rosalie Williams in my Theatre Workshop days. With *Play* I felt that whatever it was I had to offer was actually wanted.

When *Play* was over, new problems began for me at the NT. Because of Joan Littlewood's earlier influence I didn't think I could naturally fit into a classical structure. Like many actors before me, I constantly felt that every other actor in the company was better equipped for the job than I was. I also felt that some directors and colleagues at the National didn't think I was very good. I certainly had that feeling in *The Dutch Courtesan* which was the next thing I had to do. I suspected people were sitting in their little huts asking: 'What in God's name did we ask that Billie Whitelaw to come into this company for?'

Only in *Play*, as early as the read-through, did I feel we were all equal. And the production worked, which is more than I can say for *The Dutch Courtesan*. I was not very happy in this 'rediscovered' John Marston play. Most of it had to be spoken in a Dutch accent. In my insecurity I'd gone to the trouble of traipsing to the Dutch Embassy, to try and find out exactly what a Dutch accent sounded like. I was most put out when the critic Milton Shulman wrote in the *Evening Standard* that my Dutch courtesan sounded like a Welsh au pair who'd found her way to the Old Vic via Calcutta!

The Dutch Courtesan remained my one disaster at the National. I worked quite happily as Maggie in *Hobson's Choice*, and as Avonia Bunn in *Trelawney of the 'Wells'*. As for *Othello*, much more about that later.

I would not have missed working at the Old Vic for the world, but I was still not fully attuned to a normal company way of working.

As ever, I was becoming aware of the two opposing sides of my character. On the one hand I was nervous and frightened, on the other I tended to be very outspoken, what was then called 'bolshy'.

The company sometimes held meetings to discuss current problems. Michael Redgrave was not well and having a difficult time with *The Master Builder*, in which he played opposite Joan Plowright and later Maggie Smith. This led to a discussion among the actors and directors about certain things not being good enough, and about the problem of filling enough seats. I suddenly jumped to my feet, proclaiming that a National Theatre was not there to pander to commercial thinking, that things should be done for their own sake, even if it meant playing to empty houses. I felt that we should have the right to fail – surely that was the whole point of having a National Theatre.

At the Old Vic I was beginning to get the feeling that it was thought to be OK to fail, but fail only a little bit, not too much.

On another occasion I felt a great injustice had been done in the case of a sacked dresser. I got on my hind legs, and wanted to know why this had been allowed to happen. Maggie Smith would get the giggles during such meetings and say things like: 'Well, dear, nothing's perfect.' But I wouldn't let the matter rest. I called up the production manager. 'What the hell is this?' I demanded to know. 'Why have we got rid of our best dresser?' When it was suggested to me that the woman 'caused trouble', I said: 'Good for her.'

By now I think I was labelled 'D' for 'difficult'. Quite right too. I was, and still am. But I don't think anybody at the Vic wanted a young member of the company doing a 'Madame Defarge' act, waving a flag about and biting the hand that fed her.

Gradually I became a bit of an outsider. Then, as now, I thought, if I'm fired it won't be the end of the world.

I did think for a while that I was going to fit in at the Old Vic. I certainly wanted to. Then it began to dawn on me that there was a sort of power struggle going on at the theatre as to who would be the force behind Olivier's throne, and that had nothing to do with me. I was quite naive of course, and still full of romantic theatrical notions from my Theatre Workshop days. I began to get the feeling that my time at the National Theatre might well end in tears.

My personal life at this time was not happy. By now I was past my twenties. Peter and I had been married for over ten years. The initial phase – Peter's feeling that he had to knock me into some kind of shape – had long passed. If I've given the impression that our marriage was one where I was being constantly subjected to his rages, that would be quite wrong. But we were both far from happy. I thought of the marriage as some sort of 'arrangement', and floundered on, having a series of messy affairs, getting into various kinds of emotional trouble. When we were together, we were a couple of sorts, but when we were separated by work we had quite independent lives.

Professionally, Peter and I were both doing quite well; he was certainly doing more good work than before. Yet he may have felt that he should have been doing better. We had moved to Datchet, a pretty village on the Thames near Windsor, and Peter's mate Donald Pleasence, who had lived with us for many years, now moved to a house next door with his family.

I had always wanted children. For whatever reason, Peter and I did not have any. I went to see gynaecologists and all kinds of doctors. They all agreed that there was no medical reason for this state of affairs. I was longing for one of those doctors to tell me: 'The reason you're not conceiving is because . . .' and then put everything right. Nothing of the kind happened.

Though my career continued to go well, and I was never out of work, gradually I sank into a sort of hopelessness. My centre was empty, and I always seemed to be in a highly strung state.

In 1961, Tony Richardson had cast me opposite Robert Shaw in *The Changeling* at the Royal Court. On the way to my first rehearsal, I began to feel unwell. There was a very fast gramophone record going round and round in my head and I couldn't stop it. I made a detour to the surgery of an old doctor called Smithy, who was a friend of Donald's current wife Joey. He simply took the script out of my hand and said: 'You're not going to any rehearsal. Give me the name of your director and where you're rehearsing and I'll make a phone call.'

Tony Richardson never forgave me. Neither he nor anyone else (including me) would believe I was really ill. I suppose I was having a sort of breakdown. Mary Ure took over the part; shortly afterwards she left John Osborne and married Robert Shaw.

Smithy took a lot of trouble with me. After sending me straight back to bed, he told me I must rest. He also told me: 'You'll never have Peter's baby, because although you want a baby you don't want his.'

I've always known that love can exist on many levels simultaneously, each one valid in its own way. When I met my second husband I knew right away that he would be the father of any children I might have. Peter had been miscast by me as a father-figure. By this time I had also met a man I'll call 'Y', with whom I fell in love, but whom it would have been disastrous to marry, even had we both been free, which we weren't. This relationship was simply not meant for marriage, yet I would willingly have become Y's mistress and borne him children. I like to think of my feelings for Y (who is still very much alive) as an almost mystic relationship. Perhaps that's what I felt I needed.

I knew that if I was in any kind of distress, even if there had been no contact between us for six months or more, the telephone would ring and it would be Y. Invariably the phone did ring. There seemed to be some deep, undefinable connection between us. Even now, in my mind he will always remain a close friend, although I doubt if I will ever see him again.

I must have realised at this time that the main person in my childless life was no longer my husband. As the relationship with Y became ever more important to me, my feelings towards Peter changed. Soon my entire existence began to revolve around this other man, whom I hardly ever saw. This untenable situation probably contributed to my breakdown. Though on a day-to-day level Peter and I managed to get on quite well, our relationship was conducted with a thick pane of glass between us. I was simply losing touch with the realities of life, a mild form of madness I suppose.

My mother and stepfather were aware of my inner turmoil. He suggested that I went into an order of Benedictine nuns in Warwickshire, which I did. The nuns understood I wanted to sort my life out and that I had no idea how to do it. Out of the blue, Y turned up one day and the nuns let him into the kitchen. We just talked and I felt much better for seeing him.

I only spent a few weeks at the nunnery, but something did come out of it. I realised I needed time on my own. I worked up the nerve to say to Peter: 'Look, I'm not happy, I need to step back and think. Can we live apart for six months?' I had realised I was very fond of Peter, but wanted him to be my brother, not my husband. Peter seemed to be shattered by my request for a trial separation. Whatever I may have written about him, I think he did love me, as I loved him, but in the wrong way.

When I had been working at the Saville Theatre in *Progress to the Park* in 1961, Peter often came round to the stage door or we'd meet in the pub. I could tell he, too, was unhappy. I remember him saying:

'I don't seem to be able to live with you or without you. I don't know what to do.'

I still had that recurring feeling of emptiness, when the call came in 1963 from the National Theatre. The feeling engendered by the production of *Play* gave me back my confidence that I did have an emotional centre – if I could find it.

Like so many unhappy actors before me, I now decided to concentrate on my work, and to pour all my energies into my profession. I had been *promising* for too long – a promising eleven-year-old at the BBC; a promising fourteen-year-old for Joan Littlewood; a promising actress on television. When I started work at the National Theatre I became aware that, as a thirty-year-old, I was still promising, and this muddled, mixed-up creature was now going to have to get up on her two feet and be something more than promising at last.

On the Old Vic stage I would now have to slug it out with people of the calibre of Olivier and Max Adrian. With Beckett and George Devine, indeed, with the production of *Play*, I found myself in a theatrical situation that mirrored the state of my own personality. I realised that my emptiness was something I could utilise. My own inertness was of creative use and I used it.

Since then I've often said that it was never difficult for me to understand what Beckett wrote, because it always seemed to me about *me*. Doing *Play* made me feel more complete. Unconsciously I used the work as a therapy, not that I could have expressed any such thoughts at the time. But as we worked on *Play*, it began to mean more and more to me; others may have found it unintelligible.

Though George Devine and Beckett demanded a high degree of precision of working, I felt far less restricted working on this piece than I had done before. I began to sense within myself a growing feeling of freedom. I managed to touch that little flame in my centre. Actors are very lucky if they can find that more than once or twice in a lifetime. At this point I had no idea that I would ever do another Beckett play, but I was grateful to the man for giving me a certain feeling: that *Play* wasn't *finished* – until we'd worked on it. I felt part of that creativity, part of his work-in-progress.

If my first marriage was what my mother had called a 'hole-in-the-corner affair', my divorce after thirteen years can only be described as a hobnailed boot affair. To quote the politician Francis Pym, it was 'not so much the event itself, but the manner of the event' that gave me cause to grieve.

While working for the National Theatre in Chichester, I remember saying to my colleague Joyce Redman: 'I've come to the end of a long dark tunnel. After ten years I now know what to do. I think I could spend the rest of my life with Peter.'

I had worked my way through all the crises. I knew the time had come either to fish or cut the rod. I'd decided to fish and stay with Peter. When I was rehearsing in Chichester he would come down every weekend.

'We seem to be getting on much better when we just meet at weekends,' he told me. And so we did.

Yet within a few months of making my decision to stay with Peter, we were divorced. The end was very sudden. I'd been on holiday with Sheila Reid and a couple of girls from the company. Peter hadn't wanted to come along. (I was soon to realise why.) When I got back I had to start rehearsing with Laurence Olivier in *Othello*, having taken over the part of Desdemona from Maggie Smith.

One day in 1964 Peter came home and said: 'I'm in terrible trouble, I've got to talk to you.'

I looked at him and thought, oh well, I think I know what this is. You've either got somebody in the family way (I can deal with that), or you've got VD and passed it on to me (I can deal with that too). I poured him a Scotch and said: 'Well, you'd better sit down and tell me all about it.'

He said: 'I think I may be in love with somebody else.'

That was the one thing I felt I couldn't deal with. So I poured myself out a large gin and told him: 'Perhaps you'd better go and find out whether you are or not.'

There now came a strange period when Peter would spend some time with the new lady in his life and the rest with me. I was still doing his washing. I finally told him: 'Look, Peter, I think the time has come for you to decide who's going to do your laundry.' So Peter took his washing away from me, and that was the end of our marriage.

I was now fancy-free and (so my husband Robert tells me, judging by photographs of me at the time) looking better than I'd ever done in my life. In fact I was in a state of shock and uncertainty. I felt utterly rootless.

Fortunately, I'd found a few good mates in the company, and some who were indeed more than friends, who helped to get me through this period.

So here I was, unmarried and rudderless, an extremely silly, impressionable and immature young woman.

Those grey days came back to me several decades later, on a cold February morning in 1995, when I went to Donald Pleasence's funeral in Putney Vale. The night before I had spoken to Angela, Donald's eldest daughter, and with Jean, both daughters of Donald's first marriage. I had known them since 1952. This was going to be a difficult day for both of them. We all seemed to be going into a strange time-warp. Donald had led several lives, he had had many wives and many children.

I also knew that Peter Vaughan would be at the funeral. Angela had asked him, as Donald's oldest friend, to say a few words. I have to admit I was not looking forward to this reunion either. I didn't know what on earth I would say to Peter after all this time. We found ourselves facing each other while waiting in an ante-room at the Crematorium. I heard myself say: 'I think we can hug each other now, Pete, don't you?' He said: 'Yes, I do.' And we embraced with genuine warmth and affection. I was glad.

It was a strange day and a strange feeling: we had gone back – all of us – about forty years, and it was as if nothing had happened in between. This was an important day for me: not only Donald but a lot of old ghosts and bad feelings had been laid to rest.

Intermission One:
Laurence Olivier

The first thing I noticed about Olivier, when I met him face-to-face, was the fact that in the street I wouldn't have noticed him at all. Offstage Olivier looked as if he might have worked in a bank. That would be the first impression: that he didn't make an impression. Far from appearing to be our greatest leading actor and actor-manager, the director of the National Theatre, a glittering film star, the head of our profession, you'd walk straight past him.

He looked very much an ordinary middle-aged man, neither dynamic nor self-consciously actorish – except that he had an unmistakable springy walk, but that would be unmistakable only for those who knew him. At Chichester, when he came out of the stage door, crowds would often be standing there, waiting to see him, and he would be out and gone. People hadn't recognised him.

Had you been interviewing him for a job, you wouldn't have thought that this was the man who towered above his fellow creatures; you'd never mistake him for a star. Perhaps it was different when he was younger, but certainly when I first got to know him as my boss it was his ordinariness that impressed me.

Once I was a member of his company, I became aware that, though he worked all of us very hard, he would never ask us to do more than he did himself.

I was appearing in both National Theatre companies, at Chichester and the Old Vic. This meant I was constantly on the move. One day Olivier called me into his dressing-room.

'Darling girl,' he said. 'Look, we have a problem here, you've got a foot in both companies, haven't you? You're really going to have to work very hard indeed.'

As a co-worker as well as a boss, he was considerate in a professional, matter-of-fact way. As a boss he was also very concerned about *fitness*. He was anxious that we all ate properly. He made sure there was always plenty of fruit and cheese and milk and salad in the canteen. He didn't want us to stuff ourselves with biscuits, chips and half-pints of beer next door. He would say: 'You have to keep your strength up, you have to eat well, you can't act without energy, and you must get plenty of rest when you can.'

When he wanted something of you, he could be a great charmer. He knew well how to charm out of you whatever he wanted. Actors would sometimes come out of his office, saying: 'My God, isn't he marvellous, he's so concerned about me.' And they'd be clutching their National Insurance cards. One would have to point out: 'But you do realise, don't you, you've just been fired?'

He would have put it so charmingly, that no one who was asked to leave the company ever felt they'd been sacked.

We called him Larry; he didn't like being called 'Sir'. I found that difficult, as I was in such awe of him. I think Frank Finlay also called him 'Sir'.

Olivier rehearsed in trousers, braces and open-necked shirt. He certainly didn't prance around in polo-neck sweaters and designer jeans. In rehearsal he looked more like a stage manager than an actor. Yet he inspired hero-worship and genuine professional admiration in all of us.

Night after night, during *Othello*, I'd see a certain spear-carrier called Anthony Hopkins sitting in the wings watching his every word, gesture and movement. When I saw Tony like that I often thought, one day you're going to play this role yourself. And indeed he did.

Robert Stephens, our leading man, was hugely influenced by Larry on every level, professional and personal. Bob was about to get married to Maggie Smith; Joan Plowright was married to Olivier. Soon she left the NT to look after Olivier and their children. When he became ill she gave up work altogether to look after him. I was (and am) full of admiration for her. Now Joan's career is having a real renaissance, both here and in Hollywood. She has certainly earned it.

Othello was the biggest smash hit the National ever had. Then Maggie had to go off to do a movie with Rex Harrison. Possibly out of desperation, Olivier decided to let me take over. When I went to see the production, I actually had doubts about his own performance. What I saw was technically brilliant, but I could find no real emotional involvement. That being my first impression, I hoped to correct it the following night. To my astonishment what I saw was *exactly what I'd seen the night before*. Later, when I came to play Desdemona with him, I witnessed three or four performances in which Olivier was unforgettable, but only a handful of people ever saw him at his very best.

When he asked me to play Desdemona, I nearly died. I think originally Olivier was hoping Rosemary Harris would come back and play the part, which she had done before. (I had only played the tarty Bianca, for Tony Richardson on TV.) Olivier was very fond of Rosemary. She was in the company when I first arrived, but then went back to America. Olivier may have asked her if she would come back to play Desdemona, but it obviously didn't work out. So I jumped into the breach.

I hadn't had any classical training at all. I had seen very little Shakespeare, let alone acted in it. I'd done nothing in the theatre to prepare me for a leading Shakespearian part, and opposite Olivier at that! Maggie had been a big success as Desdemona. For me to play the part, opposite this rock of Gibraltar, whom I'd never worked with before, who had not even directed me at the National, left me petrified. Moreover, all the others had had three months of rehearsal. I had three weeks.

When Olivier spoke to me in his inner sanctum, I just stumbled and stuttered.

'Look,' I said, 'I don't think I can do this, I've never done any Shakespeare.'

He put his arm round my shoulder: 'Darling girl, don't you worry, you'll be quite all right. Meet me here at 5.30 tonight, after rehearsals.'

Shaking a little, I went back at 5.30. Olivier took his time with me, patiently laying down Jocelyn Herbert's many costume designs for Desdemona, until they covered the entire floor. Then he said: 'Now, darling girl, I want you to go round and round these costumes and look at them carefully.'

That gave me an insight into the way he tackled his own roles. He always claimed that once you knew what you were going to look like, seventy-five percent of your work was done. Then he said: 'Now, don't be a silly girl, go home and learn your lines.'

So I went home and started to learn the lines.

About this time, Noël Coward was to be seen around the Old Vic quite a lot. He was preparing to direct *Hay Fever*. I greatly enjoyed watching the great man go about his work. In his way Noël Coward seemed to me unexpectedly humble. I'd expected something totally different. Although I never worked with him myself, Maggie and I shared a dressing-room, and after the first night of *Hay Fever* I helped Noël Coward open bottles of champagne and pour out the drinks. I liked him enormously, which astonished me, since when I first came down from the North, people like Noël Coward and Terence Rattigan were high on the list of those who, in our arrogance, ignorance and youthful hubris, we wanted to sweep into the Thames. How wrong we were! As I write this, many of my revolutionary contemporaries are already long forgotten and there these despised 'old hat' people still are – immortals.

John Dexter rehearsed me in *Othello* with Olivier's understudy. I've already said that John and I always got on well. Like most good directors, he liked to experiment. He'd say: 'Now play this scene as though you're angry.' Then: 'Now forget that and play it as if you were in love.' Then: 'Now play it as if you're full of envy and hatred.' John enjoyed that way of working and so did I. It took all the tension out of the ordeal.

John always made me feel that he had some sort of respect for me. He was a very dynamic director, an open homosexual when homosexuality was still a crime in this country. He was undoubtedly sadistic. He went to jail for his sins, which seems unthinkable now. I found in him a raw sexual magnetism which had nothing to do with gender. One day, as we were walking down a Soho street, he suddenly turned to me and said offhandedly: 'Whitelaw, if you were a fella, I'd fuck the arse off you.'

And I said: 'Dexter, if I was a fella, I'd let you.'

I think John respected me because he recognised that whatever else I am not, I am certainly a hard worker. Albert Finney once said to me: 'I'll say this for you, Bill, you don't just take the money and run.' I gladly admit to that. On some things I work too hard and then I tend to become obsessive.

I had to work hard on Desdemona, because there was such a short rehearsal period. I felt I had to start at the bottom of the class. Once, during our dress rehearsal, Desdemona waltzes on, fanning her face, while asking Emilia where she has lost her handkerchief. Suddenly a voice roared from the back: 'You're carrying that fan like a fucking frying pan!'

It was John Dexter. I took not the slightest notice. That evening I scoured Chichester for the biggest, heaviest frying pan I could find. At the next rehearsal I came on in my wonderful white gown, waving my enormous frying pan. It practically broke my wrist. Typically, John let me play the entire scene with my frying pan. Equally typically, he enjoyed the fact that it was much too heavy to carry for a whole scene. At the end of rehearsals I heard him calling out: *'Touché!'*

I know John had a temperament that could destroy people, but for some reason he never tried to do it to me.

Olivier had worked on his part for about ten years. There are stories of the very first rehearsal, when everyone was sitting around rather nervously with their copies of *Othello*, mumbling and muttering their way through their parts. When Olivier spoke, he gave a fully finished performance. Everyone was felled. I wasn't there, so I can't vouch for the truth of this.

Olivier came to rehearsals once or twice a week to rehearse our scenes together. Quite rightly, I had to fit in with him, though there were certain things I would have preferred to do differently. With a man like that, though, you knew better than to argue. Not only as a spectator, but also as an actress, I found him technically extraordinary. It was an awesome experience to be on the same stage with him, and sometimes I found it frightening.

In one scene, Othello ends up striking Desdemona. I was standing behind him; he had thrown himself on the floor in a fit. Every now and again he'd throw those white eyes back to look at Desdemona. I always had the feeling he was throwing his eyes back in order to see exactly where I was standing.

I could never quite get away from thinking that, while giving this towering performance, he was also taking notes. Which indeed he was.

I never felt that he was genuinely immersed in his role. He was technically so polished that his performance shone like a diamond. Yet I couldn't help thinking that he wasn't personally involved. I sometimes noted from the glare in his eye, which he flashed at me, that perhaps I was standing in the wrong place, that I should come a bit farther downstage, or move towards him a bit more quickly.

He certainly encouraged me, yet no matter what I did or did not do, he was going to give His Performance. Understandably, he didn't want me to foul up what he'd worked on for so long.

When I first came on as Desdemona, which Maggie had done brilliantly, I was so nervous my voice trembled. As the play went on, I became better. On reflection I think that had you put Maggie's performance and mine together into a bottle and shaken up the contents, you would have got a pretty good Desdemona.

At this time I was going through a very rocky time privately. I felt that on certain emotional things, I could home in at a deeper level than Maggie.

My own line as Desdemona was simple and direct, as my acting lines usually are. I just played the part of a young girl who is hopelessly in love, who can see no wrong in this man, whatever he did. Nor would it have entered her head that he didn't love her as much as she loved him. For me, love makes Desdemona blind.

My first night of *Othello* was in Chichester. I realise now that I was using a form of self-hypnosis on myself. I've often done this, throwing around me a net of artificial calm, not allowing anyone to break into it. When I went up to the side of the stage before Olivier made his entrance, I stood close to him and put out my hand. He took hold of it, and nothing was said.

After the first scene, in which my voice was still quivering, I managed to get into the part's basic emotion, with which I could fully identify. I think Olivier would have preferred me to be technically a bit sharper, but it worked out all right.

I used to tell myself that as long as she stood in the right places and didn't wriggle around too much, as long as she didn't get in his light or in his way, the cat could have gone on to play Desdemona: Olivier wouldn't have minded.

Olivier was blacked up to the nines, of course. Only the part covered by his jock-strap wasn't. It took him about four hours to get himself buffed up. Jack, his dresser, put rich browny-black pancake on to his body and buffed him up with silk so that he really *shone*. Olivier was a master of makeup and he really looked magnificent as Othello. He had quite thin lips, but here he managed to give himself a large negroid mouth.

At the time, he struck me as a man getting on in years. Actually he was only fifty-seven. I thought, well for an old man you haven't got a half bad body. Two or three times a week he went to the gym. Every day he had voice lessons before he went on stage. He tried to make himself physically absolutely impregnable.

To make my own skin look 'as white as alabaster' as the Bard says, I had alabaster makeup all over my body. Once, as I knelt at his feet, I put my hand on his knee. He glared down at me: there was a white mark on his black knee! Some of my white alabaster had come off on his beautiful shiny black makeup. I felt like a naughty girl at school.

He often gave me detailed notes. He had grave doubts about the way actors from the North spoke, and I sometimes felt he wanted me to speak as if I had a plum in my mouth, the way of speaking that we – this new brigade of actors who had come down from the provinces – disliked so much. Frank Finlay, an old colleague of mine, had a rocky start with his Iago, and was frequently thought to be inaudible. This may not have been his fault. In the film version he certainly came into his own. Olivier once told me: 'All you people from the North, and Joanie has the same problem, you simply don't know how to bring your voice forward enough.' So he had me dropping my chin down. I began to feel I was talking like a monkey.

There's no time to mess about when you're in a company. I worked hard playing several parts, rehearsing others, juggling many plates in the air, travelling from one theatre to the next. After *Play*, I was doing *The Dutch Courtesan* and *Trelawney of the 'Wells'* and getting ready to do *Hobson's Choice*. I hoped Olivier would be pleased when the *Evening Standard* Awards came up, and I was nominated for Desdemona, along with Peggy Ashcroft's Margaret in *The Wars of the Roses*.

Olivier had found out that my private life was a mess, but I never talked to him about it. There was one performance on Christmas Eve which was torture for me. Peter was out in front, sitting there with his new lady friend. Afterwards he came round to my crowded dressing-room, and asked if I'd like to have a meal with them. I thought, you've got to be joking, I'm not going to sit there and have dinner with your mistress.

Larry waited for me to be alone. Then he came in and asked: 'Are you all right?'

I said: 'Yes, yes,' but he obviously knew something was wrong. He could see I was distressed, and invited me to come and spend Christmas with him and Joan. I was moved by his invitation, but didn't accept it. I went home, got up at five o'clock next morning and drove up to Bradford for Christmas Day. On Boxing Day I drove back for the next performance.

In the late summer of 1965 we were invited to go to Berlin and the Soviet Union. It was the first time the National Theatre had been abroad, a great occasion for us. We were allowed to play in the theatre inside the Kremlin. Before we left England, Albert Finney gave us some roubles and said, 'Meet you in Red Square for a coffee.'

In Berlin we had a big success. The people from the Berliner Ensemble, in what was then East Berlin, invited us to come to a rehearsal. We went through Checkpoint Charlie and one of Brecht's wives, the actress Helene Weigel, came to meet us. We went in a bus to watch a rehearsal, which I've never forgotten. It was so detailed, so incredibly *serious*. A very different atmosphere from what I was used to.

Though we were fêted and wined and dined in both Berlins, I remember I was desperately unhappy at the time, drinking far too much after the show, crying a lot, and breaking out in a rash all over my back.

Somewhere en route, we had to change planes. However the flight from Copenhagen to Moscow had been over-booked and we were told there was not room for us all. Olivier had already boarded the plane, but four of the actors were going to be left standing on the tarmac. Suddenly we saw Olivier get up from his seat and march off the plane. 'I'm not leaving my actors behind,' he said. It was very impressive behaviour. We got the seats we wanted.

The start of our time in Moscow was chaotic. The organisers had forgotten that Moscow in the middle of September can be boiling hot. All the ladies in the cast of the National Theatre had been sponsored to wear British Wool. We were sweltering! Also the sets and costumes had gone ahead of us by road and were found dumped outside the theatre, sopping wet.

Backstage, the theatre looked like a Sainsbury warehouse, which amazed me. I had thought it would be something like the Bolshoi. In fact, with one exception, our theatre had no wash-basins in the dressing-rooms. But I had a lovely dresser called Anya. I spoke Russian the way I still tend to speak foreign languages: I simply speak English with an assortment of foreign words thrown in and what I imagine to be the right foreign accent. In Russia I just added 'ski' on to everything. Somehow I made myself understood.

Laurence Olivier had the only available hand-basin because he was blacked up. He then asked for a piano in his dressing-room, because he had dropped his voice by about two or three octaves for the role, and needed a piano to make his voice hit the right pitch. What impressed us all was the fact that he had lowered his voice way beyond its natural range to play Othello, yet he retained the whole variety of vocal colours he needed for his role.

In the chaos, it soon became apparent that there was no time for a proper run-through. Poor Diana Boddington, our stage director, rushed around, demanding coffee: she had mistakenly taken two sleeping pills instead of two pep pills!

Quite exhausted, Olivier called us all together to give us a pep-talk.

'We'll get through this,' he told us. 'Just remember that we've all got to stick together.'

And we did get through it. On our first night the roof went off that theatre: Olivier was staggering. It was actually his fatigue, allied to his brilliant technique, that made him so moving. He was able to show what in my view had always been missing: Othello's vulnerability. He hadn't been able to go to the gym, he was tired, he had to do without all his usual ritualistic preparations before going on.

Clearly he had to draw on all his reserves. I no longer felt I was on stage with the rock of Gibraltar. He was too busy holding himself together to wonder whether I was pronouncing my words correctly or standing in exactly the right place.

That night Brezhnev was out in front, Gromyko was there, plus the whole Politburo. They had all come through a side door, which led directly to the Kremlin.

Our curtain call was the most extraordinary moment I had ever experienced up to then. Everyone was standing up, cheering and shouting. We were amazed. We took several curtain calls, then stood back to let Olivier go on alone. We wanted to leave the stage to him, but he kept calling me back: 'Come along, I can't keep going on stage by myself.'

The calls went on for twenty-five minutes, the length of an entire Act. I remember a little Jewish gentleman, his face all lit up. (He was out front every night, always alone.) The whole audience came towards the stage and this little Jewish man held both his arms out to us. It moved me terribly. People were throwing flowers, singly and in bunches. I was picking them up or ducking them.

Anya, my dresser, was crying; I was in tears, too, by this time. Olivier came off, asking: 'What do I do? I can't go on doing this all night.'

The manager of the theatre told him: 'They're not going to let you go unless you get changed.'

Olivier put on a dressing-gown and came on, this time holding a glass of brandy, to thank the audience.

Meanwhile I kept on getting dressed and undressed. Diana Boddington came rushing into the dressing-room to say I was wanted back on the stage. I would tell Anya: 'Quickski, back into my dress.'

At the end of *Othello* I looked like Grock the clown; all Olivier's black gunge had come off on my alabaster.

Later that night, we were greeted by our Minister of Arts, Jennie Lee, Aneurin Bevan's wife. Brezhnev sent round some sweeties for me and a book signed by him.

Typical actress! All political outrage at what the Russian people might be suffering had melted away with the applause. The biggest success I've ever been involved in happened behind the Iron Curtain – inside the Kremlin!

The moon shone on golden domes. It was like a dream – endless applause in a land of fantasy.

I remember thinking, now I know why I'm in the theatre. There's no other job in the world that could give you this feeling.

Though I knew I was really only muscling in on Olivier's huge success, I was a part of that evening – and it was magical.

Now, as I think of the state of the erstwhile Soviet Union, at the fate of its people, I have very mixed feelings about my state of elation. Would I have acted or felt differently, I often ask myself, if that 'success' had happened to me in pre-war Berlin, and I'd been fêted by Hitler and Goebbels and his henchmen?

A few months after that evening of blinding success, I was called into Olivier's office. 'Darling girl, do sit down,' he greeted me. Then he said: 'I think we'll have to let you go. We simply have nothing suitable to offer you, nothing that's worthy of you. I think you should now extend your career and expand your talent. It's been so marvellous working with you.'

And, like so many before me, I thought, what a wonderful man, what a marvellous boss, he really cares about me and my career.

I walked out, clutching my National Insurance card. I'd been fired.

Although I was a little sad to leave the NT, I could see that there was nothing for me to play in the next two seasons. It certainly didn't strike me as a great tragedy. I've got other things to do with my life, I thought.

Olivier sent me champagne and many lovely letters, and while still with the company, I eventually did spend some time with him and Joanie in Brighton. I gave him a lift there, driving him all the way down in second gear, because I was terrified of crashing the car and injuring the great man. Finally he said: 'I do think we'd get on better if you changed gear, so we can go a bit faster.'

Joan was in the kitchen, dressed in shorts, making sandwiches. I didn't want to stay the night because I'm not very good at waking up in other people's houses. I'd always rather wake up under my own roof.

A year or so later, when I was about six months pregnant with

Matthew, I had a letter from Olivier, followed up by a phone call, asking me to come back to the National: 'Darling girl, we really can't let you go,' he said. 'We do need you. Please come back and play Desdemona.'

What had happened was that both Maggie Smith and I were pregnant. Poor Larry, both his Desdemonas were expecting *and* unmarried, and our babies were due in the same week. If such a story happened now, it would be plastered all over the tabloids. Either because in those days newspapers were more discreet, or perhaps reporters were not very resourceful, the story never got out: *Othello*, the National Theatre's greatest success, had to come off – not because it wasn't doing business, but because Sir Laurence's Desdemonas were both in the pudding club.

I wrote Larry a letter saying: 'Darling Larry, thank you so much for asking me back to the National. I would love to come back, but am involved with a cultural project which is going to take me up until August and September. If you still need a Desdemona then, I'd love to come back.'

Christopher, Maggie's baby, was born on June 7th, 1967, and Matthew, my son, on June 12th. Robert Stephens by this time had married Maggie. I sent Maggie a telegram saying: 'Snap!' and got a telegram back saying: 'What *have* you done?'

I was working in Toronto shortly afterwards, on a television version of *Dr Jekyll and Mr Hyde* with Jack Palance, and had my seven-week-old baby with me. We were visiting Expo '67 in Montreal when suddenly I saw a poster of the National Theatre. They were coming to play in Montreal. I left a note for Larry at the stage door, saying: 'What a small world! By the way, my cultural project is now seven weeks old and weighs eleven pounds. Much love.'

Olivier's great ambition was to lead his National Theatre into the new building on the South Bank, but it was never to be. I felt very sad for him. I knew it was something he wanted to do very much.

Apart from occasionally bumping into him at a stage door, I never saw Olivier again – until many, many years later, shortly before he died. Joanie and I had been working together on *The Dressmaker*, a film based on Beryl Bainbridge's novel. Joan asked me round to a Christmas party at their house in Chelsea. She made sure that even though Larry was now a sick man, he always had some sort of social life going on around him.

Robert and I went to that party. When I saw Larry sitting on the sofa at the far end of the full room, I hurried over and knelt beside him. I said: 'We know each other from a long time ago. I was one of your Desdemonas.'

And he said: 'Ah yes, dear girl, ah yes.'

I suspect he hadn't the vaguest idea who I was. And a short time after that he was dead.

4

'Not I'

Nearly ten years went by before Beckett and I worked together again. But the woman who picked up the thin script of *Not I* that dropped on to the doormat, in the late autumn of 1972, was not the same actress or indeed the same person who had puzzled over the script of *Play*.

I had in the meantime become 'successful', i.e. in my 'drawing-room' a clutch of awards stood on a broad shelf. I had even enjoyed a spell of being a 'film star', working with people like Marcello Mastroianni, Donald Sutherland and Gene Wilder, and some high-level Hollywood directors. My professional life was going well. I have an image of myself at this time airily tearing up invitations to glamorous parties. I had a nanny, a chauffeur and a gardener. My life was beginning to be lived in a way that successful actresses were supposed to live. My mother was pleased with me.

I had moved from Datchet to a large house in Camden Square, London NW1, and was living with the writer Robert Muller. Robert had written two television plays for me, the first of seven. He was also the father of my son, Matthew, whose birth had been my greatest joy and changed my life completely.

My commitment to another man so soon after the end of a not very happy marriage needs some explanation. I have to go back to the earliest days of my career, my squeaky blonde starlet days, when I did a couple of TV comedy series with the comedian Bob Monkhouse.

Throughout the Sixties I stayed friends with Bob and his wife Elizabeth, a lively Irish girl with whom I got on particularly well. Liz and I often met for meals and once went on holiday to Spain together. Even after I joined the NT I spent quite a lot of time at their house in St John's Wood.

Bob was a fanatical movie buff. In those pre-video days, he often gave private showings for his friends of rare old films in his collection.

One cold February night in 1966, not long after my divorce finally came through, I was invited to one of these movie evenings. My own date was late, and somehow I drifted in the direction of a solitary man with a bald head. It was the first time I ever spoke to Robert, whom I had previously avoided like the plague.

Elizabeth had once tried to introduce me to Robert when we were having lunch at the White Elephant restaurant.

'Oh look, that's Robert Muller,' she said.

I knew this man to be a novelist and dramatist, but he was better known to me at this time as one of our dreaded theatre critics. He and Bernard Levin were known as the 'Kosher Butchers of Fleet Street'. I fled from the encounter, having twice previously escaped meeting Robert, once when he wanted to interview me back in 1953, and seven years later when we both worked for ABC TV's *Armchair Theatre*.

Yet this evening I sat down next to him. What kind, sad eyes, I thought. His bald cranium looked loaded with brains. Why, before he had retired from criticism and journalism, had he ever written those dreadful reviews?

After supper he encouraged me to talk about – me. I found myself spending the next five hours spewing out my entire life story: how awful everything had been for me during the last few months, what a mess my love life was in, the usual actress's jabber.

What a genius, I thought, to get me to talk about nothing but myself for the entire evening. Eventually he went home, but I felt I wanted to see this man again. I spoke to Elizabeth next day and asked her for Robert's address. What I didn't know was that he had meanwhile written to my home in Datchet, asking for my telephone number. Eventually we made a date to go out to dinner.

Once again I never stopped talking about myself, while I knew practically nothing about him. (A pattern which has not noticeably altered in thirty years.)

After that first date we never really parted again.

As I hadn't asked him any questions about himself, I assumed for some reason that he was a forty-year-old widower, who was living alone with his seven-year-old daughter called Sophie. I then learned that there was a Mrs Muller (soon to be ex), who was living in a great manor house on the Isle of Man with another daughter, four-year-old Clare.

Robert then told me that he had only recently absconded to

London with his elder daughter, leaving the younger girl with her mother in the Isle of Man – not a very happy solution to his marital problems, and one which was to have legal consequences. I observed that Robert must have left the island in a hurry, because all he seemed to possess was what he stood up in, a rather ill-fitting grey suit that looked as though it might have belonged to him as a school-boy. He had indeed left *everything* behind, and having abandoned his big house in the Isle of Man, he now didn't seem to have a brass farthing to his name. He was living with little Sophie in a furnished flat near the Finchley Road.

I had no money either at this time; one wasn't well-paid at the National Theatre, and Peter's token shilling a year didn't go far. Peter wanted half the money for our Datchet flat, which I couldn't afford to sell or leave. I was also paying for my mother's house and giving her an allowance.

Though at this time I was quite a well-known actress, and Robert had become a highly paid author, we seemed to be as poor as church mice when we got together. It didn't seem to matter at all. We lived on love and tinned mangoes.

All the time I'd been married to Peter, I had desperately wanted a child. When after he had left me, Peter had rung to say that his girlfriend, by now his wife, was expecting a baby, it had been like a knife going into my gut. The thought of going through life without a child was intolerable to me – while Peter was about to become a father as soon as we had parted. Yet, within a few months of meeting Robert, I was expecting his baby. Now I felt the good fairies were with me. I enjoyed every aspect of my pregnancy. I went on living at Datchet and told no one that the father of my expected baby was Robert Muller.

Robert, meanwhile, was still going through a labyrinthine and acrimonious divorce. The first Mrs Muller understandably didn't believe that Robert had met this flighty actress *after* he'd left the 'marital home'.

I was helped in my new task by Donald Pleasence's wonderful nanny Helen, who came to live in before Matthew was even born. I still regard Helen as part of the family.

Robert now got his estranged wife Eileen and little Clare to come to London. The courts obviously wouldn't have allowed him to keep Sophie, and he wanted the entire family together. He also wanted to keep an eye on his pregnant mistress. I could tell he was tearing himself apart.

With his wife and two daughters settled under one roof in London,

Robert went to stay in Hampstead with a good friend of his, the film director Wolf Rilla.

Before long, he had his ex-wife and two little girls, his mistress and a baby boy that no one was supposed to know about, all living in relatively close proximity. I have to say that I quite enjoyed the melodramatic secrecy of all this. It added drama and spice to my life.

When Matthew arrived, he at once became the centre of my life. Robert visited us every other day; he was also seeing Sophie and Clare separately and together three times a week, taking them to school, spending lunch-hours with them and weekends. At the same time he was writing his fifth novel – not surprisingly called *Love Life*. He moved between Hampstead and Datchet almost daily while solicitors drove him and Eileen further apart. Robert told me often that this divorce had been far worse than his relatively happy marriage.

When Matthew was about three, Robert and I moved with him to a house in Camden Square. His divorce finally came through, but we decided we didn't want to get married. I actually believed you could only be 'married' once; the next time it should be called some-thing else. And we felt perfectly happy as we were. Robert mean-while desperately tried to be as much of a father to his growing daughters as if he'd never been divorced at all.

There now followed a strange time. What made life difficult was that Robert only had the dreaded 'access'. Eileen knew about Robert's new son by now, of course, and still couldn't believe that she hadn't been bitterly betrayed. No emotional peace ever broke out between her and Robert. Eileen's hatred of Robert was now quite systematically passed on to the girls, which blighted all our lives. Poor Sophie and Clare became the real victims in a post-marital tug-of-war between the parents. During the two decades following their divorce, Robert and Eileen never met again, and their conflicts remained unresolved. Eileen tragically died of leukaemia in the late Eighties.

Happily, Matthew got on well with both Sophie and Clare, and they always adored their baby brother. The girls came to us in Camden Square every single weekend throughout the Seventies, and sometimes we all enjoyed this, but often the 'happy family' masquerade deceived none of us. Years later, when Sophie and Clare were young ladies in their twenties, and we still met most weekends in a Chinese restaurant, they told us that during all those years, both of them had hated their visits to us. Robert was shattered.

By now all three children are of course grown up, getting on well with one another and with us, and I'm happy to say enjoying their chosen careers.

In the light of all these events, I sometimes regard Robert, whom I love dearly, as a somewhat tragic figure. Born in Hamburg, he had a Viennese father and a German mother. Thanks to the laws of the Third Reich, he was classified as three-quarter Jewish, which meant he was never accepted either by a Christian or Jewish community. At the age of thirteen he came over to England as a boat-boy refugee. Though later reunited with his parents, he has gone through life with a deeply buried sense of loss: the beloved Jewish grand-mother he had to leave behind in Hamburg was murdered by the Nazis.

Since I have known him, it seems to me that Robert has always shied away from showing his deepest emotions. He dearly loves his daughters and his ninety-two-year-old mother (who died after I completed this book), but I've often noticed how difficult he finds it to embrace them or be embraced by them. Like most people of his background and temperament, he often feels consumed by a pro-found rage, but tends to stop short at communicating emotional pain.

I wasn't altogether surprised when, before he was sixty, a series of massive heart attacks almost killed him. Typically, he claims he only started to enjoy life after he had been so close to death. I believe him.

I find Robert, very much a Virgo, tends to make a rod for his own back. He seems to feel that he doesn't really *deserve* happiness; he compensates for this by being over-dutiful, wanting to do everything for everybody.

I've never seen Robert cry, although I've often told him there's nothing wrong with men crying. When he's in pain he prefers to go inside a shell and pretend the pain isn't there.

Like me, Robert is the sum of his paradoxes. I admire his many gifts, particularly an unfailing Continental gallows humour, total reliability, and a capacity never to appear irritated when other people pour their own worries all over him. He will endlessly listen to them, while keeping silent about his own problems. I suppose that's what attracted me to him in the first place.

If I get over-anxious about work, which I invariably do, he will stop at nothing to push all social and business problems out of my way, so that I'm free to get on with my work. Every actor badly needs such a looker-after, and I'm incredibly lucky to have a man who will always shift things out of the way, so that I can concentrate on the job in hand.

In temperament and personality, we couldn't be more different. I am open and indiscreet, he tends to be secretive. He loves music and the cinema, I never do anything to keep up with him. He reads voraciously in two languages, I hardly ever read at all. We're both curious about people, but I really prefer Nature. Rather than read a book or go out, I like to stand in the middle of a field and watch the birds.

Yet I think it's because Robert and I are such an ill-assorted couple that our relationship has lasted in harmony for thirty years. It must be admitted that we're neither of us very good at living in a conventional mode of domesticity. It wouldn't suit either of us to exist in each other's pockets. In fact, we spend quite substantial portions of our lives apart. I have my work, he has his, and often this takes us to different parts of the world. We've both found an old adage to be true: absence does make the heart grow fonder. Certainly neither of us would try to dissuade the other from following his or her own path because it might be inconvenient. We prefer to spend our lives not glued together; we offer the partner space and freedom. Yet wherever we are, and whatever we're doing, we always look forward to the time when we can get back together again.

In 1972 Matthew was just five years old. I was happy, my life was complete. I looked at my son with joy and love so often that I would sometimes wonder, what if something awful were to happen to him? What if he were in dreadful pain? What if a car knocked him down in front of the house, what would I do? And I went on to think, yes, I would have to kill him immediately, just to put him out of his pain. I simply could not bear to think of him to be in any pain, or indeed to suffer in any way whatsoever.

I was convinced that would be my reaction. Yet when one is confronted with a total nightmare one somehow finds resources from somewhere to deal with it. Matthew was not knocked down by a car or involved in any kind of accident. Yet, a week after his fifth birthday, everything was to change.

At that time I was still going through my illusory film star phase, playing opposite Elizabeth Taylor and Laurence Harvey in a film called *Night Watch*. I seem to have developed a strange sort of antenna, almost precognition, particularly where illnesses are concerned – the faculty of a witch, I suppose. On his birthday

I suddenly knew something was not quite right with him.

We have film of him rushing about in our garden, enjoying his party, but some instinct told me that something was wrong. I called Dr Freudenberg, our local doctor, who, thank God, didn't think of me as a hysterical actress or over-anxious mother, or a combination of the two. He took my maternal anxiety seriously.

One evening I'd gone up to Matthew's bedroom and found him sitting cross-legged on his bunk bed, with his hands across his forehead, staring into space. I didn't dare touch him. The next day he had a slight cold. I'd seen Matthew much sicker than this, but he looked pale and also complained of earache.

On the next Sunday morning, Matthew played with Sophie and Clare, his two half-sisters, but he seemed to be out of sorts with himself. This was most unlike him; Matthew never was a whingeing child. It also seemed to me that he kept falling asleep, and didn't want light on his face. I suspected what was happening was that he was slipping in and out of coma.

Dr Freudenberg immediately gave Matthew a small dose of antibiotics. That probably saved his life. He also took Matthew's chin and pressed it down on to his chest. I put that in my little mental medicine bag.

'If you need to get hold of me today,' Dr Freudenberg told me, 'don't hesitate.'

Helen, Matthew's nanny, asked if she could borrow the car, as her own was in dock. I found myself saying: 'No, you can't, I'll need it to take Matthew into hospital tonight.' Helen looked at me as though I'd gone crazy. Robert must have wondered too. But I knew in my gut that I would have to go to hospital with Matthew that night.

It was a practical thought. I wasn't even particularly frightened. I said to Helen: 'Oh no, of course I won't be driving Matthew, I'll be going by taxi, so do take the car.'

Matthew sat on our bed. I ran a tepid bath for him; he didn't even have a high temperature. Suddenly he cried out: 'I can't move my neck.'

A dreadful suspicion was now becoming certainty. As gently as I could, I carried him into the bathroom. He looked quite frightened now. 'I can't look down, I can't look down,' he said.

'Don't worry,' I told him, 'it's perfectly all right, you're just cold.'

He got into the bath. While I was splashing water over him, I reached out for the telephone and dialled Dr Freudenberg's number, asking him to come round again immediately.

By now I knew what was wrong with Matthew, *I just knew*. I continued to bathe him. I noticed he was crossing his legs in his bath and then couldn't uncross them. I gently straightened his legs and got him out of the bath. He was still walking with his head held up, he couldn't bend it. I put him into bed.

When Dr Freudenberg arrived he said: 'I think we should get him to the hospital.'

He wrote out a note. I asked him: 'Please tell me what it is, I can deal with the known.'

He said, 'I think it's meningitis.'

I said, 'So do I.'

Far from going into a blind panic, I thought, right, the fight is on. I was going to wrap Matthew into a blanket, but he insisted on getting dressed. He didn't want to be seen outside his house in pyjamas. *I suddenly thought of my poor father . . .*

Robert and I took Matthew in a taxi to University College Hospital. As soon as we arrived, we were told they would have to take a lumbar puncture. Because of what happened to my friend Robert Percival, meningitis was not an unknown thing to me: I also knew about lumbar punctures. I knew this was going to be bloody awful. It took about four of us to hold this small five-year-old down. I took hold of Matthew's head, and all he could do was to scream: 'Get off, get off, get off.'

We were in the operating theatre next door to Intensive Care, and Matthew screamed while the nurses tried to get the needle in between his vertebrae and spinal cord.

Suddenly I saw Robert popping his head round the door. He was waving his hand in some sort of comic desperation, mouthing words of encouragement, as though we were watching a conjuror at a children's party. I realised that the only way he could deal with this horror was to pretend it wasn't really happening. I knew all too well how he must have felt. To hear your own child screaming in pain is paralysing.

Matthew was carried back into the Intensive Care Unit. We sat and waited for the results. I already knew they would be positive.

I also realised that, had the location schedule for *Night Watch* been slightly different for that weekend, and if I'd been away from home, Matthew would by now have been dead.

That knowledge changed my outlook, my life, the entire course of my career. I knew that henceforth I would lose many friends. Not only would I not go to or give parties, I wouldn't spend a day away from home or even go out for the evening. As for work, I knew

I wouldn't go farther than a black taxi ride away from our front door.

The doctors found that Matthew had contracted a nasty form of the disease, called bacterial meningitis, but they couldn't determine for sure which one of the three varieties it was. So they treated him for all of them. This meant twelve injections a day.

I abandoned everything; I knew Robert would be ringing my agent, Joy Jameson. I wanted out of this movie, there was no way I would go back to work. I moved into the Intensive Care Unit and got a camp-bed for myself at the side of Matthew.

Matthew was tubed and wired up, and Robert and I would take turns in 'bubble-bashing', i.e. trying to stop the bubbles whenever they threatened to clog up one of the tubes.

Matthew was having so many injections that his veins were collapsing. The nurses had to take the needles out to try and find other veins. We used every vein on the back of his hands, inside his arms, in his feet, everywhere.

I don't think I ever panicked, yet once, for about ten seconds, I caught the full horror of *what could happen*. This was sucked into an invisible third eye in the centre of my forehead. I realised what real terror was. I don't think you can live very long with that intensity of feeling, without going mad. I looked at this child. In between bouts of pain, he seemed to be normal, almost happy. Yet he was dying. His nerve endings were raw and sore. Sometimes the needle would slip out of the vein, and his leg would swell up . . .

I tried to show no emotion. We were told 'the treatment' would last two weeks. By then we would have either won or lost. We would then be faced with a likely next step I tried not to think about.

We were running out of veins; there was only one more place for a needle to go – through his skull.

Dr Herman, who was in charge of the ward, spoke very frankly with us. I was grateful to him for that.

'I don't know what your religion is,' he told us, 'whether you just cross your fingers or pray, but you'd better start doing it. He may not make it.'

On *Night Watch* they called a *force majeure*, and filming was temporarily stopped. It wasn't just because of my situation. Elizabeth Taylor was having problems with Burton, Laurence Harvey had to go to hospital. I never knew for sure if he had found out he was dying of cancer of the stomach.

I only went home the odd night to have a bath. Either Robert or I stayed at Matthew's bedside all the time. Helen took her turn too.

One day a bizarre thing occurred as I sat watching at Matthew's bedside. He was still suspended between life and death, as I was called to take an important telephone call at the nurses' desk. It turned out to be from an American film producer called George George, one of the producers of *Twisted Nerve*, a film I'd made for the Boultings a few years previously.

'Oh Billie,' George George greeted me, 'listen, I'm in London and hear your boy's not well. So why not come out with me and have a meal.'

I told him: 'My son has meningitis, George. He may not live till the weekend.'

The poor man obviously didn't know what to say to that. Back came the reply: 'Oh well, come out anyway, it may help to take your mind off things.'

After a while, shooting on *Night Watch* resumed in Bayswater, not far from the hospital. The film's director, Brian Hutton, begged me to go back for two days because after that we would lose our location. I refused. By this time I must have looked like a ghost. I didn't eat, I'd lost over half a stone.

Shortly afterwards the paediatrician at UCH called me in and told me: 'I think it will make it easier for Matthew and for you if you go back to work.'

Unhappily I agreed and went back to face the camera. Every lunchtime I was driven back to the hospital to see Matthew, and every night after shooting I returned there.

While I was away, Robert sat with Matthew, drawing dozens and dozens of coloured crayon images, hundreds of drawings of fishes with multi-coloured scales, which Matthew liked. We brought a tape recorder into the unit to occupy him, and indeed to divert us. Despite what the doctors had said, neither Robert nor I entertained for a moment the possibility that Matthew would not live. *It was not allowed*.

In the hospital my relationship with Robert changed. In some strange way our energies were joined together so that they could be projected into Matthew. In doing this the three of us seemed to become one entity.

Sometimes it seemed to me that we were creating a human being for a second time.

Now back at work, I had asked that the crew of *Night Watch* would not mention Matthew's illness, just to let me get on with it. Everybody, the producer Martin Poll, Brian Hutton, and particularly Elizabeth Taylor, proved to be wonderfully sympathetic. Elizabeth never brought Matthew up at all, yet one day an enormous arrangement of white flowers arrived at Camden Square, so vast that we could hardly get it through the double doors. But while she continued to work with me, she said nothing. As for me, I couldn't speak about it at all.

One day the IVAC machine that Matthew was on broke down. When Robert told me this, I remember sinking to the floor of the Bayswater hotel where we were working. As often in moments of acute crisis, I seemed to step outside my body, observing myself from above. The creature I was watching was howling like an animal. I was so desperate, I wanted to buy another machine right away. All the production people now tried to help get a new machine. Finally we managed to find one.

Matthew had to have one more lumbar puncture to see if he had responded to the treatment. The tubes and drips had been removed; there was nothing else to do but await the result. As they took the drip away, Matthew became alive with concentrated energy. His hands were now free, he asked for a piece of paper and pencil and started to draw a picture he called 'The Show'. It shows a child, possibly himself, on a stage. There is an audience of little insects, and perhaps they represent germs. The child is jumping off the stage, jumping over the germs and leaping over the audience. I shall never forget the look on Matthew's face as he drew this with total concentration, ignoring everyone's activities in the Intensive Care Unit. Somehow he knew he'd made it.

The film was finished. Some things I had to do were not easy. Elizabeth's character had to stab me; the special effects were being made ready, and when I came on to the set I seemed to be confronted with yards of the same tubing that surrounded Matthew. When I was filming this, I suddenly found myself screaming: 'Get off me!' The director stopped me. 'I don't think those are the right words, Billie,' he said. I realised I had been yelling Matthew's words when I was holding him down during the lumbar puncture.

Matthew had been in intensive care for only two weeks, but it took many years for him to get back to good health. A pattern had started which was to continue until he was well into his teens. We never left him in the house without either one of us being there. He had been spared, but for a while he seemed to be the victim of every virus and infection going. He kept to his bed for quite a long time, staying in our bedroom where he could watch television. Strangely enough, he would never acknowledge that he'd been in hospital. He went on drawing, endlessly painting children with the top of

their heads cracked open like eggs, and horrible things spewing out of them.

Matthew would never talk about his illness or explain his drawings. Robert and I now felt that we had to bring all this out into the open for him, we had to get him to face up to what had happened, so that it should not lie buried within him.

A few weeks after he came out of hospital, I was working downstairs in the kitchen, when suddenly I heard Matthew's voice coming from the top of the stairs, screaming: 'Switch it off, switch it off!' I found him staring at the picture on the television set, almost paralysed with fear. It was some sort of hospital story. Men in white coats were moving about their business. Matthew couldn't move to switch it off.

We still had a long, long way to go. Intuitively, like an animal, I could think of only one thing to do: twice a day I ran a tepid bath and the two of us got in together. I laid Matthew across my body and gently splashed water over us both.

I had made up my mind that whatever happened to my son during this illness, I would never lie to him; I might soften the truth a bit, but I would not lie.

In hospital, Matthew had sometimes asked: 'Is it time for the hurts yet, Mummy?'

I would never say: 'No, don't worry about that.' I'd say: 'No, not yet, but it's all right, we've been through the other hurts, we'll get through these.' I tried never to make light of his illness, nor to dwell on it.

In that last respect I have probably failed.

One day when we were in the bath, and I was splashing water over him, he asked me: 'If I have the hurts, will I have to go back into hospital?'

'It's extremely unlikely, Matthew,' I said. 'At some point in their lives most people have to go into hospital but it's unlikely that you'll ever have anything worse happen to you than what's happened already.'

Tears welled up in his eyes. He said: 'I hurt here and I hurt there,' pointing to his joints in his feet. Obviously his body ached and he felt sore. It was the first time since coming out of hospital that he was able to talk about his experience. I felt great relief. Thank God, I thought, now we can really start on the process of recovery.

Throughout the next few years, we still took him to UCH every few weeks to check on his progress. The struggle was far from over.

During all this time, everything inside me ached to give up work altogether. I remember sitting with Robert opposite Professor Strang, who looked after Matthew during this convalescent period, and telling him: 'I really don't want to work again.'

He said: 'If you don't work, you will keep this child an invalid. If you want to do what's best for your boy, do what is hardest. Within reason you have to behave as if nothing has happened.'

I like to think that the closeness that Robert and I felt during these years of Matthew's recovery helped to get Matthew well again. Another thing that helped a lot over this long period of convalescence was a kind gesture from the doctor who had been on *Night Watch*. He had some connection with West Ham United, the football club. Like Robert, Matthew has always been a football fanatic. He had a set of West Ham players' photographs plastered on the walls of his hospital room. One day there was a phone call from Ron Greenwood, then the West Ham United manager: 'When your son gets better and feels up to it,' he said, 'why don't you bring him down to a practice game.'

As soon as Matthew was able to walk better, I took him down to such a practice, and he actually kicked a ball with Bobby Moore, his idol.

After that, Robert and I took it in turns to take Matthew to West Ham matches, even to reserve games sometimes. I shall be for ever grateful to Pauline Moss at West Ham for inviting Matthew to Upton Park for many, many years afterwards – and for giving us delicious teas in the directors' room after the games. It made such a lot of difference.

There is one other thing about Matthew's illness that I must mention. While we were in the Intensive Care Unit, for the only time in my life, I planned for my own death. Though I didn't countenance for one moment that Matthew might die, I actually had the pills and everything else to hand, just in case. Not because I couldn't bear to face life without Matthew, but in a quite practical, unemotional way I thought it would be better if I went with him in case he got lost if he died. When he would have to go wherever one goes, he'd be too little to manage on his own.

Afterwards I thought, what a rotten thing to do to Robert. But I decided that Matthew would need me more, because he was only five years old.

After Matthew's illness and until *Not I* arrived on my doormat, there seemed to be a long gap, filled with Matthew starting at Gospel Oak Primary School, where he received care and help from the headmaster, Mr Lendon, who had also given much thought to helping along Matthew's half-sisters Sophie and Clare. Matthew was still on the 'at risk' form, and was often off school with various illnesses, but I have happy memories of standing outside the Gospel Oak school gates, waiting for a boy to come out – a boy who was getting better and better, but very slowly.

For many years Matthew still had night terrors. He would be half-awake, half-asleep; he could hear me through his nightmare, but was unable to wake up properly. I couldn't get through to him. Sometimes he looked at his pillow with absolute terror on his face, clawing at it as though there was something there. I would get him out of bed, and he'd run all round the house. It was like something in a horror movie. It took him years to work his way through the night terrors. He continued to look pale, with dark rings under his eyes.

For about five years he never had a night's normal sleep and neither did we. I slept, as it were, with one foot and one ear out of the bed. Sometimes I would just go and sleep in Matthew's little bedroom, next to ours. Later he told us that what he saw when he had his nightmares was something like a big blob of throbbing meat that was all around him. At the bottom right-hand corner there was a little girl dressed in red. What on earth all that might have signified I have no idea. Anyway, it all had to be worked through. That was the job Robert and I felt we had to do. It took priority over careers; any social life came a long way down our list of our priorities.

When everything is brought down to basics, to a question of survival, life becomes very simple. Far from being in despair in the early Seventies, I have never felt more useful or positive. Each step forward with Matthew was more exciting than any first night could have been. I feel that if I was born for anything, it wasn't to be a successful actress or to play leading roles on TV and in the theatre; it was to get my only son through his illness.

Our social life came to a total halt. I no longer went to the theatre or the cinema. I only went out to work. Even when Matthew was better, it had become my habit to turn down invitations and to stay at home. My life had begun to revolve around domesticity and looking after my child. I made up a different story to tell him every night. There must have been hundreds of them, and I've forgotten them all.

It was five years before Matthew was struck off the 'at risk' register; that happened on his tenth birthday.

Six months after Matthew came out of hospital, and it seems much longer than that, I had a phone call from Anthony Page. He was about to direct a play by Samuel Beckett at the Royal Court Theatre. Could he send it round to me? I explained that I wasn't really in the market for working (something I fear I've automatically said for the past twenty years), but I said sure, send it round.

The script was dropped through the letterbox. I opened it up and read right through it. Anthony had said: 'As soon as you've read it, Billie, ring me back, we're very behind with our preparations. I want to know whether you're interested.'

I started reading, and three-quarters of the way through it I found I couldn't stop crying. By the time I'd got to the end of the play, seven closely typed pages later, I couldn't even speak. Anthony Page was waiting for my phone call, but I couldn't speak. Had anyone asked me why I was crying, I couldn't have told them. Looking back, I think I understand my reaction. What hit me was an inner scream, an endless nightmare that poured out of this old woman of seventy, who kept saying she was sixty. In her outpourings I recognised my own inner scream which I'd been sitting on ever since Matthew's illness began.

To me, the characteristics and emotions of all the Beckett figures I have played don't seem to be specifically male or female, old or young, rich or poor. There is a core there which we can all recognise if we take the trouble.

After about an hour I picked up the telephone and called Tony. I told him I thought *Not I* a powerful piece of work, but horrendously difficult. How on earth was I ever going to learn it, let alone play it?

'I don't think I want to say any more,' I told him, 'until you and I have worked on it for a couple of days.' But, he insisted, what did I think of it? 'Something akin to verbal vomit,' I replied, 'a mouth spouting a monologue, page after page of apparently unconnected pieces of personal information.'

Sometimes the mouth would be talking about walking in a field, then suddenly the speaker would be in a supermarket, then in a lavatory, always talking out her thoughts at the speed of thought. My only immediate suggestion was that, as with *Play*, I felt it had all to go very fast.

Tony agreed with me that we should work on it together for a couple of days. It would be a sort of mutual audition. I must admit I was half hoping this was one audition I would fail.

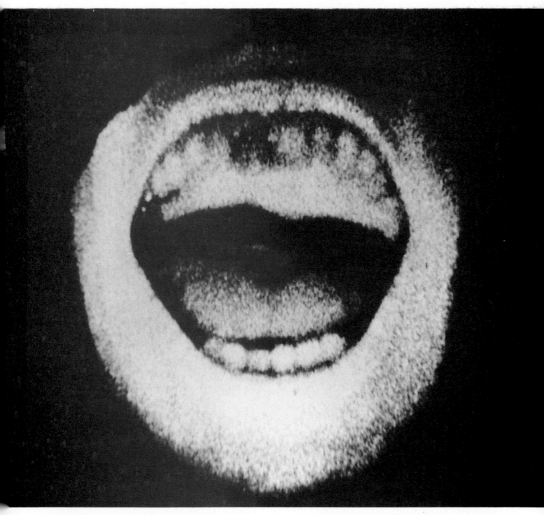

Not I – the 1972 Beckett play and performance, as Mouth, by which standard I have tended to judge all my other work.

Samuel Beckett at the National Theatre. The Cottesloe presented *Rockaby* in 1986 after I had done it in New York and before I took it to Australia.

Conducting each other. Beckett and I rehearsing *Footfalls* (which he wrote for me) at the Royal Court. It was the first time he directed me on his own.

With Alan Schneider who directed Beckett's *Rockaby*, here and in the US. A marvellous director, who died tragically in London.

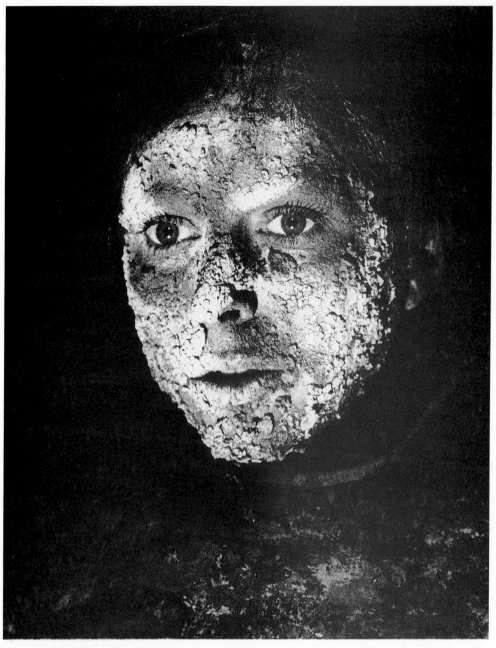

My first encounter with Beckett – my face covered in glue and porridge – in *Play* at the National Theatre. We worked together for twenty-five years, right up to the time he died.

(*Opposite*) Wearing Jocelyn Herbert's incredible costume for *Footfalls*. Of all the plays we did together, after *Not I*, this is the one I recall most vividly. It worked.

Rocking herself to death – or is she? The image from *Rockaby*, 1981, that
seemed to stay in people's minds. Strange for such a short play to make such
an impact.

(*Opposite*) 'Up to her diddies' in a mound – *Happy Days* at the Royal Court, directed
by Beckett. Mouth paid me an unwelcome visit during the preparation of this.

Samuel Beckett and I working on the television plays *Ghost Trio* and . . . *but the clouds* . . . at the BBC. Shortly after this picture was taken, I gave up smoking forever.

By this time I'd been told that Tony wanted Glenda Jackson to do *Not I*. (Later I learned that Beckett had never heard of Glenda Jackson. The fact that she was a household name and had won a couple of Oscars apparently meant little to him.) But Beckett had remembered our production of *Play*, and had told Tony that he wanted me to do it. I wasn't a fly on the wall, so I shall never know exactly what passed between Anthony Page and Samuel Beckett about the casting of *Not I*.

There certainly wasn't a single rehearsal day after I'd said: 'Yes, I'll do it,' that I didn't wish that Glenda had said yes first, and that Sam had acquiesced.

Do I really mean that?

I'm saying it to myself in a somewhat ironical manner because I knew that, even more with *Play*, *Not I* would be almost impossible to do *well*. Yet I knew it to be the most meaningful professional task I'd ever attempted. I found so much of myself in *Not I*. Somewhere in there were my entrails under a microscope.

A period of uncertainty followed. After our 'audition', Tony said: 'Well, I don't know, what do you think?'

I said: 'Whoever you choose, Tony, a decision has to be made pretty quickly. Someone should have started working on this two weeks ago.'

I didn't quite appreciate the quandary Anthony was in. Clearly he was arguing with Samuel Beckett on the phone, and couldn't quite make up his own mind. Finally, I rang Tony and said: 'Look, unless I can get down to working on this now, I can't do it at all. There is simply no more time to waste.'

That day, he said: 'Yes, OK, you do it.'

I took the script away and, for the first time since Matthew's illness, left the house. Knowing that Robert and Helen were with Matthew, I went down to the health farm at Forest Mere for a week, to get myself in some sort of physical shape, and concentrate on the play.

Beckett and I hadn't seen each other or written or been in any sort of contact, since the production of *Play* nine years previously. For a single performance at the Royal Festival Hall, I had appeared in his *Come and Go*, which I have to admit I didn't understand, nor did I take any real trouble to try to do so. Yet, according to John Calder, Sam's publisher in London, he had for some reason carried the sound of my voice around in his head – not my normal voice, but the voice I used in *Play*. Apparently, when he wrote *Not I*, that was the voice he heard.

To say that Beckett wrote *Not I for* me would not be true, but according to Calder he wanted me and nobody else to do it. This gift and challenge came at me at a time when my own mind had been in turmoil. Now I felt I was able to put that to some practical use.

I recognised that jumbled state of mind, the thoughts racing round the brain, the feeling of not being able to make any sort of decision. Do I get into the bath, do I not get into the bath? Do I run hot water into it, do I run cold water? I thought I recognised these outpourings of a crazed mind. It felt, to me, as though Mouth, as the character in *Not I* was called, was falling backwards into hell, bum first, making strange animal cries, crashing down and down, arms akimbo, looking like some sort of octopus, finally falling down and down a long tunnel, falling, falling, getting faster all the time. That's what came off the pages of *Not I*. I told Tony that I had some idea where we had to go, but that I had no idea if I could actually get there. All I knew was that it would have to go faster than anything I'd ever heard in the theatre, if possible as fast as the speed of thought, and that of course is impossible.

A lot of the work I did for Beckett from now on seemed to derive from *Not I* – consisting entirely of spoken thought, or of thoughts overheard – never presented in recognisable *dialogue*, but taking an audience into one's most private, unformed, semi-conscious, uncensored thoughts. It also seemed to me that Mouth was not going *out* to an audience; the audience had to be sucked into this rioting, rambling hole.

It certainly wasn't a case of *projecting*. Very often in the theatre one is told to project, but here the reverse was necessary. I found this to be required in most of Beckett's plays that I was to do subsequently.

Came the first reading of *Not I*. I was absolutely dreadful. I knew it would be no good asking the director questions like: 'Who am I, why does this woman of seventy keep on saying she's sixty, where is she, what the hell is "the buzzing" she hears all the time?' As with *Play*, I knew this approach wasn't going to get me very far. The words were just hooks on which to hang a particular state of mind. Much later, about another play, Beckett actually wrote something to me to that effect, in his tiny illegible handwriting on one of his postcards.

The fact that Tony would have preferred to work with Glenda Jackson never interfered with his direction. I admire him for that. He had lost the battle gracefully, and never made me feel uncomfortable.

I still didn't know whether I'd be capable of doing it. There were no other speaking characters, no interruptions, no pauses, no cues, just this one uninterrupted monologue.

In most plays, dialogue is exchanged like a tennis ball between actors. Certain key words help, like a little frog, to give you a hop into your next area. Here there was nothing like that, no help at all. I often think I'd like to see someone else have a go at it.

We were going to do *Not I* in a double bill, with Albert Finney in *Krapp's Last Tape*. Sam came over from France, as he'd done for *Play*. Before the first read-through I had written 'speed and not gabble' on my script, but I knew from the experience of *Play* that, once the engine was oiled, and the motor was running, something organic would happen: I would just stand back, the machine would take over and drive itself. Tony gave me posts to reach, words to grab at, so that the text would never deteriorate into a monotonous gabble.

At rehearsal Beckett was courteous, but a little distant. He wanted Tony to be in charge. Yet as the work continued, I started to rehearse with Sam privately.

Though we'd only worked together once, we were already developing a kind of shorthand. There is one section in *Not I* where the disembodied mouth emits a scream. I asked him: 'Shall I use the scream button here, as I used the laugh button in *Play*?' His eyes lit up. 'Oh yes, Billie, use the scream button.'

Now a strange thing happened. It seemed to me as if no time at all had passed between the last rehearsal of *Play* and the first rehearsal of *Not I*. That's fairly typical for me. I have no sense of time, a poor memory, and seem to live entirely in globules of the present. To me, life has always been a series of presences strung together on a line. I can go for years not seeing someone, then simply pick up from where we left off. Sam and I did just that. We continued where we'd left off, as if there hadn't been a nine-year gap at all.

Yet since I had last seen him I *must* have changed. I'd divorced my first husband and, on the face of it, was 'married' to my second husband, Robert. We had a son and I'd inherited two step-daughters, who were very much part of our lives. The immature girl, caught in a mismatched marriage, that he had met in the mid-Sixties had become a woman, whose life was filled with domesticity and the anxieties of motherhood. As for the writer I'd encountered in *Play*, he hadn't changed at all, though so much of the circumstances in his life had altered. In England, he was no longer considered an esoteric avant-garde writer. He had become a celebrated Nobel Prize winner, thought to be the greatest living playwright. None of this ever came up between us.

When we started to work on *Not I* in the afternoons at my home, Beckett would repeat over and over again: 'Too much colour, no no, too much colour.' By which he meant: 'For God's sake don't act.' In *Not I*, as in *Play*, and again later when he directed me in *Footfalls*, what Beckett wanted was not the acting out of an internal thought, but the internal thought itself. He didn't want anything *presented*.

His 'Don't act' instruction necessarily caused me some difficulty. Surgeons want to surge, actors want to act. An actor is usually hired precisely for the personal things he will bring to a piece.

Some of Beckett's words I found beautiful and poetic. I must admit I sometimes enjoyed acting them out. But that's precisely what he didn't want. He wanted to get to some unconscious centre. Yet the moment I started imposing myself on the text, the moment I became *aware of playing the role* I realised that I was making a *comment* on the piece, instead of allowing its essence to come through. I think I came to terms with this problem by simply concentrating on learning the lines. Then, I thought, let what happens happen.

Beckett knew, of course, that his material would come out differently with every actor, since every actor has his own individual centre. Often, when one is sent a play, the first thing that occurs to you is: 'What can I do with this to make it different?' With Beckett I learned that *you don't do anything with it*, you don't try to make it 'different', you simply allow your own core to make contact with what comes off the page. Eventually everything then falls into place, the material takes off on its own. If you allow the words to breathe through your body, if you become a conduit, something magical *may* happen. There are no short-cuts working in this way. It helped no end having Beckett there all the time. I knew I had to get to a point where an interior flame ignited, but I didn't know that when I started. As rehearsals went on, I also became aware that time was running out. I began to resent having to learn all those pages before I could start revving up my engine and get started – *not acting*.

By saying the lines over and over again, then gradually speeding up, using various repeated words to grab at, I felt after a while that something was beginning to happen.

But to be honest, the major problem remained – learning the bloody thing.

While we were rehearsing *Not I*, Donald McWhinnie was directing *Krapp's Last Tape* with Albert Finney. I'm sure Albert won't mind me saying that he and Sam didn't really get on. Very few actors did. Patrick Magee got on with Sam, and so did Jack MacGowran and Madeleine Renaud, but a lot of actors felt that certain constraints were being forced upon them by Beckett.

One night Albert rang me up: 'You seem to be getting on with this man,' he said, 'but I'm having problems. You know the way I work, I take all the different paints out of the cupboard, I mix the colours together. If they're not right, I shove them all back and take out a new lot.'

I told him: 'Albert, put all your colours back in your cupboard. Just keep out the white, the black and the grey.'

For some odd reason Sam thought Albert wasn't musical. He was quite wrong about that. Albert not only sings and dances well, he plays an excellent classical guitar. I don't think Albert would have bent over backwards to work with Beckett again, or vice versa, and they never did.

As we were coming up to dress rehearsal I was close to my usual panic. I felt certain I wasn't going to make it. I know actors always think that, but this time it was true. A few nights earlier I'd rung up Tony Page in despair.

'It's now three in the morning,' I told him. 'I've been trying to study this page for the last four or five hours, I've learned three lines. The more I learn, the more impossible it becomes.'

At the end of a night's solitary learning session, I'd try and put all I'd learned together, then pound through the lot, hoping I'd slapped on another couple of lines. But it often seemed to me that when I'd learned two or three lines more, I'd lost the equivalent number somewhere else. I thought I was going crazy.

At one rehearsal, late in the day, I found myself yelling out: 'This stuff is unlearnable. It's just impossible to learn it and be precise. *And* go at speed.'

I thought even if I ended by knowing the play, it would only prove I'm a brilliant parrot.

The trouble was, I still needed to get to the core of the text, and I couldn't do that – Catch 22 – until I'd learned it all.

A few days later I heard myself shout to the stage manager: 'I need a dwarf.' I thought I might have a dwarf with a little torch standing behind the curtain, so that I'd be able to read the text. (I was quite serious, too.) I then thought that if I couldn't have a dwarf, perhaps they'd let me have a teleprompter, like television news-readers use. I even tried to order one myself.

In the end nobody would give me either a dwarf or a teleprompter.

I just had to get on with it. Yet in learning text, I was constantly losing text.

I was now trying to do as much as I could 'off the book' and frightening myself to death. I asked to be allowed a couple of runs *reading* the play to get my confidence back, yet after two pages, and before anyone else said anything, I knew that reading was never going to work. I'd lost both speed and drive, as the eye went from page to brain and then back to mouth. I was stuck with having to get to the point where I opened my mouth, and this stuff just poured out of me, like some sort of verbal diarrhoea.

Jocelyn Herbert, the designer, was a tower of strength during this period. At the theatre I had to lean on her a lot, and also on Robert's patience at home. They never realised, I think, how much I needed them. After the first time I tried to pound through the whole text on the stage, Jocelyn came up and gave me a big hug: 'It's OK,' she said simply, 'you're winning.' She added that it was very moving to watch me struggling with my concentration, not letting go of the connecting thread between the text and my centre.

Joss also helped me with all sorts of physical things I'd never come across before. I began to understand what an athlete feels like, as he goes through training. The work was painful; my ribcage protested at having to take such little breaths. Like a singer, I had to work out exactly *where* I was going to snatch breath. I was hyper-ventilating like mad and often became dizzy, staggering round and round the stage. My jaws ached. The first time I tried a run 'off the book', I closed my eyes tight so that I wouldn't be distracted by anything visual. I didn't realise that as I spoke I was going round and round in circles. I got quite a shock when I felt a wall against my face. I thought I'd been standing still.

Another problem to sort out was what to do with all the spit that was collecting in my mouth. There didn't seem to be time to swallow my spittle. I ended up feeling like a pelican. At the beginning, until I found 'spit-swallowing places', the spittle just trickled out of my mouth. I must have sprayed the first few rows of the stalls at every performance.

One day, as I came home after rehearsal, Matthew was watching an athletics event on TV. There was an Olympic clock in the corner of the screen. I wondered if it was possible to count from one to ten in time with the Olympic clock. That became my exercise: to count from one to ten in a second. It had to be done with great emphasis, I had to grab at each fraction of a second. I finally taught myself to count from one to ten in a second, and still be articulate. That helped – it gave me drive as well as speed.

All that *Not I* consists of is a mouth; that's all the audience can see of the actress – no body, no face, nothing except a mouth half-way up, on an invisible raised stage. Downstage, on the right, there stands a shadowy figure in a djellabah. Sam used to spend a lot of time in Tangier. He was fascinated by the figures of Moroccans in their djellabahs, standing still. This figure stood stock still on the stage with a hood over his head. That was the basic image of *Not I*: the silent hooded man and a mouth pouring out words. At given moments, the Auditor (as he was called) would raise his arms, then lower them.

As he always did in his plays, Sam spent hours on the movement. The actor, Brian Miller, had no lines, but just moved his arms up and down. Sam couldn't get what he had in his mind's eye to work on the stage. This had nothing to do with Brian's competence.

In the end, Sam cut all the movement down to one single raising of the arms, a sort of gesture of helplessness. (When the BBC filmed *Not I*, Sam and Tristram Powell, who directed it for television, decided to abandon the Auditor altogether.)

Sam was equally demanding with the lighting. The figure of the Auditor was to have faint lighting over his bowed back. As for the mouth, there was light on it, but no spillage on to my face, and no beam of light 'bleeding' into the auditorium.

Fortunately, the resident lighting director at the Royal Court for all the Beckett plays was the invaluable Jack Raby.

Sam wanted *all* the lights taken out in the theatre, including the exits, the lavatories, and the aisles. There was to be no spillage of light from anywhere. Jack's lighting box was covered. Heavy curtains were drawn over the doors at the back of the theatre. For the short duration of the play, there was to be no escape from the Mouth for the audience.

Jocelyn Herbert has written in her book *A Theatre Workbook* that what Sam was after was to find out how far you can remove the body altogether from the stage, yet still end up with an intensely dramatic situation. The only way I could help was to try to eliminate Billie Whitelaw's body, then deal with what was left. What Jocelyn and Sam and Anthony were doing technically, I hoped to do emotionally.

In *Play*, I had needed something to hang on to physically, so that the tension could go somewhere. Jocelyn suggested for *Not I* that I sat in a chair, but I thought I needed to remain vertical, so that the energy could rise up from my feet, go through my body, and come out of my mouth.

To do this sixteen-minute piece I needed more energy than I have ever required before. I wanted to stand up and have it coming from me in a straight thrust, like a burst from a fireman's hosepipe, a full gush.

Jocelyn designed a makeup for me. My face was blacked out all round my nose; a couple of my teeth were blacked out, the rest stained. Albert Finney gave me a useful recipe to darken the teeth, which he had used when he played Scrooge. It consisted of theatrical wig and beard glue, and a few drops of Friar's Balsam inhalant, mixed together with cigarette ash. In those days I smoked like a chimney (I gave up in 1975), and always had plenty of ash around. I would carefully dry my teeth, which can only be done by padding the gums with cotton wool. When my teeth were absolutely dry, I painted the mixture on them. Cigarette ash isn't all one colour, so I put the blacker bits of ash over the teeth that needed to look as though they had fallen out. The rest of my face was also blacked out. An eye mask, the sort you get in an aircraft for a night's sleep, was placed across my eyes.

Jocelyn had also created a costume for me which had me dressed like an executioner (I certainly felt every night like someone about to be chopped). I wore the executioner's hood over my head and shoulders. My body was covered with a black practice leotard and black tights, and, as a final touch of invisibility, I wore a great black Dracula-like cape, and on my feet little black pumps. No flesh was visible at all. As the mask over my eyes brushed uncomfortably against my eyelashes, I also wore a pair of glasses. After I'd done a run in this crazy outfit, I found that standing up just didn't work, as it made me feel quite unsafe. (Jocelyn had been right, and later I decided to sit. But that was only after the final run.)

I stood on a rostrum high up on the stage. For an audience, the mouth looked as if it were floating in the air, an optical illusion as I was standing absolutely still.

We started the dress rehearsal. After about a page and a half, I felt myself starting to tumble over the edge of the rostrum. I clung on to the bar because I thought I was going to pass out. I remained convinced as I spoke my lines that I was tumbling off the edge of the rostrum and into the void of the theatre. I felt like an astronaut who has left his capsule. Half-way through the rehearsal I broke down.

'I'm sorry, Sam,' I kept saying, 'I'm so sorry.'

Someone turned up all the lights and came up with a ladder. Robbie Hendry, the stage manager, helped to get my mask off, and I was carried from the rostrum. I could see Sam coming down towards me.

'Oh Billie,' he said, 'what have I done to you?'

I was given some brandy and milk. I thought: 'I can't do it, it's a form of torture, it'll never work.'

Feeling disorientated, fearing I could never get through the play, I sat down with Jocelyn and Robbie and we worked out a plan. In order to know where I was, I would need an object to look at. I asked for a faint light coming out of the electrical box on which I could fix my eyes. As long as I could concentrate on that speck of light, I would know where I was. If anybody took that speck of light away, I would lose all orientation. That's when we went back to Jocelyn's idea that I must sit in a chair during the performance, with a support for my feet that I could press against.

Usually, when you're acting a part, you are given some physical movement to use the accumulated energy. Here there was nowhere for the energy to go. Remembering *Play*, we got the rod back to give me something to hold on to. I could force the energy into that.

What now happened in performances was that my head started to shake; all the energy was going into the back of my head and neck. When I was building up speed, that was the only place the tension could go. As my head started to shake violently, my mouth was juddering in and out of Jack Raby's very precise lighting, so I was given two big clamps placed at either side of my head, while I was strapped to the chair. In effect, my head was now held in a vice, clamped at either side of my temples.

The point of all this was to make sure that the audience couldn't look at anything except that mouth, as it vomited out words. If Mouth stopped, the tension in the theatre would be broken. One would have to give everyone their money back. That possibility frightened me so much that we finally worked out a special device, which may sound as if we were cheating. We put a little earpiece in my ear, going down the back of my neck and across to Robbie Hendry. By now Robbie was sensitive to all the rhythms of *Not I*. Whenever he sensed that my rhythm was changing, he would throw me a word, and without a break I would be able to carry on. I wasn't prepared to risk the entire evening by having to take a proper prompt.

Looking back on these rehearsal 'agonies', I felt that during *Not I*, I was becoming joined to Sam by some sort of umbilical cord. After work we sometimes went to relax with Tony Page at the pub next door, or the one across the square.

There then followed a short period, when Sam started to stay away from the final technical rehearsals. It's possible that he'd been told that Tony and I had wanted to work on our own – without interruptions of any kind. At the end of one rehearsal with Tony Page, after Sam and I had been kept apart for a while, Tony said to me: 'Sam's in the pub, off you go.'

I belted out of the stage door and ran into the pub, and there was Sam, sitting alone at the bar counter with his drink. I ran to him like a child, grateful for being let out of school.

I said: 'Thank God, I feel as though I've been separated from my mother.'

Sam looked at me, quite shocked. *'Mother?'* he echoed.

Perhaps he would have been happier if I'd said 'Father'. I think I said *mother* because Sam was to me the source of my nourishment. I wanted to get to that source.

I had a feeling of *déjà vu* when Sam and Tony had some kind of disagreement during final rehearsals. Like Olivier and Tynan before *Play*, it seems that Tony wanted *Not I* to go slower. I had known from the start that I would have to go at the rate of knots, ideally at the speed of thought. Sam and I never brought this up. We both knew we were heading in that direction. Nothing needed to be said.

In her book, Jocelyn quotes Sam as saying: 'When we were doing *Not I*, Anthony Page wanted it to go slower, but Billie and I won.'

Anton Gill, now a famous author and historian, was Tony's assistant at the Royal Court, and very instrumental in helping me to get through *Not I*. He took endless notes at rehearsal. Every night he gave me a stream of them, showing where I'd gone wrong.

For his own part, Sam went back to his room at the Hyde Park Hotel and wrote out page after page of notes for me in his immaculately unreadable writing, headed 'Aids to learning'.

I tried to absorb these 'aids', but found them even more difficult to understand than the play itself. I threw them into the nearest wastepaper basket. Now, when I think of all those handwritten pages condemned to the dustbin, I could weep. They would have made very interesting reading then; now they would perhaps provide help to other actors. I found one little scrap of paper a couple of years ago, and gave copies of it to my students when I was on one of my teaching jaunts in America.

Sam, by the way, thought he knew his *Not I* inside out. If I got some lines mixed up, it was like a knife going through his body. I'd hear him groan: 'Oh no . . .' quite audibly. I remember catching him out once. He had said: 'No, no, that's wrong.'

I replied: 'No, it's you who are wrong, you don't know your own play.' We both laughed.

Sam often came back to our house during rehearsal. He'd bring a present for Matthew and then sit in a big leather chair, while I squatted on the floor as we went through our lines together.

That's the way Sam and I worked for the next fifteen years. We would sit opposite each other and speak the words in unison, he in a whisper and me out loud, while we 'conducted' each other, eyeball to eyeball, his face changing expression with each phrase, just like a conductor.

During this time I must have driven everybody mad with *Not I*. I had put the whole of it on tape and wherever I went, in the car, in the kitchen, in the bath, in the lavatory, I played this tape. Robert realised I was on with the hardest job I'd ever been asked to do, and like Matthew, sometimes joined in.

After I had been all made up and was ready to go on stage, Anton Gill would come into my dressing-room in the theatre. I would then run through the whole of *Not I* twice. I needed that ritual to build up the necessary steam. I drew a small cross on the wall, then stood very still and straight, with my arm stretched out, pointing at that mark. I never took my eyes off it until Anton and I had finished. I think a herd of elephants could have come through and I wouldn't have noticed. It was a form of self-hypnosis, I suppose.

After I'd gone through the text twice, I didn't want anyone to talk to me at all until I was strapped into my seat. I'd repeat the lines over and over again. Instead of saying: 'Hello, how are you,' to people backstage, I'd just nod and continue to rap out the lines to myself. Then I'd climb into the chair and while I was strapped in I'd say to Robbie: 'Let me hear your voice,' and he'd say: 'I'm here, are you all right?' I'd say: 'Yes,' then kept burbling the text to myself. Then Robbie would say: 'Tell me when you want the curtain to go up, Billie.' I would say: 'OK, Robbie, let's go, stay with me.'

Before the first night of *Not I*, on January 16th, 1973 I went through my own sort of mantra. Strapped into the chair, I said to myself: *'Right, let your skin fall off, let your flesh fall off, let the muscles fall off, let the bones fall off, let everything fall off . . .'*

I wanted to be left with nothing but my centre, my core, which seemed to be situated somewhere around my gut – the little flame which I needed. And I thought, now keep out of the way, Whitelaw, work with what's left, don't get in the way of that, pilot your own plane, ride the turbulence. In retrospect, that may sound a bit naff, but I did say it to myself every night of the run.

About our first night I don't remember very much.

To me, every night of *Not I* was a first night. I do recall Sam coming up to my dressing-room, sitting with me while I was getting made up. At the 'half-hour' in a well-run theatre all guests have to leave, and that includes the author. Sam stood up, plonked down a carton of Benson and Hedges cigarettes on my dressing-table and said: 'Ah well, Billie, I'll leave you now.' Then he went to his chair in the pub next door. He never ever said such things as: 'That was good,' or 'You were wonderful,' or – as far as I can remember – even 'Good luck'.

At the end of that first performance, when I was unstrapped from my chair and lifted from the rostrum, my body still felt charged with the electricity that had built up through the entire performance. I felt that if anyone touched me they would get an electric shock. The ends of my fingers still tingled as I reached my dressing-room.

A few days later I heard some radio critics discuss the play on the BBC. I listened to the four of them burbling on. I simply couldn't believe that what they were solemnly discussing – this dry as dust academic nothing – was the same piece of work that I (and I hope the audience) found so hair-raising.

The notices must have been extraordinary. When I got to the theatre the following night there were queues at the box office. Later they went all the way round Sloane Square. I was told people were getting angry, because they couldn't get in. People were flying in from abroad just to see this little sixteen-minute piece. (I was being paid fifty pounds a week for *Not I*, which just about covered my car parking fines.)

One night there was a tap on the door of my dressing-room. A lady said: 'I have a letter for you from Madame Beckett.' Sam's wife Suzanne had come over from Paris to see *Not I*, but was too shy to come up and visit me. Another night the great French director Roger Blin stood at the door, and, right behind him Madeleine Renaud (she died only a few days before I wrote this) – Beckett's most important interpreter. I remember rushing about my dressing-room, like a confused, crazed Minnie Mouse, looking for something to wipe the dust off a chair so that Madame Renaud, then already in her mid-seventies, could sit down. I also tried to find some champagne, which she declined.

Early on into the run I heard that our friend Jackie MacGowran had died suddenly in New York. I sent Sam a telegram: 'From now on every performance is for Jackie.' Sam replied by return:

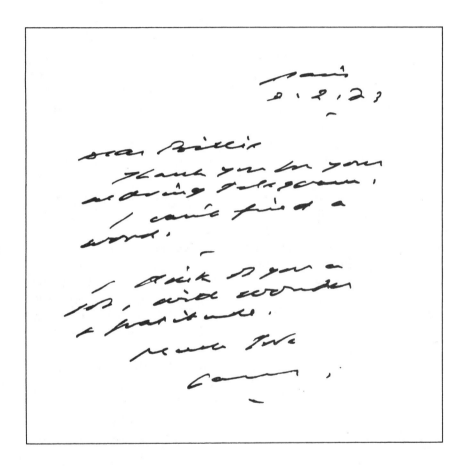

Paris   2.2.73

Dear Billie
Thank you for your moving telegram.
I can't find a word. I think of you a
lot, with wonder and gratitude.
                    Much love
                        Sam
(on the occasion of Jackie Mac-
Gowran's death)

During all this time I still had a sickly child at home. My main emotional pull was there. After the show I would belt back to Camden Square, where Robert would wait for me with my supper. It was a bit of a plus that *Not I* wasn't a long evening in the theatre. Perhaps that's why I said yes to it in the first place. I certainly turned down a lot of work during this period; it would have entailed being out of the house for too long.

I did *Not I* once more, two years later, when the Royal Court revived it in a double bill with *Statements after an arrest under the Immorality Act* by Athol Fugard, with Ben Kingsley and Yvonne Bryceland. The second time round, Robbie Hendry worked out a way of helping me to re-learn the text. He'd call me at night, when it was dark. He'd have the text in front of him, and I'd be in a blacked-out room in my house. Robbie would say: 'All right, start,' and I'd start rehearsing down the telephone.

While preparing this second run of *Not I*, I was cast in Michael Frayn's comedy *Alphabetical Order*. It was being tried out at Hampstead in 1975 and later transferred to the West End. So I was rehearsing *Alphabetical Order* during the day, while performing *Not I* at night. I'm not very competent at handling props at the best of times. I find that speaking lines even when only pouring a cup of tea can get me into a mess. In *Alphabetical Order* I was playing the head of a newspaper cuttings library, everybody's friend, and a bit of a bossy-boots who, like me, was not very good at finding things or keeping order around me.

Michael Rudman directed the play, and I was partnered by Dinsdale Landen, a superb comedy actor, and by a fellow veteran of Theatre Workshop, Barbara Ferris. During rehearsals, I think that Dinsdale, Barbara and Michael Rudman had a rough ride with me. At three o'clock every afternoon I mentally left the character I was playing, to start homing in on *Not I*. I found myself metamorphosing from Michael Frayn's librarian to Beckett's inner scream. Michael Rudman, a calm and professional director, couldn't help being a bit worried by my behaviour. I told him perhaps he'd better come down to the Royal Court to see what I was doing in my spare time.

What usually happens when rehearsals finish is that one goes over what has been done during the day, and looks at what will have to be worked on next day. Unfortunately, *Not I* seemed to erase everything from my mind. I'd return to the *Alphabetical Order* rehearsals no further forward, while the rest of the cast had progressed. Not surprisingly, I wasn't very popular with my colleagues. I felt I was letting them down. Dinsdale, who was very precise in his work, had been trying to time his lines carefully, but he never quite knew what cue I was going to throw him. Before the dress rehearsal, I apologised to the cast for my lack of preparedness. (To add insult to injury, I was nominated for a couple of awards for my performance in *Alphabetical Order*.)

I didn't realise until much later that with the two seasons of *Not I*, I had inflamed an already damaged spine and neck. Performing in that play, all the tension that went to the back of my neck also aggravated the vertigo and nausea I'd had in my early twenties. I'd come to terms with this: the damage is something I'm stuck with. In fact, every play I did with Beckett left a little legacy behind in my state of ill-health, a price I have most willingly paid.

Doing *Not I* was to have another effect: controlling and harnessing my feelings of terror during this play became projected on to other work I had to do. It made no difference whether I had to learn five lines of a voice-over or fifty pages of a play – I often became quite paralysed with fear. I felt I had some great mountain to climb, particularly when the work in hand was relatively trivial. In the family this became known as my '*Not I* Syndrome'. It seemed that whatever I was asked to do, I imagined I would have to go through *Not I* again. The play had touched terrors within me that I have never come to terms with.

All the time I performed the play, I never took a curtain call. On the very last night, without my knowledge, it was decided that a curtain call was finally due. As the applause continued, and the house lights went on, I was lifted from my chair and my cloak was taken from me.

What the audience must have seen was a backside in tights and leotard being pushed on to the stage. I turned round and blinked and the audience would see a half blacked-out face and a mane of blonde hair hanging down. Hands were pushing me further forward. I stood there like an idiot, not knowing what to do. I wanted to cry. All my professional discipline had gone out of the window. Then an interior voice called me to order: 'For Christ's sake, Whitelaw, pull yourself together, you're an actress, take your bloody curtain call.'

I did three low curtsys, one to the centre, one to the left, one to the right and then another back to the centre. Everybody in the house was on their feet. It was the most marvellous personal moment of my career.

But I had still not finished with *Not I*. The BBC decided to film it. Now we had to work out a way or making it work on the television screen. Anthony Page was in America by now. Bill Morton produced and Tristram Powell directed the television version. I knew we would have to do it while the play was still fresh in my mind, and before I had to learn the damn thing all over again.

Tristram came up with the idea, and Sam obviously consented, of *doing the reverse image from the one created in the theatre*. On the stage, one just saw the mouth upstage left, and the figure in the foreground, stage right. Tristram and Sam decided to cut the Auditor out altogether; far from seeing a little mouth like a dot on the screen, for the television version my mouth filled the entire image. It looked strangely sexual and glutinous, slimy and weird, like a crazed, oversexed jellyfish.

The TV performance of *Not I* was the only time I ever heard Sam say anything about my work, and that one time he didn't say it to my face. Tristram, Sam, the cameraman and I were sitting in a dark viewing room, watching the orifice opening and shutting on the little screen. I wanted to get out of the room. All my fears while doing the piece came flooding back. Yet there was no escape from that pulsating mouth; I knew I had to stay and not disturb anybody, so I tried not to look. I either looked down at my knees or closed my eyes altogether. I also wanted to put my fingers into my ears.

At the end of it all, out of the darkness, came one word, spoken with an Irish accent, a whisper that just managed to float across to me: 'Miraculous.'

If I've dwelled on *Not I* at immodest length, it's because this short play proved to be the most telling event of my professional life. After *Not I*, I was not quite the same person I was before. In Sam's eyes, it would seem that I could now do no wrong. Yet from an ever-present sense of insecurity and inferiority, I now often tended to go in the opposite direction. I began to feel that what I'd done on the stage of the Royal Court I could not have done better, and perhaps no one else could have done it better either. I became guilty of hubris. I often felt like that cock-pheasant that I can see strutting down our garden as I'm writing this, the posturing of a being who thinks he owns the damn place.

Some of the work I turned down in the Eighties I refused, not because I wasn't suitable for the part, but because I was scornful of it. Instead of merely thinking that I was too good to do such work, I would simply scorn it. I accepted work because it paid me good money, then became ashamed of it, and admitted that shame in public.

I remember a radio interview about a somewhat indifferent thriller

I'd done for the money. I thought myself too good to have done this. I wasn't. I now realise that feeling of superiority to be quite unprofessional. It can only lead to doing bad work. After I had spoken scornfully about this particular film, a BBC TV producer came up to me and said: 'Never run down work that you've accepted, Billie. It doesn't sound good.'

I felt ashamed of myself. But that didn't prevent the hubris from staying within me (and from coming out from time to time).

I never quite solved the problem of going too fast from being 'a brave little North Country pit pony', as I'd been described, to becoming the mouthpiece of the greatest playwright of the twentieth century. I never became quite mature enough to handle this. Part of me still clings to that pit pony, which I haven't been for a very long time indeed. Another part of me thinks I must never take on any work below the level of Beckett – no attitude for a working actress.

At a Christmas party given by the Oliviers, I ran into Alec McCowen. I've worked with Alec, and always thought of myself as being much below him in status in the theatre. Yet when Alec came up to me, he said with a little mock bow: 'Ah hello, Mrs Beckett.'

My reaction was symptomatic of an identity crisis I've tried to conceal. Alec was being courteous, greeting the lady whom Samuel Beckett had wanted in his plays. There was a twinkle in his eyes. He probably also thought that he knew me well enough to take me down a peg or two. And quite right too.

So when I come to think and write about *Not I*, I am not only filled with pride, but also some shame.

5

'Footfalls'

Just before finishing the run of Michael Frayn's *Alphabetical Order* at the Mayfair, Jocelyn Herbert became rather secretive whenever we met, saying things like: 'I think you'll be hearing from Sam soon about something or other.'

It was coming up to Sam's seventieth birthday; various preparations were being made. One night at the Mayfair, Jackie Mac-Gowran's widow Gloria came backstage with a little note from Sam.

Sam frowned on me doing commercial comedies like *Alphabetical Order*. (I felt I should be so lucky as to be doing a Michael Frayn play!) For him this was boulevard theatre. He felt I should be playing in experimental drama at the Royal Court, or the classics.

I am reminded of some time before this, when Martin Esslin, at that time in charge of BBC Radio Drama, directed Harold Pinter, Patrick Magee and me in a radio play by Beckett called *Rough for Radio 2*. At that time Sam had also written me a note, which I couldn't decipher. It looked at though it had been scrawled by a drunken spider. I knew Pat always carried a magnifying glass in his pocket, and that Martin could be described as an expert in deciphering Sam's handwriting.

The first sentence turned out to be: '*It would be good to see you any time anywhere. Just let me know the day.*'

Harold Pinter, who had also tried to decipher the letter, handed it back to me, saying: 'He loves you.'

I was a bit taken aback. I loved him, of course, but then anyone who was close to him loved him.

George Devine loved him and so did Jocelyn Herbert. So did Alan Schneider, who directed all his early plays in the States. To anyone who knew Beckett it was clear that he had that rarest of all qualities: total integrity.

Apart from his unique intellectual and artistic gifts, Samuel Beckett also had a natural quiet authority, of which everyone who knew him quickly became aware. As a director he didn't need to impress that authority on anyone; he certainly didn't need to shout and stamp about.

Once when we were rehearsing, and he was giving notes in the auditorium of the Royal Court, there were some people at the back of the stalls getting in bar supplies; others were clonking about with crates and trays; the cleaners were busy with the Hoovers; someone was yelling down instructions from the Dress Circle; others were charging down through the side aisles. Most directors would have stopped speaking and screamed: 'I'm giving notes here, will you please all shut up!' Sam said nothing; he just stood there with his head slightly bowed.

I found it fascinating to observe: gradually, without him ever raising his voice or even his head, it very soon became apparent to every single busy person in that theatre that Beckett needed silence so that he could give his notes. Gradually a hush came over the stalls. Everyone stopped what they'd been doing. It was the most extraordinary demonstration of real authority I've ever come across. What a gift, I thought.

Besides that authority and artistic integrity, Beckett also had a *moral* integrity that I've never seen equalled in anyone before or since: he had no idea how to be untrue either to himself or to his friends; he never flattered; he showed no concern whatever with the promotion of Samuel Beckett, playwright. The concept of career-building was foreign to him. It wouldn't even occur to him to say something like: 'I've got to get this play of mine on. I want to get the biggest names for it. Let's see if we can get it to New York.'

The only thing that concerned him was to get his work *right*, and if he thought he could get it right in a hut in a back street of Lower Piddlington, that's where he'd want it performed. He didn't give a damn about becoming more famous or getting more prizes, nor did he care for money. When he got the Nobel Prize, rumour has it that he gave most of the money away. Beckett was the easiest touch of all time.

Because of his authority and integrity, I soon found that he became a yardstick for one's own decisions. Whenever we were in doubt over what to do in any given situation, any dilemma, Robert and I would often ask each other: 'What would Sam do?'

That was a pretty good guide to have in a quandary, although, alas, I was far from capable of following his example.

Beckett had a horror of anything shallow, of *publicity* of any kind.

At one time, during our work together, I had given an interview to a journalist. The core of what I'd wanted to say hadn't come out at all. I felt acutely embarrassed. I showed the piece to Beckett, wanting to apologise. 'Don't worry,' he said. Then he added without emphasis: 'Never speak.'

Since then, whenever Robert or Matthew or I have done or said something foolish or self-promoting, we invariably repeat that phrase to each other, before breaking into giggles: *never speak*.

For an actor, to promote what he's doing goes with the job. Beckett never felt that. He wanted people to see his work, but he wasn't concerned to explain or sell it. For as long as I knew him, Beckett refused to talk to anyone about himself or his work. When Deirdre Bair came to write his biography, he kept his silence, saying only: 'I shall neither help you nor hinder you.' I was always aware that he depended on the sensitivity of others to get through his day. To my mind that sentence simply meant: 'I wish you wouldn't.' But she did.

Paradoxically, Beckett was quite gregarious, certainly more gregarious than I am. He'd happily go off to the pub for a pint of Guinness and an Irish whiskey with one of the electricians or prop men, particularly if that person was in some way emotionally troubled. He certainly would be happier doing that than to sit in a room full of adoring, chattering people who wanted to ask him questions about his life and work. He shied away from all that; yet he was fascinated by people's individual foibles.

As I get older, I have tended to become more and more reclusive, yet when in company, I usually chatter non-stop. This could be because I have no head for drink and am (rightly, I think) afraid of the effect a couple of glasses of wine have on me. In Beckett's sense, I'm not a private person at all. He was always private, yet not a recluse. Apart from going to pubs, he enjoyed evenings spent in the company of close friends like Jocelyn Herbert or the painter Avigdor Arikha and his poet wife Anne, Sam's neighbours in Paris. Avigdor lives on one side of the prison in Montparnasse; Sam lived on the other. Sam's flat actually overlooked the prison. While he wrote, he could hear the prisoners yelling and shouting and rattling their cups.

Personally, I never found Beckett to be a remote figure. He needed to know or feel that people were *safe* – people like Jocelyn and the Arikhas. With them he could laugh and be warm and flirtatious, and talk about football and cricket and music.

He once asked an astonished Robert quite seriously: 'Do you think my television plays are getting too short?'

He also knew that with me it was a waste of time talking about the novels of Thomas Mann or the *Lieder* of Schubert. If he wanted an intellectual discussion, he would do that with somebody else. To me, he liked to talk about Matthew and my family, or just let me chatter on.

In Paris we often went for walks, strangely enough in the vicinity of a lunatic asylum. There was a little place where he liked to sit. I would hold his hand or put my arm through his. He never withdrew his hand or felt I was being familiar. We were close, but I still felt in awe of him, although in no way intimidated. I would be aware of who this man was and what he had done. I would talk to Beckett about anything that came into my butterfly mind. I might be in mid-sentence, then see something which made me think of something else, and I'd be off on a completely new tack. Surprisingly, he seemed to find that quite relaxing, perhaps because the last thing I'd ever want to talk about was his work or its 'meaning'. He was under no obligation to find 'answers' – or, for that matter, even listen to me. It didn't matter.

I never found Beckett to be pretentious. Once he told me quite lightly over the phone: 'Oh catastrophe, catastrophe, one of the leaves has fallen off the tree in [a German production of] *Waiting for Godot*.'

He said it with irony, but he also meant it.

Like most actresses, I'll talk endlessly to anyone who cares to listen about minor trials and tribulations. I often got the impression that – like Robert – Beckett enjoyed hearing me gossiping away.

Beckett would never miss a rehearsal, but at the first night he was nowhere to be seen. In America he didn't turn up at all. When I asked him to come over to New York to see his old friend Alan Schneider's highly praised production of *Rockaby* and his own of *Footfalls*, his voice came back, filled with horror: 'Oh Lord, no.' He hated the place.

One time, while rehearsing *Not I*, I took a cassette recorder with me, which I found useful when working with Sam. He would sometimes say something, a delicate nuance, which I'd forget if I didn't note it down immediately. And often I had no time to do that. When he saw me with this tape recorder he called out: 'What's that?'

When I said: 'It's a tape,' he went white. It's the only time I've seen him near panic.

'Oh Lord, is it on?' he wanted to know.

I said: 'No, no, Sam, it's quite all right, I only put it on to record my notes.'

Paris
3.11.75

Billie
Wish you could
have been with us.
I have a little play
for you that I'd
like to put in your
fair hand.
So à bientôt I fondly
hope.
Ever Sam

Paris
10.2.76

Dear Billie
Herewith playlet. Yours
only if you like it & want it.
For inclusion in the Court
season only if agreeable to you.
Hope you are having
a good rest & feeling better.
I'll be in Paris now,
or environs. until I
go to London in april.
Love
Sam

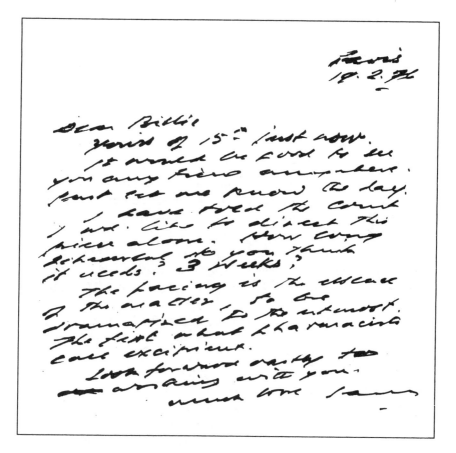

Paris   3.11.75
Billie
Wish you could have been with us. I
have a little play for you that I'd like
to put in your fair hand.
So à bientôt I fondly hope.
                    Ever Sam

Paris   10.2.76
Dear Billie
Herewith playlet. Yours only if you
like it and want it. For inclusion in
the Court season only if agreeable to
you. Hope you are having a good rest
and feeling better. I'll be in Paris now
or environs until I go to London in
April.
                    Love
                    Sam

Paris   19.2.76
Dear Billie
Yours of the 15th just now. It would
be good to see you anytime anywhere.
Just let me know the day. I have told
the Court I would like to direct this
piece alone. How long rehearsal do
you think it needs. 3 weeks?
The pacing is the essence of the
matter. To be dramatised to the
utmost. The text: what pharmacists
call excipient.
Look forward vastly to working with
you.
                    Much love Sam

139

He hated to have his voice recorded. I don't know why. A great pity, because he read his own work and that of Yeats better than anyone I know.

I found Samuel Beckett to be a kind and caring man. Though I never ever heard him make a 'political' remark, he had a powerful understanding of, and compassion for, his fellow man.

He seemed to have unlimited patience when put upon by strangers, yet when it came to his work he would be – like any artist – totally single-minded.

During rehearsal I've often seen him throw up his head in despair and mutter: 'Oh Lord, that's dreadful.' Beckett's audible 'Oh Lord!' moan was something I became quite familiar with over the years.

'Will you never have done? (Pause) Will you never have done . . . revolving it all? (Pause) It? (Pause) It all? (Pause) In your poor mind. (Pause) It all. (Pause) It all.'

In the note he had sent via Gloria, Beckett had mentioned that he had 'a little play' for me. He didn't want to send it. He wanted to give it to me personally.

This 'little play' from Beckett was called *Footfalls*. 'Yours only,' he wrote later, 'if you like it and want it.'

I read the play and thought I couldn't make much sense of it. I had no idea about the play's tempo. Flying into a panic as usual, I got in touch with Sam in Paris. (No one had his telephone number.) Once I'd got the tempo into my head, I would know the area I was working in. I told him I must come over to see him.

We met in Montparnasse.

He said: 'Come on, we'll go and have a meal.'

By this time his eyesight was not very good, certainly not in the dark. I was expecting him to put his hand out to hail a taxi. As he led me down the steps of a Métro station, I was still wondering about a taxi. He simply said: 'No, no, here we are.' I thought it extraordinary that he would want to go by tube, since it wasn't easy for him going down all those steps.

He looked extremely well at this time. He'd got rid of that awful scrubbing brush hair; the old raincoat had gone too. He was in fact very smartly dressed. He wore a soft polo-neck sweater and a ginger-coloured jacket. He looked better and more cared-for than when we had done *Play*, a dozen years previously. Like many men, the older he got the more attractive he became – at least as seen through a woman's eyes.

We came up the steps of another Métro station and went into a bistro, where he was obviously well known. The place was full and we started talking. He was primarily concerned with my character's *movements*, not the words. I felt that *Footfalls* was going to be different for him: he was interested in something other than his text.

He ordered some food and wine. He usually asked for liver. Then he got up and started to walk up and down between the tables. 'It's the movements,' he explained, 'the movement is most important, the way you hold your body.'

Sam felt that directors didn't always grasp what he was after. The shining exception was Alan Schneider, whom he trusted absolutely. But I have never had to act in a Beckett play without him being there to guide me even if, in later years, it could only be done on the telephone.

What I wanted to know most, at that initial meeting in the bistro, was the exact rhythm of the piece, the tempo. Beckett said: 'Slow, and get slower.' Then he reiterated that the main thing was to get the movements right, the changing of the body's posture as the play progressed, as though the character was turning slowly inward.

In the crowded bistro, he now started to show me exactly what he meant, taking seven paces this way and seven paces back, making sure I wouldn't start on the wrong foot. Interestingly enough, no one around us took the slightest notice of all this. I wasn't embarrassed either. We would go back to the table, have a mouthful of food and a sip of wine, then get up again, walk up and down between the tables, talking animatedly. As far as we were concerned, the restaurant could have been empty.

That was our first rehearsal. Though he was going to direct *Footfalls* himself, I realised why for most of his plays, Beckett writes such incredibly detailed stage directions – with maps and diagrams, showing exactly how one should walk, how many paces to take this way or that. He did this in the hope that his intentions concerning the staging of a piece should be absolutely clear. (Now that he's dead, some directors feel all that can be disregarded.)

The pacing was a most important aspect of *Footfalls*. He drew diagrams of the seven or nine paces (depending on the size of the stage) the character has to take. One had to take care to start with the correct foot – the upstage foot. If you got it wrong, when it came to the *wheel* at each end, you'd get your feet all tied up. The actual *wheel* was important to Sam – as were *all* the movements.

Like *Rockaby* later on, *Footfalls* was divided into sections or stanzas. With each stanza, the solo character's movements get slower, slower, slower. There is a short epilogue, a final section. When the lights come on again for this, there's *nothing* there on the stage, nothing. Then the lights go down for the last time. The woman in the play has disappeared, evaporated, dissolved like smoke.

The play is about a woman of indeterminate middle age, dusty and old before her time, pacing up and down a strip of carpet. She is caged in by this one little strip. She's not even pacing around the room, she's confined to *one specific area* of the room, and there she has been pacing up and down, or so it seemed to me, for 999 years, unable to break out of her compulsive, narrow rut – the strip of carpet is now bare. She's having a conversation (which may be going on in her head) with her mother, obviously an invalid, who can't be seen but is heard to speak in the next room. The woman, May, or Amy as she's later called, has the appearance of a spectre. She is looking after this invisible but audible mother, who may be real or not.

The play's movement, the pacing up and down seven or nine paces to the left or to the right, is the physical substance of the play. Sometimes the woman just stands still. The stillness and the silences are as important as the words, and just as important are her clothes which over the years seem to have rotted as they cling to her. May seems to be in the process of disappearing like smoke, of becoming more and more inward, the movements getting ever slower, the body gently spiralling inward as the play proceeds – towards nothingness.

When, with Sam's help, I came to grips with *Footfalls*, there was something else that wouldn't let me go while I was studying the play – a family tragedy.

At the top of my text I've written: 'She was never properly born.' That was something Beckett had said to me about a lecture he'd heard Jung give in Paris. Jung was talking about the case of a young woman. He used the expression that this woman had never been properly born. Perhaps that was the case with May in *Footfalls*. This caused certain shocking echoes in my mind.

My sister's twenty-one-year-old daughter had recently committed suicide. She was found ten days after her death, holding on to a tree, tangled in barbed wire, having taken an overdose of sleeping pills. I hope I'm not upsetting my sister by referring to this, but I admit that all the time I was working on *Footfalls*, I couldn't help thinking of Linda's final collapse, of not being able to go any further . . .

That thought pursued me until I finally spoke to Sam about it. I told him that the last time I'd spoken to Linda, her voice had sounded so strangely slow and empty.

Sam was very interested. He asked: 'What do you mean?' I repeated that, in retrospect, her voice had sounded as though she'd already done the final dreadful act – emotionally and spiritually but not yet physically. That thought haunted me throughout the production of *Footfalls*.

During the rehearsals that followed quite soon after my visit to Paris, I asked him the only question I ever addressed to Beckett about any of his plays: '*Am I dead?*'

He thought for a second, then said: 'Well, let's just say *you're not quite there.*'

I understood this. The woman existed in that ghostly spiritual half-way house between living and not living. I've often thought that when you die it can't be possible to exist at twenty seconds past one and be non-existent at twenty and a half seconds past one. There has to be some sort of passage or transfiguration, a period when the body gets the message that it's dead: I used that in the play. I was aiming for conveying a period between dying and grasping the message you're no longer *there*. Not that we ever discussed this. With Beckett, a good rule of thumb for starters is: 'If it ain't there, don't do it.'

Jackie MacGowran once asked him: 'Am I asking a question in this line?'

Sam said: 'Has it got a question mark at the end of it?'

Jackie said: 'No.'

Beckett told him: 'In that case, you're not asking a question.'

By now Beckett and I had our own aforementioned shorthand. I didn't have to ask: 'What do you mean, *not quite there?*' I knew what he meant.

Another note I remember him giving me early on was: 'You're too earthbound. I want a voice from beyond the grave,' and of course, once again, the perennial 'too much colour, too much colour', i.e. 'Don't act.'

His words were spot-on acting notes. Without these notes I would have been lost. Later, when he could no longer travel, Sam's phone calls to me for radio and television plays were like a substitute rehearsal. I was able to say to him: 'There's always some little thing you tell me on the telephone that gives me the key to the entire part.'

From the start I had assumed that Sam wanted me to do *Footfalls* at the Royal Court. In fact, he was upset that I'd talked to the people there about the play. I have no idea what other plans he might have had for it.

In his letter he had said: '. . . *perform it where you will.*' Perhaps I had misunderstood this. Possibly he wanted this play to be done somewhere else.

I just handed it over to the Royal Court for their celebration of Samuel Beckett's seventieth birthday. *Footfalls* was to be programmed with Pat Magee doing *That Time*, two compatible, complementary, bizarre pieces.

We rehearsed at the Royal Court. It was the first time we'd worked together with Sam as sole director. Needless to say, Sam would not do a play without Jocelyn Herbert. For *Footfalls* she designed the most extraordinary costume I've ever worn on the stage: it really was 'a faint tangle of pale grey tatters'. Like May, this costume was *never quite there*. It grew, it became organic, starting with bits of old lace and things Jocelyn had picked up in various markets. She dipped these bits in different shades of grey, then tore them to give the costume depth.

As I wandered about in it, Jocelyn would come up and tear off a bit here or add a bit there. The making of this garment was typical of the production, part of *work-in-progress*.

Working through the script, I noted the insistent rhythm of the words, the scratching sound of the feet (Jocelyn had put emery boards on the soles of the pumps), the swish to the train of the costume, which Jocelyn lined with taffeta. When I walked, that slight swish had to be heard when I wheeled at the end of my walk. Though the footfalls had ceased, there would be this swish, like the playing of a drum with a brush. All this worked almost like a trio – sound of voice, scrape of footsteps, the brushed drum-beat.

The lighting by Jack Raby was also part of a developing creation. Sam was trying to convey something that was in his head, possibly a dream, something ghostly, mystical, *not quite there*.

For me, as for him, *Footfalls* was to be an entirely new creative experience. Sometimes I felt as if he were a sculptor and I a piece of clay. At other times I might be a piece of marble that he needed to chip away at. He would endlessly move my arms and my head in a certain way, to get closer to the precise image in his mind. I didn't object to him doing this. As this went on, hour after hour, I could feel the 'shape' taking on a life of its own. Sometimes it felt as if I were modelling for a painter, or working with a musician. The movements started to feel like dance.

Beckett moved my fingers, perhaps no more than half an inch this way or that, then he would stand back. If it didn't feel quite right he would correct the pose. Strangely enough, this didn't restrict me at all. More and more I felt that my movements were being choreographed. At other times I felt I was being painted with light. Then it seemed as if Beckett had taken an eraser out of his pocket to brush away what he didn't want. Having done all this detailed direction of movement, he would sometimes rub it all out, so that what grinned through (as they say in the wallpaper trade) was something never strident but faint, i.e. something that was not quite there.

Working with Beckett on *Footfalls*, I began to feel like an extension of his hands. Within the context of this required precision, I enjoyed a feeling of freedom. Whenever the shape and the movements were finally right, I found that a surge of energy would start to go through me. It had taken ages to get to this point, but when we had reached it I knew it. It became the only possible shape. I knew when the shape was not right, because my body felt dead, lifeless.

I made a slightly off-centre *curling* shape, the head at an angle, the waist at another angle from the body, the spine slightly twisted. When this creature moved, it could only move in a certain pre-destined way; the body had its own laws. Whenever Robert saw the play, he was reminded of a sad old dinosaur. In *Footfalls* I sometimes felt like a walking, talking Edvard Munch painting.

Beckett was trying something new. He was no longer merely directing text. Sometimes he had doubts; once, when he came to the house, he muttered to Robert: 'I'm not quite sure whether the theatre is the right place for me any more.'

The walls of the theatre, he felt, were perhaps no longer the right arena for what he was trying to do.

Footfalls may have been the most important work we ever did together. It excited us to be working on this play. Beckett looked at his best; he obviously felt energised by directing on his own. He wasn't involved in any conflict with anyone, certainly not with his leading ladies (Rose Hill played the non-visible mother). Most of his time he devoted to the attempt to create the play's movements, and the strange ghost-like atmosphere, the not-quite-thereness of it. He wanted the pace to become slower and slower, until the play and the woman finally disappeared.

At one point I told him: 'Sam, if I go any slower I'm going to grind to a halt. I'm going to bore the audience to death.'

'Bore them to death,' he said. 'Bore the pants off them.'

And I thought, I'm doing this under his instructions, on his head be it, it's his play.

Often, when directing, Sam would use a specific word when he wanted a pause – like a bar's rest in music. He would say: 'Recover,' and I would know what he meant. I would disengage, and allow a beam of relaxation to enter my consciousness, so that I could recharge batteries and then carry on.

Academically, I didn't understand all of *Footfalls*, but I felt I understood it emotionally. When I got to the part where Amy suddenly turns into May (I assumed it must be the same person), I broke off briefly to say: 'I'm not quite sure what this means. Does it matter?'

Sam didn't bother to explain; he just said: 'Make it ghostly.' Or he would say: 'Make that very quiet, then take it even farther down.'

I took it down to almost nothing, yet at the same time gave it as much physical energy as if I were screaming. I opened my mouth wide enough to belt out a scream. I gave it all the energy of a Shakespearian roar, but produced only a thin cry: 'Amy, Aaaamyyy . . .'

Beckett liked that. His direction was often as basic as that: 'Slow. Quick. Ghostly. Make it ghostly.'

We developed a private joke which made me laugh and stayed with me throughout our relationship: at one point May says that she's 'dreadfully un . . .' I turned that into a sort of spiralling howl. From then on, 'dreadfully un . . .' became a password between us. One morning when I greeted him: 'Morning, Sam, how are you?' he replied: 'Dreadfully un . . . this morning, Billie, dreadfully un . . .'

During the prayer 'Holy Mary, mother of God', I found myself chanting the line like a choirboy whose voice hadn't broken. I allowed the 'Amen' to taper away – like smoke. I was trying to convey a feeling that this creature who was 'not quite there', was beginning to evaporate . . .

As the play progressed, I began to feel more and more like a 'thing' of the spirit, something that was vaporising as we went on. Smoke has a tone and a rhythm. Sometimes it whirls around, sometimes it almost disappears, only to start whirling again in a gush, before disappearing in a diminuendo into nothingness. I felt *Footfalls* was gradually disappearing in our hands, until finally, in the very last section of the play, a very pale light is thrown on the floor, and there is – nothing: the lighting has become paler and paler, the woman looks like smoke, and finally she disappears. That is the image Beckett wanted to leave one with, and it's presumably why he wrote this play.

I said to Sam: 'We should rush out and put a little pile of Fuller's Earth there . . .'

Between the various sections of *Footfalls* there is a blackout, which greatly relieved me, because as I bent over in my dinosaur-like pose, my nose always started to run like a tap, dripping on to the floor

with the consistency of tears. I had a grey hankie tucked down my bosom, and during the blackout I was able to blow my nose without making a sound – at least 'none that could be heard'. I shoved this grey hankie up each nostril and sniffed backwards very hard. By packing my nostrils I avoided any noise. Then I could start the next section.

Footfalls opened at the Royal Court on May 20th, 1976. It was as Sam wanted it. In New York, nearly a decade later, under Alan Schneider's direction, it found a new, enthusiastic audience.

Martin Esslin once wrote: 'There is usually some image in a Beckett play that one takes out of the theatre, and which remains with one for the rest of one's life.' With *Footfalls*, the image of a tangle of grey tatters, gradually vanishing, had an extraordinary effect on some people.

Sam, by now far from well, asked Walter Asmus to direct the play with me for TV in Stuttgart. This production was a true interpretation, yet to me it seemed like a photograph or copy of the original. When I saw it on TV, it looked too distant to me. Sam wanted to see my eyes throughout. When I turned I always 'swirled' my face into the fading light. At least that's how it worked on the stage.

Seeing a revival of *Footfalls* in London in 1994, I felt deeply depressed. The very talented director and actress obviously felt that they had to 'do something' with the play. The production had May wandering about, not only all over the stage but upstairs into the dress circle. Yet, in the dialogue, the line occurs: 'I say the floor here, now bare, this strip of floor, once was carpeted, a deep pile.'

During a discussion on BBC Radio's *Kaleidoscope*, the presenter commented how well the play lent itself to being 'opened up'. What a sad misunderstanding! Just the reverse is required: the play spirals inward.

Beckett didn't write this play for actors to 'experiment' with. The plays were, in themselves, experimental. He wanted them to be done as he wrote them. To him, the speaking of the lines was only a small part of the whole work. If you throw out his detailed stage directions, you lose the play. An actor and director should have faith in what's on the page, and that comprises both the text *and* stage directions.

6

'Happy Days'

After we had done *Footfalls* at the Royal Court, Jocelyn Herbert had it at the back of her mind that Sam and I should do *Happy Days*, with him directing. I think Professor Jim Knowlson, Sam's biographer, who is in charge of the Beckett archive at Reading University, was also in on this plan.

Beckett and I talked about the possibility of doing *Happy Days* together for about a year (1978–9) before we started. He wanted to direct it right away, which was almost immediately after Peggy Ashcroft had done it at the National in 1977, with Peter Hall directing.

I told Jocelyn I didn't think we could do it so soon after Dame Peg; it would appear disrespectful to our greatest actress. It might have been all right for Joe Bloggs to do it somewhere in the back of beyond, but for Beckett to come over to do it in London would be like a slap in the face of the National Theatre. Beckett agreed that we should leave it for twelve months.

When the time came, I dutifully, rather than joyfully, went off to read *Happy Days*. Even on an occasion like this I could not bring myself to read a play before rehearsals had actually been set. I knew very little about *Happy Days*, except that it was the play in which Brenda Bruce had been buried up to her neck in arid earth.

Now, as I began to read, I was immediately struck by the thought: how on earth could this man have written the story of my life so long before he knew me? Instinctively, I felt the play showed the universal human task of *getting through the day*. To me, this meant sometimes having to hang on by one's fingernails – just to survive. And who is to say that what we do just to get through the day, such as acting in a play, or having a coffee morning, or going to a cocktail party, or writing this book, is more or less significant or typical than poor Winnie's desperate, pathetic ways of getting through her day in *Happy Days*. Filling in the time between 'the bell for waking' and 'the bell for sleep' is what her life amounts to. Sometimes it satisfies her, sometimes it doesn't. Sometimes she is filled with happiness about her activities; occasionally – like all of us – she has to dodge despair.

That's how Beckett has etched Winnie's life – buried up to her waist, and later up to her neck, in arid earth. To me, this seemed a perfectly legitimate way of dramatising the way one spends one's life – which is all we've got.

Winnie empties her bag, but never too quickly; *she has to make it last*. She doesn't want to use up too soon the various options available to her during one day. And while she does this, she babbles away – as I do.

It wasn't difficult for me to grasp any of this. For me, getting through the day meant acting for a living, pretending every day to be *other people*, while also being a wife and mother.

By now, I knew enough about working with Sam to realise that to turn up at rehearsal without knowing my lines would be a waste of time for both of us. I wanted to use the seven weeks we had together to *work* on the play – not as a means of learning my lines. I knew I'd have to learn all those 'Oh wells' and 'Ah wells' littered about the script, and in their correct order – every dot, every dot, dot, dot, every comma and semi-colon.

I went upstairs to the top floor of our house and made myself a cosy bed-sit out of a spare room, which I called my 'snug', a place where I could just sleep and eat and read. Next door was a kitchen. That took care of my fuel: endless cups of tea. Every morning I had breakfast with Robert and Matthew. Then I gave them a hug, fled up to my snug, and drew the curtains.

I had a copy of the play on the bed with me, and as a starter put the whole play on tape, over two hours of it. If I woke up in the night, usually with some of the lines racing through my head, I would stretch out, press the button on my cassette recorder and check them out to see if I'd got them right. I couldn't go back to sleep if I didn't. I spent three months like this. I tried not to abandon my family, but working on *Happy Days* must have tried the patience of everybody around me.

As always, when I'm trying to learn accurately, I became more and more nervous as the first day of rehearsals drew near. My back went into spasm, my head began to spin with blind panics. I had pinned a calendar on the wall which told me that by such-and-such a day I had to get to page 27, to page 38 a week later. Sometimes on this calendar I scrawled 'Help' in large red letters, because I seemed to be for ever going backwards.

As with *Not I*, when I'd learned one page and was able to rattle that off, I found that when I tried to add some more and then put it all together, I had erased what I had already learned. At least I thought I had.

Towards the end of this period I became aware of something horrible happening inside my skull. I couldn't lie flat on the bed because a large mouth had started to grow across the back of my head, and when I put my head down, the mouth kept trying to scream. I knew there was no mouth there, but nevertheless that's the way it felt.

I went to see Eric de Payer, a man I'd consulted before. He was about seventy and had been a Latin scholar. He had given all that up to teach the Alexander Technique of body relaxation. But he was more than that – a natural healer, and, like Beckett, he was one of those people I had an immediate rapport with. He got me to stretch my various muscles and helped to ease my tensions. He told me that I was very tired, because I was trying too hard.

'But I've still got such a long way to go,' I told him.

Sometimes when I was with him, I went into a deep sleep. He would then just go off, leaving me to rest for an hour or so. He never woke me or said it was time for me to go.

At one point I rang Brenda Bruce. I asked her how on earth she ever learned this damn thing.

'I suppose once you've learned *Happy Days*,' I said, 'you can learn anything.'

'No, no,' she said, 'after *Happy Days* I felt I could do *nothing*. I've never recovered. Even after all these years.'

Before I started working with Sam, I had a couple of word-runs with Robbie Hendry, who was once again Sam's stage manager. By the time Sam arrived, I could juggle with the text. At the Royal Court a young man called Roger Michell joined us. He had just come down from Oxford; his first job was to be Samuel Beckett's assistant!

It had taken me three months, but when Sam first came to rehearsal at the Irish Club, just off Sloane Square, I knew *Happy Days* inside out and back to front, or thought I did. With Sam came the lighting designer, Jack Raby.

Sam and I quietly started to go through the play together, *to speak it together*. After a while I heard Roger ask Robbie: 'When are they going to start rehearsing?'

Robbie told him: 'They've started, this is it.'

We just sat there on two kitchen chairs, whispering the lines and 'conducting' each other, eyeball to eyeball.

Sam said the play was a sonata for voice and movement. By that he meant that everything was precisely timed – like notes of music.

I had no problem with the rhythm of the play, but got into my usual mess with the props I had to handle. They are essential to the play: taking a toothbrush out of my little bag, cleaning my spectacles, taking my handkerchief out of Winnie's cleavage – all had to be accurately timed, fitting not just a specific word but *a specific syllable of a word.*

Jocelyn and Sam had dressed me like a soubrette, with strapless top, a feathery thing over one shoulder, a silly little hat with a feather in it on top of my back-combed straw-on-a-muck-cart hair. My makeup comprised bright red lips, crudely put on, red dolly rouge on my cheeks and a lot of eye makeup. A demure, middle-class lady I was not.

Sam had told Jocelyn exactly how he wanted me to look. I told them I had a strapless bra at home. That was used. Jocelyn covered it with pink satin and black lace. The hat was similarly pink, decorated with black lace and feathers.

Roger observed the progress of our unusual rehearsal method. I thought it had all started off well. I felt properly prepared. Then, gradually, I began to get the familiar feeling that other actors working with Sam had experienced. As we went on, getting more and more precise, I had a sense of starting to roll backwards.

Not only were all the details of his direction incredibly precise, he had also begun to rewrite as we rehearsed.

With Beckett rewriting is not as it is with other writers. 'Oh wells' would become 'Ah wells', some 'Ah yeses' became 'Oh yeses' and vice versa. If I got these wrong, I could hear Sam groan with anguish in the front row of the stalls.

That didn't put me off at first. I knew him well enough to ask him if he would mind very much sitting a little farther back in the stalls, so that his groans wouldn't put me off my stride. I knew that it caused him physical pain to hear someone say 'Oh well' when he had finally decided on 'Ah well', and I tried to explain that my brain was not like a piece of paper, where once you'd written on it, it would stay for good.

It was becoming hard going. Squatting in my mound for over two hours, and looking out at the audience, I couldn't always tell where to direct a certain line.

'I want to ask you a technical question,' I said to Sam. 'Where shall I look on this next page?'

He said: 'Inward.'

I said: 'Of course. Inward.'

I understood that Winnie, too, has moments when she just drifts inward and into herself.

At one point in rehearsal Sam said, in a sort of aside, that he didn't think *Happy Days* was really a very good play. This upset me a lot. Hell's bells, I thought, I'm putting in all this work, turning myself inside out, trying to give him what he wants, and now he says he doesn't like the play! In my heart of hearts I thought it was because I was so bad. All I wanted was to please him. I blubbed all this out to Jocelyn, who was, as always, supportive. I think she must have said something to Sam, because after the first night I had a contrite letter from him.

However, for me things began to go from bad to worse. Having started by knowing the play inside out and back to front, I now began to forget it. The harder we worked, the less I seemed to remember. The two-and-a-quarter-hour virtual monologue was in danger of reducing itself to a technical problem about whether I said two 'Oh wells' on page 36 or two 'Ah wells' and one 'Oh well' on page 37.

Robbie could see I was getting into a state. 'What am I going to do?' I asked him. 'I'm getting worse and worse.'

I went in to see Stuart Burge, at that time running the Royal Court.

'I'm going to pieces,' I told him. It was something that had never happened to me before when working with Sam.

Stuart wondered if he should perhaps take over direction of the play. I wouldn't have that. I knew I'd rather have the whole thing cancelled than do that to Sam. Yet something had to be done.

Jocelyn had begun to worry; she knew Sam always had dreadful problems with actresses going to pieces on *Happy Days*. I rang Peggy Ashcroft: 'I'm going mad,' I told her. 'I don't know what to do.'

'You've got to ask him to leave, dear,' she said. 'He's impossible. Throw him out.'

I said: 'I can't do that.'

She said simply: 'Well, you'll have to.'

Robbie and I decided I needed forty-eight hours on my own. I had to get out from behind my rehearsal table and chair and all the things I felt were restricting me. I needed to free myself. All I wanted to do was to stand on that stage and yell the words out up to the gallery.

I'll never forget Sam's sad look when Robbie told him what we'd decided, and the way he tried to seem unconcerned as he came up to me and said, almost cheerfully: 'Well, Billie, I think perhaps it would be a good idea if I just left you on your own for a couple of days. Just go through this on your own a bit with Robbie, then we'll meet again on Monday.'

Then, with his back to us, his head and shoulders bowed, he slowly walked along the length of the stalls. Somehow I was reminded of a Lowry painting. I felt my heart was going to break. And I remembered Sam walking towards me when I broke down physically during rehearsals of *Not I*, when he'd said: 'Billie, what have I done to you?'

This time I just watched him walk slowly away from me – out of the theatre.

All I wanted to do was to cry. Yet as soon as he'd gone, I said to Robbie: 'Right, let's get out from behind this table, throw the chair away, and let me yell this stuff up to the Gods.'

I had my forty-eight hours on my own, and managed to get rid of my tension. When Sam came back on the Monday, I felt better.

As rehearsals continued, I also got slightly irritated when Sam seemed to spend as much time with Leonard Fenton (who played Willie) as with me – a typical actress's reaction.

I wanted to say: 'Look here, Leonard's only crawling round this damn mound and has a few lines. I've got two hours of dialogue!' How infantile!

During a rehearsal lunchbreak, there was a moment that moved me very much. I was standing in the wings watching Sam, a long, thin figure without an ounce of spare flesh on him, crawling round and round the mound of earth on the stage. That entire lunch hour he spent in deep, deep concentration, playing Willie, crawling round and round and round. I couldn't take my eyes off him.

Which reminds me of what another actress, directed by Sam in *Happy Days*, told me. He had read the entire text of *Happy Days* to her. 'I'm sure there was only one perfect Winnie ever,' she ended her story. 'That was Beckett himself.'

As we came to the final rehearsals, Jack Raby perfected his lighting. It became very fierce. I think he was waiting for me to protest. The lights got brighter and hotter still. They seemed to burn my eyeballs through my eyelids. Finally I couldn't stand it any more and spoke up.

'I was wondering when you were going to complain,' Jack said. 'I've used everything I've got on your face.'

I like to think that Sam's production of *Happy Days*, which opened on June 7th, 1979, was a success. Certainly all the reviews were excellent. During our very limited run at the Royal Court the place was packed out.

It was Sam's only production of the play in England. Later he was to say that my Winnie was child-like. Odd little bits about my Winnie made him laugh: the telling of the story about the small girl climbing underneath the table and undressing her dolly, probably all very Freudian and sexual; the way I did the Mr and Mrs Shower or Mr and Mrs Cooker story, which I spoke with a broad cockney accent. I enjoyed the freedom of doing it that way. It was never analysed or discussed between us, but I always had the feeling that the story, and the line: 'What's she doing? he says – what's the idea? he says – stuck up to her diddies in the bleeding ground?' were Beckett's comment on the audience – as much as to say: 'What's that bloody actress doing up there on that stage, buried up to her waist, and then up to her neck, in earth?'

My own thoughts on such lines were, who's to say that what she is doing is more or less significant than people sitting out there in the auditorium, watching us do it?

I think Sam wanted me to lighten the part. On a line like: 'The earth is very tight today. Can it be I have put on flesh, I trust not,' I wriggled around as though I'd put on a bit too much weight. Sam gave me a note about that: 'Winnie wants to float up, she's bird-like.'

Being on the stage as Winnie felt a bit lonely. Willie was there with me, but I couldn't see him. I felt I had to have something of my own in the mound. I filled it with all the rabbits I'd been collecting for thirteen years ever since Robert started calling me 'Miffy'. I had soft toy rabbits, pottery rabbits, wooden rabbits. I managed to find places for all of them in my mound. Then, when we started the run, I also shoved poor Roger Michell in to be my prompter. On the odd occasion when I needed a prompt I couldn't always hear him. Sometimes I kicked him hard – not unlike the way Winnie kicks out at Willie. Poor Roger never complained. It must have been very hot and uncomfortable for him down there, surrounded by all those rabbits.

Whenever I waited for the prompt, I just stared out into space. I'm sure Beckett scholars regarded these pauses as something terribly significant. (Mind you, there were moments when I did stare into space as part of the characterisation.)

The general reaction to the production was not quite as intense as it had been for *Not I* – nobody had ever seen anything like the endlessly babbling Mouth – or indeed for *Footfalls*, where Beckett had attempted something entirely new.

Also, of course, *Happy Days* had already been seen a number of times, and the run at the Royal Court was too short for me to make the play absolutely my own. I only became fluent with the sonata towards the end of the run.

It was the last time Beckett directed me in the theatre. He told me more than once: 'I'm not going to work in the theatre any more, Billie, I haven't got the energy for it.'

Looking back, I think Sam found doing *Happy Days* a strain. The two of us hadn't lost our appetite for working together, but it must have depressed him a bit that, like every other actress who had ever attempted *Happy Days*, I had become distressed during rehearsals.

I suspect Sam was a bit sad – not necessarily with me, but possibly with himself. Perhaps I'd made him feel that he'd failed as a director. He was upset because he'd upset me.

When he got back to Paris he wrote me a sweet letter, apologising: he should never have said during rehearsals that *Happy Days* was a bad play.

By this time the BBC had started filming everything Sam and I did together. Tristram Powell, who had directed *Not I* for television, which had pleased Sam so much, now directed *Happy Days*. We had planned for two weeks' rehearsal, but then I went down with flu. I had a temperature of 103. For the filmed record of *Happy Days* I didn't rehearse at all.

I consulted a famous throat specialist. Actors called him the Chorus Girls' Friend because he considered it one of his perks (if you were a woman patient) to give your left breast a little squeeze as he poured something down your throat. It didn't offend me, it made me laugh. I called in on him on my way to the TV studio for the recording, knowing I only had this one afternoon to do it. He gave my backside some sort of cortisone injection to stop me from coughing, to enable me to make *some* kind of sound.

I got through the first half of the play, then I started to cough. We were running out of time. Jim Knowlson rang up his own doctor. He gave me another strong concoction to take. Somehow we got through it.

Perhaps because I'd had no rehearsal and was still running a temperature, and there were so many details to worry about, I was relatively unafraid. When Tristram Powell said: 'All right, Billie, do it,' I said: 'All right, off we go,' and I didn't stop till it was over. I hope I managed to retain all that Sam had asked me to do in the theatre.

Working like this in the TV show, I remembered some of the

performances Olivier had given as *Othello* when he'd been too exhausted to go to the gym or do his vocal exercises, when – in my opinion – he was at his best.

Looking at it after fifteen years, I feel the filmed version of *Happy Days* isn't all that bad. As I write this, I'm also thinking, at the moment I seem to have lost heart for acting, yet part of me likes to believe that one day before I die the fire may be rekindled: I'll be able to re-learn this wonderful, incredible part, and just once more perform it somewhere where it's never been seen before.

I have one treasured memory of working with Sam on *Happy Days* that seems the right way to finish this chapter. The play ends with Winnie softly humming to herself to the chimes of a musical box. Beckett scholars tell me that Sam had originally wanted Winnie to sing 'When Irish Eyes Are Smiling'. But, in the play's definitive version, it's the waltz duet from *The Merry Widow* that she sings.

When we came to it, Sam asked me: 'Do you know this?' I answered yes, but he insisted on singing it to me – from beginning to end – in a frail, quavering voice.

I felt so moved that when I sang it at the end of the play, I always tried to do it exactly as I heard it when he had sung it to me. He never knew that I was impersonating him, as I sang so softly:

> *Though I say not*
> *What I may not*
> *Let you hear,*
> *Yet the swaying*
> *Dance is saying,*
> *Love me dear!*
> *Every touch of fingers*
> *Tells me what I know,*
> *Says for you,*
> *It's true, it's true,*
> *You love me so!*

Intermission Two:
Writers

I am practically illiterate. I try to avoid writing letters; when I do write something I make a spelling mistake every third word. I very rarely read, preferring to potter about the house, listening to Radio 3 or 4, or Classic FM. If it's fine, I sit in the garden and watch the birds. If I do pick up a book, it is very likely to be about the life of a composer, and I've been known to read a book I'm interested in in one gulp. Yet without words, and without writers, I wouldn't be anywhere in this (or any other) profession.

I married a writer; my closest professional relationship was with a writer; my closest friends are writers. Yet I have read only a couple of my husband's novels, hardly any of Beckett's prose, certainly not more than two or three plays by Shakespeare. I have an uneducated, possibly unprejudiced taste, which allows me to enjoy both trashy show-biz books and Greek Tragedy, without there being a great deal of difference to the enjoyment I derive from them.

The writer who was probably more involved than anyone in kicking off my career – by inventing a certain character from me – was Alun Owen. We both came along just at the right time. When I got a couple of awards in 1960, it was for the work I'd done in Alun's plays.

This was just after Sydney Newman had come over from Canada to shake up what was then ABC Television, and British television drama in general. I had already seen some of the Canadian TV dramas he had produced, and found their realism streets ahead of what was then being shown on British TV. Sydney was a brilliant bully, who matched writers with directors, letting them build up a body of good work together. He partnered Alun Owen with Ted Kotcheff, Philip Saville with Harold Pinter and then Robert Muller,

Charles Jarrott with Leslie Sands and Bill Naughton, among others. Sydney and his team changed the face of British television drama. People stayed in on a Sunday night to watch *Armchair Theatre*, and discussed the plays the following Monday and Tuesday.

I was the heroine in the Ted Kotcheff and Alun Owen team, along with Tom Bell – always a startlingly good actor. We worked together on a play called *No Trams to Lime Street* (now wiped, alas). Alun was, I think, the first writer to bring to our TV screens 'romantic leads' with strong Liverpudlian accents. Up to this time Northern accents were relegated for use by funny charladies, chirpy typists – in other words, as comic relief.

In 1960, it was considered quite revolutionary to have love scenes played with Liverpool voices. (Now of course one hardly hears anything else.) Audiences expected leads to talk like Noël Coward and Vivien Leigh. Alun's second play with me, *Lena, O My Lena*, has been miraculously preserved (God help me – I thought I was dreadful), and is frequently repeated. It does look a bit old-fashioned now. I want to put my head in my hands whenever I see this neurotic performance of thirty years ago. But I'm sure series like *Z Cars*, *Softly Softly*, and even soaps like *Coronation Street*, partly developed out of the *Armchair Theatre* revolution.

Alun, Tom and I also worked together on the stage. A play we did for Theatre Workshop, *Progress to the Park*, later transferred to the West End. This was a Liverpool Romeo and Juliet story, Protestant v. Catholic, and most critics praised it for being exotic and new.

Alun and I knew each other well, also our ways of working. I never asked him if he wrote specifically for me, as Beckett and Robert were to do later on. We were just part of a particular group around at a certain time. I think I might have been a bit put out if *Progress to the Park* had been played by anyone other than me. In a musical version of *Progress to the Park*, Rachel Roberts played my role, because my singing voice wasn't good enough.

Like Harold Pinter, Alun had been an actor before he became a writer. He was Liverpool-Welsh or Liverpool-Irish, depending on whom he was talking to. In fact, he was Liverpool-Welsh, but he had the actor's desire to please. He married when he was very young, sixteen or seventeen. Thirty years passed before I saw him again, at a party given for Ted Kotcheff by Clive Exton, another of Sydney's protégés in the Sixties.

Ted who had come back from Hollywood, a millionaire film director, wanted to see his old friends for a get-together.

I almost didn't recognise Alun at first. Decades had gone past, but, after a hug, it was as though we had worked together only the day before.

Alun never told any of our gang how to do our jobs, but he was always on hand at rehearsals. As an actress I marvelled to have someone writing dialogue that came so naturally out of my mouth.

Before there was Alun Owen, in my early twenties, I tended to be cast as a funny cockney secretary with big breasts, who filed her nails and said: 'Gor blimey', or I was the tweeny below stairs. Alun allowed me to play a woman as opposed to a parody of one, and I was able to identify with the character. Before it became the norm, he had the facility of writing about 'ordinary' people and their problems. The parts Alun wrote enabled me to use my own experience of life. The lines he gave me were the sort of thing I said in real life. Alun's writing opened me up as an actress, and helped to give me an identity that enabled me to play other modern roles. He was, I suppose, the British Paddy Chayefsky.

One of Alun's plays for Armchair Theatre, *After the Funeral*, had no part for me in it and proved to be a big success. The story goes that after the play was done, Sydney Newman cried out triumphantly: 'And this time Alun did it without Billie!'

Alas, in what Sam Beckett would call 'a bit of synchronicity', Alun died, aged sixty-nine, while I was revising this chapter.

This is where I must mention another writer, who was not a playwright at all, but who contributed to the creation of my professional persona. In the late Fifties and early Sixties, Kenneth Tynan was our most influential drama critic. I think Olivier took him on board at the National Theatre as literary manager because Ken was in the forefront of those in the theatre who demanded radical change. I have a feeling that Ken must have had a hand in getting Olivier to bring me to the National. Tynan did much to change our perception of theatre, though I must confess I could never take him quite seriously. He was a somewhat fluttery, hysterical man with a stutter. This made me nervous in his company because I suffered from the same affliction. The first time I saw him stuttering and spluttering was at the rehearsal of Beckett's *Play*, where he thought we all went much too fast.

Ken had an odd way of holding his cigarette – not between his index and middle fingers, but between his middle and ring finger. This gave him a somewhat effete air, although it was no secret that he had an eye for the girls. To me, at this time, for all his revolutionary left-wing views, he looked a bit of a toff, at the same time foppish and very grand. He had nothing in common with me, wasn't my kind of man at all. Nor was I his kind of lady. But Ken doffed his hat towards the likes of me – whom he considered to be the rising working class in the theatre.

When the company went to Moscow (see Intermission One) Tynan and Albert Finney returned to London early. I was at Moscow Airport to see them off. As their flight was being called, they were still standing at the end of a vast check-in queue. Tynan was becoming more and more jittery. He spluttered and twitched; his arms and hands always seemed to me to be too long for his body. Suddenly I saw him grab his passport and leap into the middle of this endless circular queue. He waved his passport, baying at anybody who cared to listen, that he was B-b-b-British and had a p-p-plane to catch.

I almost peed myself with laughter. Here was our great left-wing intellectual asking for, no, *demanding* preferential treatment, in Soviet Russia of all places, because he was British.

Poor Ken died far too young; the British theatre would never have made such strides without his writing and preaching.

Two young writers I felt at home with (yet somehow in awe of) were Keith Waterhouse and Willis Hall. Very early on in their careers they wrote *England, Our England,* the revue that John Dexter directed at the Princes Theatre, with music by Dudley Moore. Keith and Willis came from my part of the world. Though they had already achieved considerable success with *Billy Liar,* they were neither arrogant nor strident, but modest and rather shy. They had already developed that rare talent – of taking neither success nor failure very seriously.

One thing that has stuck in my memory about *England, Our England* was the first-night party at the White Elephant. At this time Willis was married to Jill Bennett, who later married John Osborne. Jill was already sitting at the company table. As I approached, she simply froze me out. I was too embarrassed to be angry. Bloody hell, I thought, I'm playing the lead in this damn thing, and here I am standing in the middle of this posh restaurant with egg on my face. I just wanted to get out. Fortunately, Stanley Baker, who was at a neighbouring table, gallantly came across and asked me to join his table.

I found it difficult to take to Jill after that, although I admired her as an actress. My friend Elizabeth Monkhouse, who had been to the first night, said to me: 'I wouldn't take it to heart, love. She's been bitching you all through the show.'

In 1970, I worked with another Northern writer, David Mercer, who, like Ken Tynan, died far, far too early. The director David

Jones rang up from the Royal Shakespeare Company, to ask me if I would transfer with David Mercer's *After Haggerty* to the Criterion Theatre. Frank Finlay, an old friend from the National Theatre, played the lead. By now I was no longer the frightened little thing with a chip on her shoulder, who could be frozen out of her first-night celebration.

I already knew David Mercer's work. I held him in great respect, though in my internal cupboard I had put him in a drawer marked 'Intellectual Writer'.

I took to him straight away, though he didn't seem to want to get involved in the rehearsal process. One night he stormed into the theatre, a little the worse for drink, and, for some reason, insisted on going on the stage. In the corridor I threw myself between him and the wings. I told him if he wanted to get on the stage he'd have to knock me out first. Had I not stood in his way he'd probably have lurched on to the stage to make a speech.

After the performance we went out and had a Chinese meal with Robert and his director friend, Peter Zadek. Neither of them seemed to notice that David was in some sort of emotional pain. I knew what was wrong: he was desperate for a drink. I said to Robert: 'For God's sake, get this man a drink.'

In *After Haggerty* I played a tiresome young American revolutionary. It was the writer Alan Brien's then wife Nancy who helped me with the New England accent. Even so, I felt the part to be virtually unplayable. I tried to ease up on the character's hysteria, but David Jones wanted me to give it all the energy I could muster. This creature was yelling and shouting from the moment she came on. I wish there had been time for me to go a bit more deeply into the character, but we opened 'cold'. I didn't have the luxury of a pre-London tour.

We had quite a decent run at the Criterion Theatre. I remember one afternoon lying down, after a matinée, when I felt something crawling across my belly. *Cockroaches!* The entire dressing-room had to be gutted because there was an infestation of them.

David Mercer had a child by a French woman. They had Daddy's Place in London and Mummy's Place in France and they visited each other, a style of living Robert and I had found quite attractive before we moved together to Camden Square. After the birth of his child, David seemed to calm down and for a time he actually stopped drinking. It was shortly afterwards that he dropped down dead.

I met John Osborne for the first time when I went to audition at the Royal Court Theatre. He was a small-time actor and stage manager, very slim, keen, and helpful, not yet *the* John Osborne, and especially kind to nervous actors who came to do their auditions. This early John Osborne is certainly far removed from the dragon who wrote dreadful things about his friends and ex-wives.

Unfortunately I was never asked to appear in any of his stage plays. When the BBC did a TV revival of *The Entertainer* with Michael Gambon and me recently, he wrote in the *Spectator* that he hated all of it. Never mind, Robert and I liked and admired him enormously.

In the Sixties, I briefly came across yet another John Osborne in, of all places, Acapulco, where he insisted on behaving outrageously with his consort of the time (and later wife) Penelope Gilliatt. Telling the paparazzi to go and get stuffed, while at the same time making themselves so available around the hotel swimming pool, they challenged the photographers to buzz around them even more, or so it seemed to me. Clearly a high old time was had by all . . .

Listening to the radio this Christmas Day (1994) I hear the announcement that John Osborne has died on Christmas Eve.

Like Alun Owen and John Osborne, Harold Pinter emerged from obscurity in the Fifties – as an actor. I first met Harold in Datchet in 1960. Donald Pleasence, who'd just had his first real West End success in *The Caretaker*, was now my next-door neighbour. I had already seen some of Pinter's television plays. They struck me as quite extraordinary and (in the case of *The Lover*) very sexy. Certainly they were quite unlike the naturalistic plays that Alun Owen and I had worked on in Teddington.

Whenever I met Harold at Donald's, he always appeared to be dressed in a uniform of black trousers and sweater and seemed somewhat unapproachable. I was quite frightened of him, and remained so for many years. Recently, after we'd known each other for ages (and acted together in Beckett) I told him: 'You know, Harold, I've been frightened of you for thirty years. I'd like to get rid of this fear.'

Harold *almost* smiled. At Donald's funeral we embraced, and for the first time I felt totally at ease with him.

Harold obviously enjoys acting, just as John Osborne did. Together with Patrick Magee we worked in a radio play by Beckett called *Rough For Radio 2*, about which more later. Patrick was at his most brilliant, using his croaky stream-of-consciousness voice, which worked so well in Beckett's work. I don't think Harold or I were all that good, nor, I suspect, did Beckett like what we did.

Over the years I seem to have worked with most of our leading playwrights, usually during the very early parts of their careers. One of these was Michael Frayn, whom I first met when we were being interviewed together on a radio programme. Because of my work with Beckett, the interviewer had dropped me into a totally untenable intellectual slot. I was left high and dry and had to let Michael do most of the talking, which he did charmingly.

Michael and I met again when Michael Rudman, the young American director who was running the Hampstead Theatre Club, came to see me in 1975 with a Michael Frayn comedy called *Alphabetical Order*. Reading it made my toes tingle with delight. I loved Michael's unpretentious humour. I was never frightened of him at all, although he comes from a quite different background than my own. I've always thought him warm and very accessible.

I could easily identify with the part he'd written, a scatty lady who worked in a newspaper cuttings library, and was about as efficient as I would have been doing her job, a collector of lame ducks, who never realised that she herself was the lamest duck of them all.

I regret that it was the only time that I worked with Michael. However, quite recently, nearly twenty years after *Alphabetical Order*, I worked with his stepson Tom in a television film about disabled people called *Skallagrig*. Michael and I met again, and I found him as friendly and courteous as ever, warm and open, with no 'side' at all – a good man and a fine mind.

In my own estimation I bracket Michael with a similarly gentle and vastly talented writer, Christopher Hampton. Though enormously successful now, and powerful in the film industry, Christopher remains warm and modest. I always feel I can give him a big, welcoming hug.

I first met him in the mid-Eighties when I was cast by Peter Gill in *Tales from Hollywood* at the National Theatre.

The play had originally been commissioned by Gordon Davidson for his Mark Taper Theater in Los Angeles, where I've appeared a couple of times. The idea for it had first germinated when Christopher stayed with Gordon at his Santa Monica home, the house where Salka Viertel had written most of her friend Greta Garbo's films. It was that house which, just before and during the last war, had become a centre for European intellectual refugees who had fled from the Third Reich to make a new start in America – people like Bertolt Brecht, Heinrich and Thomas Mann, and Lion Feuchtwanger.

Gordon became increasingly involved with the history of this house. He asked Christopher to stay there and write a play about its history. Not long ago, while I was spending the day with the Davidsons, he showed me the little Wendy house in his garden.

Bertolt Brecht had once lived there. When Christopher came to live there, he became steeped in its atmosphere. He said he could almost feel the ghosts of the place coming alive, and that he longed for the walls in Gordon's dining-room to speak to him. Out of this feeling came *Tales from Hollywood*, for this is where, strangely enough, these European intellectuals had ended up.

I played the ex-Berlin barmaid Nelly Kröger-Mann, the great Heinrich Mann's unbalanced wife, whom he loved dearly, but who was despised by Thomas and the rest of the Mann family because of her background. They all regarded her as a common trollop. Nelly had the proverbial heart of gold and nursed Heinrich for years, though she herself became unhinged by homesickness and alcohol, and eventually committed suicide.

Nelly's background was not at all unfamiliar to me. Robert had once wanted to write a play about Nelly, and had told me quite a lot of her history and that of the Mann family. He had also adapted Heinrich Mann's most famous novel *Man of Straw* for the BBC. This introduced Derek Jacobi to British television audiences. So I didn't come as a total stranger to the uprooted Mann family in California.

Nelly was a woman who, though she loved her husband dearly, became increasingly angry that he was old and failing. She wanted him to be as strong and dominating as he had been during the gregarious life they had enjoyed in Berlin. In Hollywood, Heinrich was poor and totally at sea, trying to earn a crust at Warner Brothers, and growing senile.

The highlight of *Tales from Hollywood* was a birthday party, at which all the snooty intellectuals had assembled to pay homage to Thomas Mann. Nelly must have felt about this bunch of people rather as I did when I first encountered London's theatrical society. I'm sure Nelly's response was as superficially dismissive as my own.

Genuine and open-hearted, Nelly couldn't find anyone with warm or genuine feelings among Heinrich's family and friends. How I could identify with her!

At the climax of the party, Nelly comes into the crowded room, holding a birthday cake aloft, with all the candles lit up – stark naked. For someone of my age – I was fifty – to come on nude at the National caused a bit of a stir. During rehearsals neither Christopher nor the director, Peter Gill, ever discussed this nude scene with me. They must have had a hell of a lot of trust in me. No one apart from the costume designer knew what I was going to do till the first dress rehearsal. I jibbed at showing my pubic hair, so I sent the whole thing up slightly by wearing a waitress's tiny frilly apron, the size

of a small hankie, with long ties that went over my hip-bones and
a bunny rabbit bow at the back of my bum.

After the first night, a well-known (female) casting director rang
me and exclaimed: 'My dear, *you* – a centrefold! I've been thinking
of having my boobs done, too.'

I was outraged.

Unlike most professional actresses, I seem to need a point of personal identification in the parts I play, something that recalls to me
an incident in my own life. When I had to play this scene I recalled
the time when I first came to London. At a party I'd drunk a glass
too much, feeling, as usual, ill-at-ease and out of my element. I was
standing by a table on which stood a lot of empty glasses. I was
thinking, what do I have to do to get just one honest reaction
from this lot? I took all the glasses off the table and smashed them
on the marble floor, one by one. No reaction. Nothing. So I followed
this up by hitting the host across the face. After smacking him about
four times, my very polite host, an actor, finally hit me back. I con-
gratulated him for showing me the first genuine emotion I'd encountered all evening.

All that had happened decades ago, but now I managed to use
those feelings for playing Nelly Kröger-Mann. There was a lot about
her that I understood only too well.

Altogether *Tales from Hollywood* was for me one of the most
satisfying productions in the theatre. Moreover it gave me the chance
to play opposite Michael Gambon, one of my favourite actors, whom
I first met during his spear-carrying days at the Old Vic.

Christopher Hampton and Peter Gill worked together very har-
moniously, and throughout rehearsals I found Christopher very
encouraging and buoyant.

Some readers may think I've spent too much time in the theatre
being frightened, or belly-aching, so I'm very pleased to say that
another production which gave me a genuinely happy feeling was
the epic *The Greeks* at the Aldwych for the Royal Shakespeare
Company.

Unfortunately, my mother died towards the end of the rehearsal
period for *The Greeks*. Mum was eighty by then and hadn't been at
all well, but I'm glad she lived long enough to see her only grandson
grow up happy and healthy.

Probably the best contemporary play I've ever done was written
by Peter Nichols for the Royal Shakespeare Company. It was called
Passion Play and was about a middle-aged, middle-class couple in
crisis. The couple is played by *four* people, one pair of actors playing

the husband, another pair taking the part of the wife. One couple lead lives as seen by the world around them; the other pair perform the same couple's secret inner life, the existences they try to conceal. Eileen Atkins and I shared the part of the wife, Benjamin Whitrow and Anton Rodgers played the husband.

Most playwrights I've known have suffered from anxieties about their work. Possibly people like Michael Frayn and Christopher Hampton find it easier to conceal their neuroses. Peter Nichols would admit, I think, that his latent paranoia shows a bit at times. Paradoxically, Peter and his wife, a brilliant painter, are very effervescent people socially, enormously entertaining, and I think probably happier than most theatrical couples. Yet in 1980 towards the end of the successful run of *Passion Play*, after its allotted six months at the Aldwych, two members of the cast didn't want the run extended. I thought the play was unique and worth fighting for, and in fact I fought hard for its run to be extended. When *Passion Play* received the Evening Standard Best Play Award at the Savoy, Peter got up to receive his prize, and I was astonished to hear him tell the assembly in so many words that his play could well have continued – had the actors not wanted to take it off. One got the impression that the actors had sabotaged *Passion Play*. I must say I felt a bit hurt by this, but Peter realised he had inadvertently hurt me and felt sorry about it.

Perhaps not quite in the same superior class as *Passion Play* was *Molly*, a play I had performed in 1978. I think Simon Gray would now agree that it's not among his better works.

The subject matter of *Molly* had been treated earlier in a play called *Cause Célèbre* by Terence Rattigan with Glynis Johns. It's the story of a woman who is living with an older, deteriorating husband in a remote part of Canada. Rather like Nelly Kröger-Mann, she hits the bottle because she has no real life with this old man. A seventeen-year-old gardener comes into the household, and the woman starts an affair with the boy, who ends up killing the husband (played by T.P. McKenna). All this was based on a true criminal case. The woman went to the electric chair, taking the blame for the boy.

For Simon this was a very untypical subject, but he'd written a demanding part, an alcoholic who seduces the boy on stage. (I wouldn't let my young son come to see the play!)

Molly was performed at the Comedy Theatre at a time when Vanessa Redgrave was more than usually politically active in the theatre. Over an issue which I have quite forgotten, Vanessa wanted to bring out all the casts in the West End on strike. I didn't have a great deal of time for this, believing that actors have enough of a hard time getting work, without millionaire actresses hauling them out on strike.

The flying pickets came out, and one night they appeared at the Comedy Theatre, shouting at the arriving audience that there'd be no show tonight. This made me so angry that, half dressed, I leapt out of my dressing-room. I ran down Panton Street and along the Haymarket, grabbing members of the audience and dragging them back to the theatre. Most of them dodged this madwoman in a dressing-gown, to hail taxis and disappear.

'If just seven come back, we'll play!' I yelled above the London traffic.

Like me, T.P. McKenna was in a rage, but he is less volatile. (On this occasion I would seem to have been on the wrong, i.e. the right-wing, side!) Enough people responded that night and the curtain went up.

Later, when I got home, I rang up our local radio station, something I shouldn't have done, because I was far too agitated to put our case rationally.

Simon Gray is a playwright who gets deeply involved in a production of his work. He simply wouldn't leave *Molly* alone during rehearsals. There were the usual disagreements during the pre-West End provincial tour. I couldn't settle on any specific interpretation. At Cambridge, Simon turned up at breakfast, and we would go off to sit on the banks of the Cam to argue about his play.

During this tour, something I'd not experienced before was happening: every night I was giving a totally different performance. What I did depended on the last person I'd spoken to.

One night Robert came to see the play in Richmond. Afterwards he asked me: 'Why are you playing a demented lesbian in a mackintosh?' So for the next performance I changed everything again, and tried to soften the character, who had become far too strident. Simon came round and said, 'I wish your husband had come round a little earlier.'

I became very fond of Simon and remain a great admirer of his writing, though I have to say: a silent laid-back observer of his own work he's not. But I quite like that. I think Simon is the only other person I've met who shares my own constant sense of guilt. During one rehearsal I said to him: 'Why do I always wake up feeling so guilty?' And his face lit up with a sense of recognition.

I feel very privileged to have worked on so many new plays by living playwrights, rather than appearing in revivals of works that are hundreds of years old. I suppose ever since Theatre Workshop, I've wanted to be involved in the creative process with writer and director, as opposed to doing Lady Macbeth for the umpteenth time, wondering what actresses A, B, C and D had done with that part since the year dot. Mind you, I have to say that nearly *all* plays are new to me. It's most unlikely that I will have seen or read any of them. But I like working on new material, and have been incredibly fortunate working with some of the best minds in the contemporary theatre.

One eminent writer I got to know by walking through quite a different door: Edward Albee. We had a great mutual friend in Alan Schneider, who directed most of the early Beckett plays in the United States.

In the spring of 1990, the University of Wisconsin in Madison held a week's conference on Alan's work, at which I was invited to speak.

Most of my time in Madison I spent with his widow Jeannie, and Joy Small, Alan's Girl Friday, and with Edward Albee. Meeting Albee was fortuitous because I'd desperately wanted to talk to him ever since, in 1987, I'd had my shot at playing Martha in his best-known play, *Who's Afraid of Virginia Woolf?*

Alan had told me this was the play he wanted to direct with me. On one of my very first visits to the theatre in London I'd been lucky enough to see the original production of this play, and was held spellbound. While working with Alan on *Rockaby*, I remember asking him if he'd ever seen that wonderful production.

'Well yes,' he said, and smiled. 'I directed it.'

When David Thacker asked me if I'd come to do a play at the Young Vic, of which he was then in charge, we settled on *Who's Afraid of Virginia Woolf?* The play is about George and Martha, an unhappily but indissolubly married couple. George is a rather ascetic university professor; Martha is the daughter of the Dean of the university. The play, now a classic, is about the couple playing out their raging neuroses and aggressions in front of an audience of a visiting younger couple. George and Martha lacerate each other verbally until they draw blood.

After I'd agreed to play Martha, David and I sat down to discuss at great length who should play George. We both wanted Ronald Pickup. Unfortunately he was unavailable. We settled on a highly experienced and distinguished actor from the Royal Shakespeare

Company, Patrick Stewart. Out of the habit I had developed while working with Beckett, I went away to our little country cottage in Suffolk and started to learn most of the part up-front. I also discussed various aspects of the play with Jeannie Schneider. As always, she was enormously helpful.

I was a bit thrown at the start when David said the play would be staged in the round. I felt this would make it far more difficult for all of us to create the play's *trapped* feeling. I tried to persuade David to do it with an apron stage, or with a thrust stage, but both he and Patrick were in no doubt: In-the-Round was the right way. For me, that may have been the beginning of a feeling of being at odds and out of synch with both leading man and director.

As rehearsals proceeded, something happened to me that reminded me of a similar situation on *Happy Days*: after a few weeks I felt I was starting to roll backwards. In *Happy Days* it had been possible to put things right; this time I felt things going from bad to worse.

Patrick is physically very strong and athletic, and he was incredibly fit, not only younger than me, but certainly in better shape. I have never been blessed with great reserves of physical energy and try to guard them like gold dust when I'm working. I find I have to draw on nervous energy when my strength starts to run out. Possibly because he never had an abundance of physical energy himself, Beckett (when I worked with him) seemed to understand this. We would rehearse for two thirds of the day, then I would sleep, and then I'd be able to quietly absorb the work we had done. This division of work and rest was an ideal way of working for me. Perhaps in that way my work with Beckett had spoiled me, as he would arrange rehearsals to suit my own energies and needs.

Now, as rehearsals continued, I felt Patrick getting stronger and stronger and fitter and fitter, while I watched myself becoming a worn-out rag. What should have been a battle of heavyweights became unbalanced. I also felt disheartened by what both David and Patrick thought to be a necessary activity – endless discussions about certain aspects of the play. The answers to some of these problems were, to me, as plain as the nose on my face. Maybe these discussions were a valid exercise, but I wasn't used to pulling something about that was obvious to me, and began to feel that I had nothing to contribute.

This analysis of the play would sometimes go on for hours. The question came up over and over again whether George and Martha actually had the child they constantly talked about, or whether it was an invention for their game-playing. It seemed to me glaringly obvious from reading the text that there was no child, though I can quite understand that David and Patrick regarded their debates as a necessary part of the rehearsal process. Yet, after a while, I found it destructive. Finally I said to Patrick: 'Look, if you want to believe that they have a child, go ahead and play it like that. As for me, I just don't think they've ever had one, and I'll play it like that.'

That must have sounded like heresy to the others. Yet I must say I've often played a part with my own private thoughts possibly diametrically opposed to what was in the head of my partner. To work that way can sometimes make absolute sense to me. In real life, what can we ever know about what the person one is talking to is really thinking? I tried to get hold of Albee in America to ask his advice, but unfortunately we never made contact.

One evening after we'd been rehearsing for hours, I felt so exhausted, I just wanted to lie down and die. At which point Patrick decided he wanted another run-through. I couldn't believe my ears. I didn't know how I was going to get through this. On impulse I did something I'd never done before, of which I'm now ashamed. Like those tempting glasses on the table at my first London party, I picked up the script and slung it along the entire length of the rehearsal room. That did at least one thing: it gave me the necessary shot of adrenalin to carry on rehearsing.

During the second half of the rehearsal period, I began to feel that I was quite seriously beginning to unravel. I wondered again if I had been spoiled by working with Samuel Beckett, who never ever stopped to debate the meaning of a play or a particular line. We concentrated on the music of the lines and by some grace of God and little fairies we were in harmony. I just tried to get on with creating the atmosphere the author had indicated on the page.

Yet I mustn't be unfair. We weren't doing Beckett, we were doing Albee. Also I mustn't give the impression that I never wish to discuss a play I'm in. Once, during the TV production of *The Entertainer*, Michael Gambon screamed at me: 'For God's sake shut up, I want to get on and rehearse.' But here the recurring 'problem' of the child seemed to me as plain as a bloody pikestaff: this couple had no child and the killing of the fantasy child at the end, which had me in tears at every performance, was indeed very much like the murder of a real child.

I never managed to make my view comprehensible to Patrick or David, and slowly retreated into my corner.

The best way for me to re-charge my batteries whenever there is a break in rehearsal, or at lunchtime, is to lie absolutely flat on the ground. Some actors like to relax by going to a pub or the canteen. I prefer to lie flat, with a pint of milk and a leg of chicken. I can burn up a whole afternoon's fuel by chattering and gossiping during the lunch hour.

I'm dwelling on the problem of rest, because this production demanded a great deal of energy input from two leading actors. It seemed to me that the more energy Patrick was able to give out (for which I envied him), the more he seemed to gain in stature over me, which wasn't necessarily right for the balance of the play.

What I didn't realise is that privately Patrick must have been on a high throughout the rehearsals. He was wheeling and dealing for a job that would take him to the States, and into the show-biz stratosphere, a job which would make him a household name and a multi-millionaire. He was to be Captain of the spaceship *Enterprise* in *Star Trek: the Next Generation*!

What an insecure lot we actors are! I had to be reassured by my husband and my son that they wouldn't be too ashamed of me, if I walked off the stage half-way through the first night. They would love me, they assured me, no matter what I did.

The first night came, and I managed to get through it and, in fact, through subsequent nights. The notices were good for us all. To the world outside it must have looked as though we were a big success, but I was deeply unhappy.

There now began a lot of talk with backers about a transfer to the West End. I noticed, however, that whenever this subject cropped up, there was a strange hush of embarrassment all around me. I put this down to my paranoia. I wondered if my doubts were caused by a feeling, shared between Patrick and David, that they couldn't bear to work with me any longer. Patrick's then wife, Sheila, a well-known movement and dance teacher, whom I had known well from the Royal Shakespeare Company, came backstage one night. I went to greet her cheerfully, but she seemed to look straight through me.

I again thought this was because I'd made life such hell for everyone during rehearsals. Later I realised that Sheila was embarrassed. While I was babbling about a transfer, she knew it could never happen. Patrick was off to Hollywood.

This may have contributed to the heightened excitement in Patrick's performance. We actors don't leave our private lives entirely behind when we walk through the stage door. However hard I tried, I could never match Patrick's elation.

During the run of *Who's Afraid of Virginia Woolf?* many people came to see me backstage. David Jones, who'd directed *After Haggerty*, could see I was distressed. When I told him: 'I don't know what the hell's happened to me, I have totally lost my confidence,' he said something very wise: 'It sometimes happens that an actor loses his place between the director and another leading actor, and can't find his way back.'

I think that's what happened to me during *Who's Afraid of Virginia Woolf?* But I didn't just feel I couldn't find my way back with David Thacker and Patrick Stewart. I began to feel there was no longer a place for me in the theatre at all.

What little confidence I had left broke up in the second week of the run. Half-way through a performance my mind went an absolute blank. I could have been on the moon.

To have a sudden crippling sledgehammer blow of stage fright isn't unusual for experienced actors. I've been on stage with Laurence Olivier when it's happened to him. Here it occurred to me half-way through a sentence, but this time I felt no help could be expected either from David or Patrick. They weren't able to say: 'Don't worry, it happens to us all, forget it.' Far from being sympathetic, I suspected they were probably angry with me for my lack of professionalism. I certainly didn't feel embraced by comfort or warmth.

After that, my mind went blank every night, whenever we came to that one point in the play. We managed to get through it, of course, by Patrick getting me on to something else that followed. But my confidence was shot. The fact that I went on to spout long speeches when Martha is alone on stage made no difference. My entire evening started to revolve around this one line half-way through the play. The production became the ultimate actress's nightmare for me.

Since then, except for my one-woman Beckett evenings, I've never set foot on a stage again.

This débâcle sets the scene for my Madison meeting with the writer of *Who's Afraid of Virginia Woolf?*, Edward Albee, a couple of years later. During the conference we sat side by side. I was able to admire his razor-sharp wit, his gift of cutting through a maze of argument to go straight to the heart of a debate. At the conference he was constantly saying things that, over the years, I've often longed to say but for which I've lacked the right words. He would often get up and simply say: 'Oh, I see,' then cut the ground from under some pompous speaker. It was a spectacle I enjoyed watching.

I felt that he would be supportive and sympathetic, so eventually

I told him about my daunting experiences with his play.

'Am I crazy?' I asked him. 'Surely there is no child, is there?'

'Of course there's no child,' he said, 'that's the whole point of the play.'

In retrospect I should have gone along with the others at the Young Vic, *pretending* there was at least a possibility of a real child. By now, I'm convinced they were debating the point as an exercise, and were quite justified in doing so. Yet at the time it seemed to me to be a waste of precious energy.

I still wasn't used to getting up and talking to a room full of academics, but this was what I'd been asked to do here – to talk about my work with Alan Schneider.

That afternoon in Madison, Wisconsin, with Jeannie Schneider and Joy Small at my side, I suddenly found myself sidestepping into an entirely new career.

What irony! The play I had wanted to do ever since I saw it those many years ago, and which the original director wanted me to revive with him, broke my confidence. Yet that same play's author also helped to give it back to me – to use in quite a new and different way. He gave me a big hug and I felt forgiven – I certainly felt a lot better.

Joy and Jeannie told me that afternoon that, whether I liked it or not, I would from now on have to go and spend some months of the year in America to talk to university students, particularly about all the work I'd done with Beckett over the years.

But that is another story.

7

'Rockaby'

O ne afternoon in 1980, while working on *Passion Play* at the Aldwych, my telephone rang. A man with an American accent introduced himself as Danny Labay, and asked me if I would appear in a new Beckett play in Buffalo. *Buffalo? Labay?* Another Beckett nut, I thought to myself. (There are quite a few of them about.) Or perhaps an over-enthusiastic American academic.

I was very wrong. My life was about to take a new turning.

I had never acted in the United States before. Though I'd made a few American films, they had always been shot in Europe.

The play that the unknown gentleman (who turned out to be Daniel Labeille, head of the Drama Faculty at the University of Buffalo) offered me was called *Rockaby*. Dan had written to Sam some time ago to ask him if he would 'please write a play for my university'. To Dan's astonishment, Sam wrote back saying: 'I hope this meets with your approval.'

Attached to the letter was *Rockaby*. Sam's favourite director, Alan Schneider, would present the play in Buffalo, along with a short story called *Enough*.

The piece was sent to me. It was even shorter than *Footfalls*. I couldn't quite work out the tempo, but knew it would have to go slowly. However, from past work with Sam, I knew that there is slow and slower and graduations of slowest.

I spoke to Sam about *Rockaby* on the phone. As usual he gave me the one decisive note I needed. He wanted the play to have the quality of a lullaby. He also said I was not to be afraid to make it sound monotonous.

Rockaby is a one-act, one-woman piece for an old lady dressed in black Edwardian clothes, with grey hair, on which rests a little black hat (again, as in *Happy Days*, with a little feather in it), who rocks backwards and forwards in her old rocking chair, listening to her own repetitive thoughts. She only speaks a few sentences out loud. The rest of the lines are recorded on tape – they are her last unspoken thoughts, as she rocks herself to death. (Or does she?) Alan tried to get as close to *white sound* as possible when we recorded this tape.

The unnamed woman's last thoughts are repeated more or less verbatim in three stanzas. The voice gets slower; the movements of the rocking chair become slower; the light on the woman's face becomes fainter and fainter, until in the end everything stops.

The play's structure reminded me at once of *Footfalls*. In fact I discovered quite a number of things in this late Beckett work that I recognised from previous plays we'd done together.

I had to explain to Mr Labeille that I couldn't come out to America immediately, as I was working for the Royal Shakespeare Company. That didn't seem to discourage him. During the final week of the run of *Passion Play*, he arrived at my front door, together with Alan Schneider, and an American documentary film-maker that even I had heard of – D.A. Pennebaker (who had made *Don't Look Back*, the famous film about Bob Dylan on tour). With them, they also brought a young stage manager and Chris, Pennebaker's wife, who did the sound for his films.

As we sat down, Alan asked, in passing as it were, if I minded if Penny hung around for a while to take some film. Of course I didn't mind. However, as Alan, a youthful and enthusiastic sixty-three-year-old Ukrainian-American, and I started to rehearse our project, I began to feel slightly self-conscious: for the next few weeks Pennebaker's camera hardly ever strayed from me.

We rehearsed at our home in Camden Square. I must confess I sometimes showed off a bit in front of the ever-present camera. I also said certain arch things I wouldn't have uttered without the camera being there. Thank God, Penny cut all that actress's artifice out of his final version. All the same, the rehearsals took on a slightly schizophrenic edge: I didn't always know whether I was supposed to concentrate on Alan's direction or whether we were collaborating with Penny to make a good documentary. Finally I had to ask Alan and Danny: 'How long is Penny going to be around, so that we can start rehearsing?'

They both grinned and looked a bit sheepish. I realised that *Rockaby* wasn't just a production for Buffalo. I suspect money had to be raised, and one of the main draws for the backers was this documentary: Alan and myself rehearsing a Beckett play from the first reading to the opening night – something that had apparently never been done before. When I realised this was the deal, I stopped showing off and got on with the work.

I liked Penny and Chris, and got used to their presence: everywhere I went Pennebaker was close behind me, or more usually in front of me. I wouldn't have been surprised to find him at the other side of the door when I went to the loo. Certainly, when in the evening I came running down the steps of the Aldwych Theatre, Penny's camera would be in position. When I returned to my dressing-room after the show, he'd be waiting for me.

When it came to our last night at the Aldwych, Penny filmed me as I waved goodbye to Peter Nichols and the director Mike Ockrent. I didn't even have time to go to the last-night party. My last night in London was spent packing; we were set to leave for New York early next morning.

Looking back, the rehearsal period at home in Camden Square had been a very happy process for me. Alan possessed the enthusiasm of a teenager. I loved his open, eager face; he was very practised and patient with actresses' egos. If I was determined to do something other than what he had intended, he'd say to himself: 'Well, OK, let her, that way she'll be happy. If I try to make her do it my way, she'll only be miserable and won't be able to concentrate on the things that really matter.'

Alan had been very close to Sam. They were in harmony when they worked together, even when, as in *Rockaby*, they worked apart. Alan had directed the first production of *Who's Afraid of Virginia Woolf?* and also the only movie Sam ever wrote, called *Film*, with Buster Keaton.

For Alan's sake, Sam actually went to America for that, but he hated the place. 'Never again,' he once told me.

To me, Buffalo was a great adventure, though we almost didn't make it. The flight from New York to Buffalo with Alan was the closest I ever came to an air crash. There was snow and ice everywhere. Lake Eyrie was frozen; even the waves turned to ice. As we lifted off, the plane skidded. Everyone screamed. I looked sideways at Alan. He was clutching his seat, his knuckles showing white, his wide-open eyes staring straight ahead. I don't think he was breathing.

Is this it, I wondered?

Somehow the plane retrieved its balance. Had the wing tipped a fraction more to one side, the plane would have exploded.

We made it, but there had been other problems to overcome. Initially, American Equity had refused to let me work in the States.

It was thought the part in *Rockaby* could be played by an American actress. Sam wrote to them more than once, pointing out that he had written this play (and indeed other plays) especially for me. Would they please be kind enough to let me in to play in *Rockaby* in Buffalo? The answer was always no. Finally Equity relented. I was never to find out why.

When I got to my enormous dressing-room in Buffalo, Pennebaker's camera went back into action. I took things out of my makeup bag and arranged them on the dressing-table. He cut from this to Winnie doing almost the same thing in *Happy Days*. He even managed to juxtapose my own comments as I unpacked my makeup with Winnie's remarks as she paws about in her handbag.

I took out a pot of my mother's Pond's cleansing cream which I always had in any dressing-room I worked in. Penny caught me looking at this little pot with great affection, giving it a little kiss before putting it down. This exactly matched Winnie's taking out and kissing the gun in *Happy Days*.

The Buffalo opening consisted of me (as myself) reading *Enough*, then performing *Rockaby*, filmed by Pennebaker as the climax to his film. Like most American university theatres, the Buffalo theatre was very grand and well equipped. Naturally I had thought to myself that we were going out to the sticks, a typically British attitude. I soon found out that Alan was giving the production all the care he would have invested in a production on Broadway or the West End.

I have a feeling Alan could have made a fortune in the commercial theatre, but he wasn't much interested in that. He was always on the lookout for new and offbeat pieces of writing by people like Beckett and Pinter and Albee, work that he wanted to do even if it meant doing it in some place at the end of the world. He would often have three or four productions on the go at the same time, usually off-Broadway. Yet when he died, all the Broadway theatres dipped their lights.

In Buffalo, during the final rehearsals, I was to encounter a new Alan Schneider. When things weren't going quite the way he wanted them backstage, Alan would have one of his temperamental brainstorms. I would hear him yelling and shouting at the top of his voice. Yet this temperamental side of him was never used to destructive ends. There was nothing neurotic or calculating or sadistic about Alan's outbursts; they came straight off the top of his head. When the time was right he could be a real taskmaster. Everything had to be exactly the way he had it planned, or – in this case – as he thought Sam wanted it.

Alan had to work very hard to get this production absolutely right the first time round.

As with most of Beckett's shorter works, the play *Rockaby* looks deceptively simple. It isn't, of course.

I've often been asked to set up *Rockaby* somewhere: it's a one-woman play after all, it's short, all it needs is a rocking chair. I've always had to refuse. The play can't be performed without minutely designed lighting. Also, the chair can't be any old rocker. It rocks *on its own*; the actress's feet never move. This can take hours to set up, and requires a special mechanical device with someone at the back of the stage with a ratchet and a monitor.

To Sam and Alan, these technicalities were essential elements of the play. *Rockaby* must have a certain disembodied, not-quite-of-this-world look, akin to a surrealist painting, if it is to work.

Should a young director ever take it into his or her head to do a simplified revival of *Rockaby*, doing without the myriad lighting cues and the chair's complicated rocking mechanism ('all the actress needs to do is just rock backwards and forwards'), I have to disillusion them.

It is the fact (a) that the chair is rocking on its own; (b) that the woman's feet never move; (c) that the dialogue sometimes comes out of the actress's mouth, sometimes out of space, and (d) that the disturbing effect of the play's ending is achieved by very precise lighting changes, that gives *Rockaby* its unearthly quality.

Another difficulty is Sam's insistence that the actress keeps her eyes wide open for a very long time. I found this particularly hard, as I tend to blink a lot. When I look at some old movies I've done, I seem to be blinking all the time. My eyes are weak and sensitive to light.

At the Buffalo dress rehearsal I had to look out-front with a blinding spot on my face. I tried to look just underneath the light, but that didn't give me much comfort. My eyes became unnaturally dry.

Once again I had to hunt down a doctor who could help me. At a local hospital, an ophthalmic surgeon told me: 'You have no tears whatsoever in your eyes. What on earth are you doing?'

When I told him, he said I should try and keep my eyes closed for as long as I could. He didn't know *Rockaby*! Frequently Alan yelled from the back: 'Your eyes should be open at this point, Billie!'

'I know they should,' I'd yell back, 'but this light is making me blind.'

I was given some drops, but at the first performance, and even later on, my eyes hurt like the devil. In the *Rockaby* documentary, I can see my eyeballs trying to roll backwards. Obviously there's no such thing as an easy Samuel Beckett play.

It had not crossed my mind that this (to me) 'provincial' production at an Eastern university of two short Beckett pieces would be the first of many trips I had to make to America and other parts of the world to perform this bill. Alan's production went to the East and West Coast of America and to Australia, and also opened an entirely new kind of life for me, which I have already referred to briefly – talking to young people about working with Beckett.

Reading this section back, I am aware that I may be giving an impression that my work with Beckett was always an *ordeal*, that during any production of his plays I was in the position of a victim.

It wasn't necessarily so.

There were hurdles to be jumped over, but that was all part of the challenge. My somewhat plaintive attitude is probably due to a flaw in my character: whatever part I accept, I am invariably overcome by an element of blind panic. By the time the first night comes round, this panic has subsided. I begin to feel that from now on, it's all in the lap of the gods.

I do realise, though, that I'm not easy to have around during the rehearsal period. I think Dan Labeille found this to be true. During *Rockaby* rehearsals he said to me: 'At one time, early on in our relationship, Billie, I did think you thought I had horns.'

Actually I found working with Alan Schneider and Dan Labeille very stimulating and I enjoyed our time in Buffalo.

Robert came out to join me, bringing Matthew with him, who by then was thirteen years old. In the foyer of the Buffalo theatre, an exhibition of Beckett memorabilia had been arranged, for which Alan contributed his prized collection of Beckett's letters to him.

Alan and Sam were both great letter-writers. Sam was unbelievably punctilious in keeping up his correspondence. No letter to him ever went unanswered, and his correspondence with Alan obviously meant much to him.

From Buffalo we went straight off to New York to do the Beckett bill of *Rockaby* and *Enough* at the La Mama Theater on the notorious Bowery.

It surprised me that the production of a new Beckett play off-Broadway was regarded as an important event in New York. The critics came. So did Irene Worth, who had done so much Beckett in the States before me, and was most generous in her attitude to me.

Albert Finney came to visit, and next day took me out to lunch at the Russian Tea Room, where we joined Michael Caine and his wife. Albert asked what I wanted to drink. I asked for a Buck's Fizz – called a Mimosa in America. To my astonishment, Albert ordered Dom Perignon and I watched him mixing this most precious of champagnes with orange juice. 'Bloody hell, Albert,' I told him, 'what a waste.'

Albert had also come to see me backstage at La Mama. He found that in my enormous barn of a dressing-room there were no flowers. The following evening, when I walked in, I was stunned: the room was filled with flowers and plants. I looked at the card: 'Dearest Billie, these flowers are for your dressing-room, love Albert.' That was nice.

Despite these intimations of New York success, it was down to the lower depths of the Bowery every night – hardly the most salubrious of venues. The street outside the theatre was littered with drug addicts, veterans from the Vietnam war, who had just been dumped on the sidewalk. Seeing those poor sods, after drinking Dom Perignon Mimosas and finding roomfuls of flowers, put things into their proper perspective for me.

In the second week of July 1982, Robert, Matthew and I went away for a short holiday in the South of France. We stayed in a well-known restaurant, which had rooms as well.

Robert had been working very hard on a German film. I felt he needed a rest.

On July 14th, France's national holiday, we went up to the mountains to see our friends, the novelist Thomas Wiseman and his wife Malou, who lived a few miles away, near Grasse.

We enjoyed a lovely big lunch of paella. Afterwards we swam in their pool. It was a warm, pleasant afternoon. Before it got dark, we drove back to our restaurant. I was at the wheel.

Suddenly Robert complained that he thought he had indigestion. Being the witch I am in matters of health, a big 'danger' lollipop went up in my head. Lord knows how or why, but I *knew* it wasn't indigestion. I stopped the car. Robert said he needed a little walk, he'd be fine after that. Yet when we got back to the hotel, I immediately rang Tom and Malou to ask if they knew of a cardiologist. Robert was getting cross about the fuss I was making, but this was Quatorze Juillet. I didn't want to be trapped on a national holiday with a sick husband who needed immediate help.

I was quietly certain that Robert was about to have a heart attack, and felt no great emotion about this. In fact, I thought of it as a re-run of the way I felt when I knew Matthew was about to be diagnosed as having meningitis. I determined to get a cardiologist to Robert at once.

The doctor arrived, a friendly, plump, concerned man, slightly harassed, but not at all upset that I'd called him out on this of all days. He told Robert to lie still and relax. To me, he said I was to call him immediately if we should need him during the night. Then he left.

Robert lay quietly on the bed, not unamused by the thought that one was waiting for a heart attack as for a country bus. There was nothing to do but to carry on. I ordered champagne and changed into evening clothes. I kept an eye on Robert while Matthew and I idled in the sunset on our idyllic terrace, eating smoked salmon goodies and drinking champagne – not at all the way one would have written the scene had it been in a play or movie.

After we'd finished our gourmet meal, which we also had on the terrace, Matthew went off to bed. I sat with Robert, who wanted me to give him a detailed description of the meal he had missed.

Then it happened. Robert felt a burning pain in his chest and all the way down his side. I called the cardiologist, and asked him to get back quickly. He arrived, looking very hot and now a bit anxious, as if he had had to suffer too many patients collapsing on him on the fourteenth of July.

By this time Robert was in agony. The doctor couldn't give him an injection until he had swallowed various pills or tablets. Robert was indeed having a massive heart attack. The doctor showed more concern than Robert, who said that dying was a not uninteresting, possibly unique, experience. Meanwhile either the doctor or I accidentally dropped the vital pills and were scurrying and scrabbling under the bed to try and find them. Robert got the giggles despite his pain. We finally found the pills and pushed them down Robert's throat.

'Visconti got dying so wrong,' Robert said, obviously thinking of *Death in Venice*. 'It's pure farce.'

Throughout this harrowing night, none of us reacted the way one thinks one is going to react. In fact, most of the time we were laughing and giggling. It all felt quite absurd – this sudden catastrophe, though we both knew Robert could be dead within the next five minutes. All I knew was we had to move *fast*. Perhaps we laughed in order not to have to think about what was happening.

By now it was one o'clock in the morning; the hotel restaurant was closed. It was difficult to get a telephone line to work. Finally an ambulance arrived. The ambulance men looked very solemn. Robert asked them for the football results of the day.

By the time the ambulance had reached the nearest hospital, Robert was no longer laughing. He was told he would have to stay the night. His mood had changed; he was convinced that all the doctors in the hospital were drunk and incapable. He claimed they were breathing alcohol and garlic fumes into his face, which he found not to his liking. I was sent home. What remained of the night, he spent wide awake in a darkened room.

The following morning a doctor and two nurses came, and discussed in excited Gallic whispers how and when the patient could be transferred to a specialist cardiac hospital in Nice. Robert kept hearing one of the nurses exclaiming several times, loud enough for him to hear: 'Mais c'est trop tard!' which encouraged him no end.

Some time later I got a phone call to say that Robert had been transferred to an Intensive Care Unit in Nice. Tom and Malou drove me there. I was allowed to go into the ward but I had to gown up first. I walked along corridors, where trolleys stood at all sorts of angles, with people asleep or groaning in pain. I had never seen anything like it. It felt like being in the middle of an episode of MASH.

In the ward there wasn't even a semblance of order. It looked as though there had been a plane or rail crash. There were far too many beds, all standing at odd angles, with tubes running along the floor and hanging from the ceiling. People were moaning and crying, others looked already dead. There were children in there too, also men who, even in their close-to-death state, looked very well off. They had obviously been brought in from their holiday yachts, and now lay almost naked, except for fashionable primrose yellow shorts and Rolex watches around their wrists.

In the middle of this chaos I discovered Robert, who was allowed to have three minutes with me. I think I mumbled something totally fatuous through my green mask, like: 'Well, you've come through the wood.' Then I had to turn and leave. I started to laugh uncontrollably.

'It's like MASH in there,' I kept saying, 'I've never seen anything like it.'

It was touch and go. Robert had another couple of heart attacks in my absence, but the second one happened while he was already in the operating theatre. As the doctors had nothing to lose, and it was indeed almost *trop tard*, they did what was then an experimental emergency operation: they slashed his groin and put a tube through his body up to his heart and inflated a bubble in one of his arteries. Robert was only given a local anaesthetic and could watch his survival (or absence of it, as the case might be) on monitors.

He recovered very slowly. For two weeks he was as weak as a kitten. They wanted to send him home on a private plane, but finally the doctor sent him (and us) on an ordinary flight. They roped off part of the plane, and put a stretcher along several seats, with Matthew and myself sitting close to him, and the doctor at his feet.

Miraculously, Robert recovered completely. Eighteen months later, a cheerful French doctor called us, wanting to know if Robert was still alive. Indeed, he wanted to be told where his 'papers' could be studied. The case had been so interesting; they had done this particular operation only three times before, and had only decided on it that time as there was nothing to lose. Now the doctor wanted to see how the experiment had worked out for the patient.

'It worked out fine,' Robert told the cheerful doctor. 'You're talking to the patient.'

I have tried to report this account of Robert's heart attack with a light hand. Robert would be furious if I didn't. But after all this time I feel that if ever there should be a reckoning at the end of my own life, the only thing of value I have to offer is that Matthew's and Robert's lives were saved. Had I not been on the spot with my witch-like precognition when Matthew had meningitis, and Robert complained of 'indigestion', both my son and my husband would have died. At least I can offer that at Heaven's gate, or wherever else I am to go.

Whenever Robert and I refer to that exceptional Quatorze Juillet, we tend to laugh about it. As I'm writing this, I'm almost laughing again. In some way it was a very positive thing to have happened. It had a very good effect on Robert's attitude to life, and also on our relationship. I now feel I want to let Robert do whatever it is he wants to do; we both feel he's living on borrowed time.

The first thing he did when he was better was to fly on his first trip to Hollywood, to visit friends and to stay at the Beverly Hills Hotel, and then to travel to New Mexico, Arizona and Texas on a Greyhound bus.

I want Robert to feel free and to enjoy his life, whether we are together or apart, and I think in that I have succeeded. Anyway, twelve years later he is busier than ever, and happier than I have ever known him.

*   *   *

A few months after my first New York adventure and Robert's brush with death, the National Theatre asked Alan Schneider and myself to do *Rockaby* and *Enough* at the Cottesloe.

Alan and Dan Labeille came over, bringing the beautiful Edwardian dress for *Rockaby*, which belonged to his university in Buffalo, and which the National Theatre managed to lose – for Dan an irreparable loss.

Sam came over from Paris. This time, we were therefore able to rehearse in his presence and with his help. He seemed to be happy with *Rockaby*, though I was nervous about doing *Enough* again, with good reason. I wasn't very good because I didn't fully understand what I was doing. The story made a contrast with the ghostly *Rockaby*, but meanwhile I had found out that Sam hates his prose to be read out as theatre.

I promised Sam that I'd never again try to read another of his stories in public. It wasn't a difficult promise to make: I think I need a character to hide behind.

I've since given excerpts from Sam's plays, and have put together an evening of excerpts of work we had done together, but I have never again attempted to read his stories.

For the opening of *Rockaby* in London, the Cottesloe was packed. People were standing at the back of the theatre and even the director of the National, Peter Hall, found he couldn't get a seat. Robert, who knew Peter from the time when he had been a critic and Peter ran the Royal Shakespeare Company, was happy to offer him his own seat. People seemed to want to see *Rockaby*.

This may have sparked something off in Alan. Shortly afterwards he was back in London with a new idea. Could we put *Enough* and *Rockaby* together with a revival of Sam's original production of *Footfalls* for a full Beckett evening in New York? Alan had already decided on the venue, Theater Row on 42nd Street, where a new theatre was about to be opened next to the Harold Clurman Theater. The idea was that our première would coincide with the opening of this new theatre. I would christen it the Samuel Beckett Theater.

When Alan came over to rehearse, I was still playing in *Tales from Hollywood*. History repeated itself. As with *Passion Play* and the Buffalo trip, we finished the run of *Tales from Hollywood* on a Saturday night, and on Sunday morning we flew off to New York. This time there was no D.A. Pennebaker to record the event.

At JFK we were met by the producer Jack Garfein. He was accompanied by Agapi, the younger sister of Arianna Stassinopoulos. In a younger incarnation we had known Arianna as the girlfriend of Robert's close friend Bernard Levin. We met the couple quite often. She accompanied Bernard when he came to visit us in a very modest little *Gasthof* in Austria in the mid-Seventies. A few years later Arianna had become a celebrity in her own right. She wrote books, and in London fronted a quasi-religious Californian sect called Insight.

In August 1978 she organised her spectacular 'Levin is Fifty' birthday party in the South of France, where we happened to be staying at the same time. Bernard was visibly in love with Arianna. I remember marching her up and down the lobby of the Carlton Hotel in Cannes.

'Never mind giving him a party and flying in guests,' I told her in my customary bossy manner. 'If you love this man, give him a baby.'

She replied: 'I want to see if something works. If it does, Bernard will never be the same again.'

What I was watching was Arianna passing on the teachings of her guru John-Roger. It seemed to me a kind of exercise. I was a bit alarmed and glad that Robert had an appointment in Hamburg; we left the day before the party.

After the publication of Arianna's controversial Maria Callas biography, Robert said: 'I think Arianna has a Maria Callas complex.'

I had been given quite another vision by Arianna's personality. I thought I detected in her a Jackie Kennedy complex.

Not altogether mistakenly, as it now turns out, I felt that Arianna had her eye on the White House.

But to go back to the man who – with Agapi Stassinopoulos – welcomed me to America, Jack Garfein. Jack had been married to the beautiful film star Carroll Baker, who had appeared in Robert's television play, *The Paradise Suite*. So Jack didn't know me, but he had met my husband. I had been warned (and not only by Carroll) that Jack, to put it mildly, sometimes tended to get over-excited by his projects.

I was to grow very fond of Jack. He was a concentration camp survivor. It wasn't always easy to come to grips with his behaviour – an odd mixture of generosity, sensitivity and somewhat eccentric business methods.

Most of the time he seemed to be oblivious of the chaos he created around his person.

As young Agapi greeted me with flowers at the airport, she handed me an invitation to her famous sister's cocktail party, apparently given in my honour.

I was shocked to see that this party was timed to start on my opening night, two hours before the rise of the curtain! I must have looked a bit dubious at this welcoming present.

Sounding perhaps a little like an Edith Evans impressionist, I explained to Agapi that I *never* attended cocktail parties, and certainly wouldn't do so on my own New York opening night. Whenever they were given bad news, the Stassinopoulos sisters had trained themselves to ignore it, merely to smile serenely.

On the way to the Algonquin Hotel, I asked Jack if we could pop into the shining new Samuel Beckett Theater, so that I could conveniently drop all my costumes and makeup there.

'No,' he said. 'Don't you bother yourself, Billie. We'll see to all that later.'

I thought it a bit odd that we should lug all my theatre stuff to the hotel, rather than install it in my dressing-room, but decided to let it pass.

When I arrived for a first rehearsal at the theatre next day I realised why Jack had diverted me: *the Samuel Beckett Theater was still in the process of being built.*

There was an auditorium of sorts, but when I asked to see my dressing-room I found there wasn't one. Somewhere in a basement area there were indeed *plans* for a dressing-room. Indeed I found a couple of cheerfully grinning workmen laying down cement, and drilling holes in the wall. Wooden boards had been laid across the wet floor, leading to an unfinished lavatory with a wash-basin. So this was New York's famous Theater Row!

Still jetlagged, and overcome by the horror of it all, I collapsed on to a wooden bench outside the unfinished lavatory and tried to withdraw into sleep. All I wanted to do was to get out of New York, back to London, to be with Robert and Matthew.

Lying among the wet cement and wooden boards, I must have muttered something about getting the hell out of this town, and on to the first plane home, because I suddenly heard Alan Schneider shouting and yelling.

'Just tell everybody she's flying back to London today!'

Rehearsals were clearly out of the question. A while later I turned for help to Jack's number two, Jonathan Curillo, a young man I found to be caring and considerate and, like almost everyone one meets in the New York theatre, a mile high on enthusiasm and optimism. Even unsuccessful actors and actresses appear to be in love with their jobs, however menial. Waiters and waitresses all seem to be expecting to be discovered at any moment – it's all part of the inimitable New York atmosphere.

Back at the hotel I rang Jeannie Schneider.

'I can't even rehearse,' I told her, 'let alone open in this chaos.'

I then told Alan we'd have to postpone the opening. My American agent (who was also Alan Schneider's agent) was asked to confront Jack Garfein with the intention of taking him apart. Jack, apparently accustomed to total delirium around him, probably just listened contritely. Another Jack Garfein débâcle loomed, yet this man of chaos had many lovable sides to him. He could be so optimistic and open-handed. He was also a brilliant movie director; his film *End as a Man* was a directorial *tour de force*. Jack thrived on adventure, confusion and risk. He needed them, like food and drink and oxygen.

Having made clear that I could hardly open in a non-existent theatre that didn't even have a dressing-room, Jack reassured me: all would be well. And, indeed, I was to find that overnight the place had been made almost habitable.

My dressing-room now looked like one of those prefabricated houses we had during and after the war. Someone had brought in an armchair, hung up my clothes, put up my photographs and posters, and laid out my rabbits and knick-knacks. The cement was almost dry; they'd installed a pretty dresser called Mary for me, who wanted to become an actress, and was studying at Jack Garfein's acting school on Theater Row. In my absence Mary had raided my suitcase and put all my stuff in some sort of order.

I'm sure Alan had warned Jack that unless they made this place cosy for me, I'd be off to London before opening.

Alan and I started rehearsing. I got used to my surroundings and found my sense of humour. The new theatre was intimate – ideal for Sam's work – holding about 150 people, and painted entirely black from floor to ceiling.

It came to the first night: February 16th, 1984. I was due to stand outside the theatre to make a brief speech to declare the theatre officially open. As I put on my makeup, I waited for the familiar sound of an audience entering. I became aware of a deathly silence.

Nothing was happening. It was the same sort of ominous silence I remembered from the night the flying pickets were sent out to stop a performance of *Molly*.

I wondered what the hell was going on. Why wasn't I being called? Why was there no audience? There was just this empty house, my dresser Mary, Sybil Lines, who was playing the voice of the mother in *Footfalls*, and me.

Like Dorothy Parker, I thought, what fresh hell is this? as I hurried through the empty auditorium to the front of the house.

I found quite a number of people on the sidewalk on 42nd Street, *just waiting*. I thought I recognised familiar faces. I felt I had to be positive. Possibly, all my repressed hysteria over the last days of rehearsal came bubbling up in me. In any event, I couldn't remember a single person's name. If I did think of a name I attached it to the wrong person. I think I introduced Ruth Gordon to her husband, imagining she was Jessica Tandy, or possibly it was the other way round, who can tell? I got myself into one dreadful mess after another. Did I really say: 'Miss Gordon, have you met this wonderful actor?' thinking I was introducing her to Hume Cronyn, as I held out my hand to Garson Kanin. And was it Ruth Gordon who told me very nicely: 'Yes, my dear, we have met, we're married.'

Robert has since claimed I even introduced Glenn Close to her co-star Jeremy Irons, both appearing in Tom Stoppard's *The Real Thing*, saying: 'And this is a young lady who's doing very well in some theatre up the road.' But I do believe that to be an outrageous calumny.

I seemed to be in the middle of a New York cartoon. Nobody seemed to be surprised or alarmed by my cascade of *faux pas*. Meanwhile, I was growing increasingly anxious and angry that all these eminent people of the theatre were being kept waiting on the sidewalk. Why? Nobody seemed to know what had happened. Only gradually the rest of the audience began to arrive. I've always had a sneaking feeling that half the audience had been hijacked to attend the future Mrs Huffington's cocktail party.

It was high time for the curtain to go up, and I was getting more and more agitated, as people continued to make long speeches in praise of Samuel Beckett. Finally I turned to Alan Schneider: 'Come on,' I said, 'let's get this show on the road.'

He explained that I was expected to speak next, to name the theatre. So I turned to the crowd and said: 'I'm going to keep this short, folks, because I think it's about time we took the curtain up.'

I then told the assembled celebrities that I should really have a bottle of Guinness in one hand, and a bottle of Irish whiskey in the other, and that we should raise both to Samuel Beckett and then smash them against the wall to give this theatre a real launch.

Unfortunately we had got neither of those bottles available, but even without the props I still managed to launch the theatre, before rushing back through the auditorium and backstage.

Luckily the chaos had taken care of any first night nerves I might have had. I still couldn't believe that an entire first night audience had been to a cocktail party, while Ruth Gordon and Garson Kanin, or was it Jessica Tandy and Hume Cronyn (or both?), had been left standing on a cold night on 42nd Street. I clearly had much to learn about the way things are done in New York.

I can hardly remember getting through the first night. At the end lots of flowers were thrown on to the stage by Arianna and Agapi from their seats in the front row.

I had the feeling that I was just rattling through my first night performance in New York, and that we were in for a dreadful flop.

I had done these plays before, of course, and knew there was interest in Beckett's work in America. I wanted the evening to work for all of us who were involved in the production, for Alan Schneider and Jack Garfein, for Sam, who was far away and not really well, and for Rocky Greenberg, who had done a wonderful job on the lighting. I knew the end of *Rockaby* could be very moving, but if those last moments of the play were to work, it was due to the subtlety of the lighting rather than any acting.

When the show was over, I started wiping the gunge off my face, and put on a dressing-gown. I remember I had nothing on underneath except a pair of knickers. We then just sat around, with cans of Budweiser, waiting for the papers: the great American tradition. How often I had seen it in the movies!

I didn't think there would be that many notices. How could there have been time for long reviews to be written when we had started so late? I expected the odd snippet, perhaps something later in the Sunday edition of the *New York Times*. I doubted if critics like Frank Rich and Mel Gussow would give us more than a few lines.

Still, we all waited, as tradition demanded, about twenty of us, squatting outside my dressing-room backstage in that unfinished building site. I continued to take my makeup off, as everything suddenly went very quiet. Jack was standing on one of the wooden planks, his body slightly rocking, as he started to read out the first line of Frank Rich's review in the *New York Times*.

'It's possible that you haven't really lived until you've watched Billie Whitelaw die . . .' it began.

I sat on the cold floor, grateful that we'd got through the craziest first night I'd ever experienced. I was quite content with that.

Robert later told me how moved he was by the sight of Jack Garfein – holding up that newspaper, trying to control his voice as the impact of Frank Rich's very long notice sank in. Jack had clearly had his hour of fame and success, but it had long since passed. He had suffered some dreadful blows in his professional and private life. Now he was reading words, written by the butcher of Broadway, that would mean that all his dreams were coming true at last. The review was a catalogue of praise, not only for Samuel Beckett, but also for the production and for me. And the other reviews were in the same vein.

Backstage, everybody was now getting drunk, not on alcohol, but on excitement. Looking back, I can't say that at the time I was really bowled over by it all. My life and happiness didn't depend on a notice by Frank Rich. I thought, well, that's nice, good – it's worked, tomorrow we'll go and do the second night.

I hadn't quite reckoned with what *success* can mean in New York. Over the next few days I was to find out. All hell broke loose.

I had always scoffed at that absurd phrase: 'The phone never stopped ringing.' Now this is exactly what began to happen to me at the Algonquin. Journalists were queuing up for interviews. They wanted to have breakfast with me, they wanted to invite me to lunch, the publicity people were in seventh heaven. Their messages arrived on the hour every hour. Every radio programme in New York was asking for me, every chat show, every New York magazine. Photographers were queuing up in the lobby. I was even asked to be on TV news programmes. I felt people had taken leave of their senses.

The theatre couldn't hold the people who wanted to get in to see this new sensation, this 'hot ticket'. There were queues crawling all the way down the seamiest part of 42nd Street.

When I came into the theatre for the second night, Jack had already wallpapered the entire foyer with blow-ups of the notices, floor to ceiling. It did look impressive.

At the risk of sounding arrogant, I have to say that I had received good notices before, and had always thought, well, thank you very much, I've managed to skate over another bit of thin ice without being rumbled.

Maybe it's because I've been around for a long time, but to me a first night has always meant you win a few, you lose a few, and on to the next. *This* reaction to a few good notices was something I couldn't understand at all. Why was everyone getting so excited?

A smash in New York (even off-Broadway) is unlike a success anywhere else in the world. Everybody now wants a piece of you, to share in this phantom called success. It did go on a bit. Jack doubled the prices of the seats, we had garden chairs running down the aisles, we couldn't accommodate everybody. People were queuing for returns. Mel Gussow, Clive Barnes, Andrew Porter, Benedict Nightingale, Richard Corliss and Barbara Lovenheim followed up with feature articles.

I thought that would be that, but the heat didn't let up. The luggage boys and the news store man at the Algonquin were all agreed we had a 'hit'. I thought, good Lord, they do get excited here don't they, and waited for things to simmer down so that I could get on with the run.

But things didn't seem to calm down. I was glad I had Robert and Matthew with me during the first few days, to help me keep my sanity. I still felt I wanted to rest and recover and then work. For the first few days Robert had protected me from other people and from myself, then he had to take Matthew home.

I had always known that American ballyhoo wouldn't agree with me. Had I done what young British actresses tend to do, to make for Hollywood the moment they've had their first success, I reckon within a couple of years I would have been dead.

I understand why successful American actors have minders and an entourage. I also started to appreciate why some people who taste American success become addicted to it, and can no longer bear to live without it. I can also understand why they take to drink and drugs, and why they can't bear to have the carousel stop. As for me, I'm afraid it filled me with fear and trembling.

While still doing the show in New York, I was flown to Los Angeles to appear there at the Mark Taper Theater – for just one day.

My attitude must have been very hard to understand, and was probably interpreted as ingratitude. I must have mortally offended Gordon Davidson, who runs the Mark Taper Theater. It was Sunday, and he had thrown a lunch party for me. But we were performing that day and I had told him: 'Please don't do this for me, I can't be there. I can't have a big lunch and then go and do the show.' He clearly didn't believe me. About midday he called my room.

'Where are you?' he asked.

'In bed resting,' I told him.

'But Billie, everyone's here.'

'But I did say I wouldn't be there,' I told him.

I now realise that was very bad behaviour indeed. I shudder with guilt every time I think about it.

I expect that somewhere in me there is a sneaking envy for actors for whom success only has a positive effect. I'm thinking here of Anthony Hopkins, the old spear-carrier from the Old Vic, who had an alcohol problem. It was only after his ascent into the show-biz stratosphere that he managed to come to terms with this. Success and adoration have done him nothing but good. Yet I know myself.

I can only work in an atmosphere of comparative tranquillity. I've always known that where more than half a dozen are gathered, that's where I don't want to be. I'm probably afraid of my own immaturity, my own excitability. I'm afraid of getting wound up.

Meanwhile Beckett, and our show on 42nd Street, were the talk of New York. 'Everybody' wanted to come to see the show. I was happy to meet Liza Minnelli again, whom I had mothered when, aged twenty-one, she played her first big film role in *Charlie Bubbles*. She was starring in the play *The Rink* around the corner, together with Chita Rivera, who became a friend when she starred in *West Side Story* in London, and danced on my lawn in Datchet. Chita went home as soon as the show was over, and I recognised and appreciated that need. Liza came to see the plays at the Samuel Beckett Theater. Afterwards she grabbed a lipstick, and wrote on my dressing-table mirror: 'So who's Amy?' a reference to my character in *Footfalls*, who half-way through the play changes her name from May to Amy.

By now it was the middle of winter, and there was snow everywhere. A frail but undaunted Katharine Hepburn came to see me backstage. She'd broken her ankle and had a metal pin in it. She was so concerned about the weather that she sent a car to take me back to my hotel. I thought, what incredible thoughtfulness. Joel Gray, who had played the Master of Ceremonies in *Cabaret*, came round. Another night it was Mike Nichols, to ask if I would have dinner with him. Force of habit made me say: 'I can't, I've got a matinée next day.' He must have been stunned. However, a few days later I did have dinner with him and his wife, together with William Hurt and Jeremy Irons. I was then able to explain to him in my prissy way that I only went out for a meal if I wasn't working the next day.

One night the door opened to my dressing-room, and there stood John Dexter, who I knew had been very ill. He was no longer the up-and-coming director I'd known in London twenty years previously. In the meantime he had been running the New York Metropolitan Opera. He threw down his walking stick, and came to embrace me. I was in tears, touched that he should bother to come and see me when he had been desperately ill. Not very long after our reunion, he was dead.

On another night the theatre was visited by the Shuberts, the big bad wolves among New York theatre-owners. I expected ruthless and icy businessmen. Then this rather shambling big fellow came up to me in my dressing-room, which he nearly filled with his bulk, and found he couldn't say anything to me. He just stood there, moist-eyed.

I said: 'You were moved, weren't you?'

And he said: 'Yes, I was.'

I took his hand and gave this great bear of a man a big hug and a little kiss. I suppose I could only do this because I knew my life and future didn't depend on him.

Jack Garfein now thought his big moment had come. The Shuberts had visited his theatre. One of them had gone backstage to see Billie. It was the moment to *move*. His little big success was about to turn into a *smash*. He started to drag me all over New York. He wanted desperately to find a new, bigger theatre for us. I know he meant well, but it all seemed quite crazy to me. We went to meet people who had put on *Zorba the Greek* with Anthony Quinn. We even went to meet Anthony Quinn himself. Jack thought his backers might be interested to put money into transferring our esoteric little show. Jack started to take me around various other theatres, huge Broadway houses that were either dark or about to become empty. It was all becoming ludicrous. To my mind, these theatres were totally unsuitable for Beckett, but beset by his gambling fever, Jack would say: 'But Billie, look at the people we're turning away every night! It's got to go to a big theatre.'

He just didn't realise there is no big money to be made out of Samuel Beckett. That wasn't the way it worked. We'd done well, but I knew it would be right to leave it at that.

Every night I rang Robert in despair. I also called Jeannie Schneider and told her I was going crazy. I didn't know what to do. Jeannie told me to do what I felt was in my heart; that would be the right decision.

'If you want to stay in that little theatre where you are, don't move.'

I told Jack: 'Please, let's not go on charging all round New York, looking for a bigger theatre. Let's just do the run here until I can go home.'

I could read the disappointment in his eyes, but he knew he wouldn't be able to change my mind.

By this time I just wanted to go home. New York had been a marvellous experience, I wouldn't have missed any of it for the world. But it had confirmed to me what I had always known: that this high-powered lifestyle was not for me. I need domesticity, tranquillity and a bit of solitude.

A friend of mine, Penny Perrick, working for *The Times* in London, was visiting New York at the time. We spent some days together. I told her I hadn't been geared for this circus, I had thought it would be like the Royal Court in London. You went in, did the show and that was that. I hadn't brought anything but jeans and a sweater, plus one dress. Penny lent me her best dress. When she got home to London, she wrote an article for *The Times* about this unexpected event on 42nd Street, that had turned a British actress into the latest New York sensation. I often think that if she hadn't written that generous article, not many people in England would have known about Beckett in New York.

Before I could go home, I did a week of Beckett in Los Angeles, again at the Mark Taper Theater, together with two excellent Beckettian actors, Alvin Epstein and David Warrilow. The whole of Hollywood seemed to have taken over the theatre. At dinner I found myself sitting between Jane Fonda and David Selznick, Jr. A friend in New York, Helen Bishop, had realised I would need clothes for this event, so she lent me the right things from her wardrobe. I'd got to know Helen through her husband, Professor Tom Bishop, a friend of Sam's from way back. It was after this dinner that Harold Clurman's widow, Stella Adler, beckoned me over to her table to tell me: 'You must stop doing so much Beckett. You're too young to be working this close to death.'

I had first visited New York as a fluttery little film-starlet, to promote the film *No Love for Johnnie*. I thought I hated America. I judged New York to be dirty, commercial and superficial.

After the McCarthy hearings I had thought of the States as semi-Fascist. Everything seemed to be gauged by money values. Mind you, a lot of New York still is like that. But decades have passed, and I've got to know another side of America. My visits to the universities there have changed my jaundiced views of the United States. It's become a place of which I'm very fond, not a symbol of show-biz success, but a place where I can do work I enjoy.

I always look forward to my trips there. I find people, particularly in less exposed places than New York and Los Angeles, to be positive, helpful and optimistic, and loving their work. And every Christmas when I come to write my cards, I discover that I now have more friends there than in this country.

Intermission Three: Directors

Some years ago, when Gill Pyrah interviewed me on the radio, she asked me about discrimination against women working in the higher reaches of my profession. I said I hadn't come across any discrimination, and probably followed that up with a remark about never having been a feminist. She drew in her breath, taken aback by my politically incorrect attitude.

Everything that happened to me in my early career, all the little pushes up the ladder, involved women in executive positions. The person who introduced me to Nan MacDonald at the BBC in Manchester was a woman. Nan MacDonald gave me my first break when I was eleven, and if anyone can claim to have 'discovered' me, even earlier, it was Esmé Church. A little later I was given another haul up by a high-powered woman called Joan Littlewood. When I was eighteen, Denise Roylance, Nan MacDonald's PA, introduced me to Dorothea Brooking, who was in charge of BBC Television's *Children's Hour* in London. This led to my first appearance in a television series, *The Secret Garden*. The first important thing that happened to me in television was working in a much-lauded dramatised documentary, *Patterns of Marriage*. This, I admit, was written by a man, Ted Willis, but it was produced by a woman, Caryl Doncaster. Chloe Gibson gave me my first West End job, in a play she directed, R.F. Delderfield's *Where There's a Will* (in which I never got to the West End).

In view of this personal history, it was a long time before I was made conscious of the sorry role dealt out to women in show business. Even in the early Fifties, I was completely unaware that women were deprived of promotion opportunities.

It was only after I had become an adult that I started to work with men directors. Of the dozens I've worked with, the one that sticks in my memory is Ted Kotcheff. He was the first director I felt involved with on a creative journey – just as when I think of writers I've worked with, I always think first of Alun Owen. We were all in the same *Armchair Theatre* 'team' at ABC Television at Teddington. I felt part of Ted Kotcheff's repertory company.

I've always needed a strong director. I want a director to give me the confidence to go down a blind alley. Like a frog, I need someone to pat my bottom, someone who can get me jumping.

When I look at a script, I often don't know where to start. Alternatively, I can think of ten different ways of approaching a role, but can't decide on the right one.

What I need is a director who, when I'm in doubt, can say: 'Try that road, off you go.' Once I know the road I'm on, I can build from there.

Many actors I've worked with – Donald Pleasence for one – prefer to be left alone to find their own way in a part. I need someone to confirm for me whether I'm on the right path or not. I find it difficult to work with a director who has elected to fool around, play the clown, make jokes to relax the cast. After a while, I find that irritating. I don't apologise for taking my work seriously, probably too seriously. Though Ted Kotcheff let me have my head in some ways, in those early days he moulded what talent he found, and proceeded to give it direction and shape. The fact that he was a volatile man didn't worry me one bit. I certainly didn't take offence if he yelled at me: 'You're not going to play it like that, are you?'

In Ted I recognised something I could home in on – creative energy. Ted liked to break the rules; I felt I didn't have to act to an expected formula. That made me feel free.

Since those early days I've sometimes had to go up to a director at the start of rehearsals and say: 'Look, I seem to be making a dog's dinner of this part. Have faith, don't despair, *I'll get there in the end.*'

I've watched many an actor come to rehearsal with a performance already mapped out in detail, while I'm still floundering after more than a week. Which doesn't mean I don't try to contribute every last ounce of my own energy to a rehearsal. In any production there is a pool of energy floating about. Whether good, bad or indifferent, I believe an actor has one obligation at rehearsal: to put what energy he has available into that pool.

In any cast I've worked with, you can always sense if an actor is 'walking' it, or, as they would say today, telephoning his part in.

You can feel the energy being drawn out of the pool; that means his fellow actors have to put more in.

With the first play I ever did in London, I jumped in at the deep end: a Feydeau farce, *Hotel Paradiso*, with an incredible cast headed by Alec Guinness, Irene Worth, Martita Hunt, Douglas Byng and Frank Pettingell. Young Kenneth Williams and I played the sidekick sweethearts. Osbert Lancaster designed the clothes, and our photographs were taken by an eager young man called Tony Armstrong-Jones. The director was Peter Glenville. I saw Mr Glenville very much as a director of the old school. Strikingly handsome, an actor himself, he always came to rehearsals immaculately dressed, as though he were off to Ascot in the afternoon.

He was a sort of elegant ringmaster, yet totally different from a member of what was then the modern school – like John Dexter. John c-r-a-c-k-e-d the whip with the energy of his body. Peter Glenville cracked it delicately from the wrist. I always felt he should be rehearsing with a long cigarette holder in his hand. (And maybe he did.)

Another early theatrical experience was with Toby Robertson, who directed Ian Bannen and me in the world premiere of Eugene O'Neill's *A Touch of the Poet*. We first did this at the Dublin Festival, then took it to the Fenice, an incredibly beautiful theatre in Venice which looks like a miniature version of La Scala, Milan.

I think Toby was in despair with me. Presented with very long speeches, I could only start by bumbling and groping my way through at rehearsal. (I have always found acting to be like wrestling with an octopus. You no sooner get one tentacle nailed down to the ground, when another tentacle jumps up to slap you in the face.) Those long poetic O'Neill speeches frightened the hell out of me. At one rehearsal Toby came up to me and said, shaking his head: 'You really have no method of working, have you?'

I had to admit that I hadn't any method. Eventually though, I managed to get there and give a performance of sorts, and I think Toby was quite pleased.

For all his sadistic outbursts and scapegoat-seeking, John Dexter and I worked well together from the very beginning. I had respect for him; he in turn respected the fact that at rehearsal I worked damn hard. John often reminded me of a football coach – what he couldn't stand was an actor who didn't put his two penn'orth of hard work into the project.

The distinguished theatre director William Gaskill, whom I had known since he was in short trousers at the Civic Theatre, Bradford, had the unenviable task of directing me in *The Dutch Courtesan* at the Old Vic. I shall never know what Ken Tynan was thinking about when he resurrected that piece.

Although I have always admired Bill's work, and felt he was a childhood friend, we were a mis-match theatrically.

After I had done a scene he would shake his head.

'Wrong,' he'd say, but not go on to explain why he thought what I had done was wrong, or what else I might try.

I'd go off and come back, trying it a different way. I'd get the same reaction: 'Wrong.'

In the end I was just doing *anything* that might please him. I would have happily come in dancing on my little pinky or juggling plates in the air. I would have blacked my face up or painted purple dots all over my face – just to make Bill Gaskill say: 'Right.'

But Bill continued to shake his head: 'Wrong.'

The whole company was watching me go through this agony. I found I simply had nothing left that I could pull out of the bag for Bill. Meanwhile, the part of Francesca had gone entirely out of the window. Finally I went up to Bill and said: 'I don't know what the hell I'm doing any more. Help!'

He said: 'I'm not your father. A director is not a father, you have to find the part for yourself.'

A company member, young Johnny Stride, finally came to my rescue. I can't remember exactly what he said, but it made no difference anyway. I was destined to be a bloody awful Dutch courtesan.

I've worked with two theatre directors – Peter Hall and Mike Ockrent – from entirely different generations, who, from an actor's point of view, seemed to have one thing in common.

I was only about twenty-two when I worked for Peter's company at the Oxford Playhouse. We weren't given contracts, but all verbally agreed that we wouldn't leave before six months were up. (As far as I can remember, the very first person who had to leave was Peter Hall!)

Peter and I used to meet on Paddington Station to commute to Oxford and back, and he would always quite openly and charmingly talk about himself. He felt that things were going just too well for him. He often said to me: 'You know, I'm just waiting to be rumbled. I'm waiting for it all to fall apart.'

This was before he was offered the job of running the Arts Theatre Club in London, where he introduced Samuel Beckett to despairing

London audiences. It was a career move he had to make. Peter has always managed to be in the right place at the right time. Actually I don't believe that has anything to do with luck, only with character.

I think Peter's diaries show him to be an extremely honest man – about himself. Three decades after Oxford, when I worked on *Rockaby* at the Cottesloe, Peter came to our house in Camden Square and I found him to be totally unchanged, telling me the same things about himself as he had done thirty years before. I reminded him about his fears when we were young. Sir Peter shook his head and smiled. He was still waiting to be rumbled.

My memory of Peter as a director at the Oxford Playhouse is of a young man with a big scarf round his neck and shoulders, just sitting there doing nothing – or so it seemed to me.

Mike Ockrent, who directed me in Peter Nichols' *Passion Play* at the Royal Shakespeare Company, was very similar in his method. To be directed by Mike in this very complex play felt to me like being back in Oxford in the Fifties. Mike would just sit there in front of his actors, and *apparently* do absolutely nothing. And yet – startling and innovative things were happening on the stage. I think he found me a bit taciturn and reclusive, but as he is now in the top league of international directors, I'm sure he doesn't give a damn.

Not long ago Robert and I were in New York and went to see his production of *Crazy for You*. This Gershwin musical gave me the most joyous evening I've spent in the theatre for years. So when doing nothing, Mike must have been doing everything. And Peter Hall, with his big scarf around his neck, ended up running both the RSC and the National Theatre. He got a knighthood very early on, and now has his own company, which seems to put on a new play in the West End every month.

When he asked me to perform in the last two productions at the National Theatre I had to turn him down, which made me feel miserable. Following my problems with *Who's Afraid of Virginia Woolf?* I was at this time going through a crisis of confidence in my acting. I just rang up his secretary, hoping I wouldn't have to talk to him. Had I written and told Peter why I felt I couldn't face going on stage, he might well have changed my mind, and got me through those productions, and thereby restored my confidence.

In David Jones, who asked me to do *After Haggerty* by David Mercer when it transferred to the Criterion Theatre, I found a most encouraging director, though looking back I feel I might have given him a better performance.

On her first entrance the young American revolutionary that I played has to scream: 'Haggerty, Haggerty, if you don't open this door I'm going to shove your goddamn baby through the keyhole,' and the character carries on from there.

I would have liked to delve a bit more deeply into this character and energise it afterwards. David, however, seemed to want this powerhouse energy element above anything else.

What I liked about David Jones was a talent not all directors possess: he gave one the impression that he liked the actors he worked with, always encouraging them to go that little bit further, while being sympathetic to 'actors' nerves'.

Another RSC director for whom I cherish the most enormous respect and affection is John Barton. John is a scholar and an academic as well as a director. A very quiet, untidy man, he seems not in the least concerned with career-building – or so it has always seemed to me.

While directors with a fraction of his talent have become household names and millionaires, John seems to go on doing the work he loves, while wearing the same old knitted cardigan with holes at the elbow. When I worked with him on *The Greeks* he reminded me very much of my stepfather, who also liked to wear the same old cardigan for as long as I knew him.

In rehearsal, John was always calm and concentrated. His task in *The Greeks* (Aldwych, 1979–80) was enormous. He and Kenneth Cavander had adapted the entire story of the house of Atreus. *The Greeks* ran for twelve hours and we performed it on three consecutive evenings. On Saturdays we did the entire twelve hours. You would see a bunch of worn-out actors dragging themselves through the stage door of the Aldwych at eight in the morning. The curtain had to go up at ten. By the time it was all over, at eleven o'clock at night, we were all flying high on adrenalin.

John, a wonderfully patient director, never ever lost his cool with this enormous cast and understood the different paths the various actors had to tread before arriving at a performance.

We all played many parts in *The Greeks*. I was Artemis and Andromache (whose husband Hector is killed and who sees her baby snatched from her arms, his brains smashed). At the end of a long evening I came on as Athene, the goddess of wisdom, sliding down a cloud of dry ice. Still choking on this, I had to make a very long summing-up speech.

At the start of rehearsals I remember giving John my little speech: 'Look, trust me, I feel this speech is beautiful, but I'm going to start from zero. I'm just going to speak the lines and do no more than that. Then, gradually, I'm going to let it grow, and we'll see what happens.'

The speech and the part, the play and the whole sequence of plays, seemed to work out. The speech patterns of the piece fell into rhythms of three; this helped me a lot when it came to Athene. For the first months of rehearsal I just tapped that out in my head, with both part and culminating speech taking on a colour of their own. The role I enjoyed most in *The Greeks* was a Member of the Chorus. I enjoyed building up this non-existent character, imagining her as some sort of pre-history peasant, with pelts of various animals and strings of onions around her belt.

During *The Greeks*, when Agamemnon comes on in the equivalent of an enormous gun carriage, I had to say a few lines to him. Whenever I got to this sentence, the words didn't want to come out of my mouth; it was just one word that beat me. A whole twelve-hour play had carved itself on my mind, yet this one word had become the most dangerous moment of the cycle for me.

At the dress rehearsal I begged John: 'Please help me, I can't sleep any more. I know whenever I get to this one word my heart almost stops.'

John just spoke two words: 'Cut it,' he said.

There are many good directors who would have said to me: 'Sorry, darling, but that's the line. Say it.' John released me from having to say that one blocked word, and the entire play and my performances fell into place for me. After that, I was able to enjoy all twelve hours of *The Greeks*. (I've often wondered over the years why that one word in one particular speech was blocking me. Was it because in the original Greek the speech was meant to have been spoken by a man? So that in my subconscious, it didn't ring true to me?)

What was sad about *The Greeks* was that (rather typically) it was eclipsed in some people's minds by Peter Hall's rival production of *The Oresteia* at the National which followed quite soon afterwards. For all its good press and crowded houses, *The Greeks* didn't have the long run that John deserved. I remember the great actress Elisabeth Bergner, about eighty at the time, who had sent me a golden rose for the first night, exclaiming: 'Why are they taking it off? It still has an audience! It's a sin to take off a play which still has an audience. And what a waste of money!'

When my mother died during rehearsals of *The Greeks*, John wasted no energy being dramatically over-sympathetic. With all the crises whirling around him, he told me: 'You must go up to your mother's funeral.'

I belted up north, dressed in a black velvet tracksuit. It was the only black thing I could lay my hands on. I came back to work within twenty-four hours.

I suppose I'm fond of people like John Barton and Samuel Beckett because they so clearly have an immutable inner centre, an integrity that is unassailable.

When he directed me in Christopher Hampton's *Tales from Hollywood* at the Olivier, Peter Gill ran the National Theatre Studio. Although I was nearly fifty-two at the time, I had the feeling that Peter treated me a bit like a student. He was most probably quite right to do so (although it did irritate me at times), but he could clearly spot an actor without any classical training. Instinctively he knew how to prod me into directions he wanted me to take.

Some actors object to being given detailed instructions as to how certain lines should be spoken. Peter liked to tell me quite precisely how he wanted my character, Nelly Kröger-Mann, to pronounce certain words. Instead of letting me say 'dog' in the cockney accent I'd used before, he insisted I say an exaggerated 'dawg'. We spent quite some time on this 'dawg'.

Peter made me give a broader performance as Nelly Kröger-Mann than I would have done without his guidance. Vocally I sounded quite crude, and sometimes I felt he was laying on me a rather gross performance, but perhaps that was his valid way of trying to break down my vanity – the actor's number one enemy.

In films, as in the theatre, nothing ever happened to me 'overnight'. No film director handed me a large part in a movie because my face was right. No film director ever 'discovered' me.

For my first picture I had to bring on a tray and serve it to the leading lady who, if memory serves me right, was called Marie 'The Body' Macdonald. Both tea and tray were shaking like mad in my hand.

For my next few films, I never had more than three or four lines to speak. I worked on some real humdingers, which memory has happily obliterated. For young actresses in British films of the mid-Fifties it seemed to be obligatory to run around in briefs, squeaking in a high-pitched voice, preferably with a 'common' accent.

Both here and in America, a few people seem to remember a film called *Make Mine Mink*, for which I have to thank Robert Asher, who cast me opposite Terry-Thomas. The only serious film I was asked to do at this time was *No Love for Johnnie* with Peter Finch. Ralph

Thomas directed it, and probably gave me my first opportunity in films to etch out a characterisation.

Earlier in my film career, in 1954, an American director called something like Joe Bloggs said he wanted to see me to have a word about a film he was directing with Dirk Bogarde and Alexis Smith, called *The Sleeping Tiger*. My part was very small, and I was surprised how encouraging and kind both the director and Dirk Bogarde were to a raw beginner. As for 'Joe Bloggs', he turned out to be Joseph Losey, who had come to this country as a victim of Senator McCarthy's idiotic committee.

I met Joe a few times with Dorothy Bromley, who was then his wife, and whom I got to know better after she and Joe had parted. I have a memory of Dorothy and me swimming in the private pool that went with each room of our hotel in Acapulco. We drank champagne while a servant threw hibiscus flowers over us – not the kind of scene two working-class girls were used to.

I found working with Joe Losey very enjoyable, and I find it difficult to imagine why, long after his death, he tends to be depicted in print as a monster. There may have been negative sides to Joe Losey, but I can't say that I ever encountered any of them.

As with the writers I've mentioned, I seem to have come in at the very start of many directors' careers. I worked on the first movies made by Albert Finney, Stephen Frears and Peter Sellers.

Peter is another artist now characterized in books as an unspeakable villain. He cast me in the first feature film he directed, *Mr Topaze*. We got on very well and I found him very easy to work with.

While working on another movie at the same studio, I had the chance to watch Stanley Kubrick directing Peter Sellers in *Dr Strangelove*. I observed Peter having to do a very long speech, where his arm keeps on shooting up in a Fascist salute.

I noticed that whenever Peter stumbled, or forgot one of his lines, which happened frequently, Kubrick just threw him the next line. Sellers kept still, then carried on, leaving it to the editor and director to put it all together. I thought to myself, what an un-neurotic way of getting an actor through a three-page speech!

Much later I met Peter Sellers again at a dinner. In fact, it was Robert and I who introduced Peter to Liza Minnelli. Peter behaved rather outrageously that night. Liza kept looking at me, as if to ask: 'Hey, is this guy putting me on?'

I told her I wasn't sure, but if I were her I'd watch it. Anyway, they went home together that night, the beginning of a big, if short-lived, romance.

When Albert and I worked at the National, he mentioned that Shelagh Delaney, who had become famous with her play *A Taste of Honey*, was writing a screenplay. They were thinking of me for the part of Lottie, the hero's wife and mother of his little boy.

I've always felt with *Charlie Bubbles* that if you had woven Shelagh Delaney's and Albert Finney's careers together, you'd have a pretty good idea of what the film was about. I am astonished that after so much early success both are still sane people.

There are obviously some people who can deal with the sudden rush of fame – the excitement, the party-going, the publicity, the adulation, the demands from the press, *the big money*. In my young days there was no 'big' money to be made by an actress – a bit like footballers, who in my early days, were on a twenty pounds a week limit. Now, if they're successful, they become – like young actors – millionaires.

I'm actually glad it's worked out that way. My stint in New York proved what I had always known about myself: I haven't got the temperament for handling Big Money or Stardom. I suppose that's why I've only ever wanted to be moderately successful. I realise I've gone through my entire career with the brakes on. I have turned down more parts than I care to remember, everything from Hamlet's mother at the National to the lead opposite Peter Sellers in *Only Two Can Play* in my younger days.

Sometimes even now I find myself saying: 'No thank you,' for no good reason at all. Yet putting the brakes on myself may have been my salvation – both as an actress and as a woman.

I've known Albert Finney for nigh on forty years. Years ago we even had a brief affair, but it got in the way of our friendship and our work. Anyway, I wasn't really comfortable in the back of his Rolls, which usually had to be driven by a chauffeur round the outskirts of Chichester because it was too big to go through the town centre.

When Albert, a kind and generous man, worked on *Charlie Bubbles* with me, he starred and directed, and his stand-in director was a beginner called Stephen Frears – now one of the few really bankable British directors in Hollywood. Stephen supervised all the scenes when Albert was in front of the camera, wearing his actor's hat. He used the actor, Alan Lake, who later married Diana Dors, to rehearse the scenes with me when he put on his director's hat and went behind the camera. Then, when we started shooting, Albert would come on the set, and Alan would step down. Stephen meanwhile kept an eye on things behind the lens. I noticed then that Albert always consulted Stephen. He certainly knew talent when he saw it.

What I admired enormously about Albert as a director was his honesty. On the first shooting day he told the crew: 'Look, I've acted in films, but this is the first one I've ever directed. I'm going to need your help. If you have any suggestion that you think is better than what I'm doing, just tell me. If I'm asking for things that are imposs-ible, tell me; let's try and work it out.'

Though he was already a very big film star on both sides of the Atlantic, Albert never threw his weight about. He liked to get every-body on his side, and he succeeded.

On *Charlie Bubbles* he did have some moments of anxiety, but the only time he communicated them to me was after we had shot our first scene together, which was also the first day's shooting. Sitting next to Albert during the rushes, I could see he was deeply depressed about something. I naturally assumed it was my fault, that I'd done something wrong. Later when we went up in the lift, Albert could barely speak to me.

I burst into tears all over Stephen, who turned out to be the perfect assistant, later ringing me to say I shouldn't take any of this to heart. This had been the very start of filming, and Albert was more anxious than any of us. I should have realised: this was Albert's first viewing of the first scene that had been shot by him as a first-time director.

Throughout the film, Stephen proved to be a pourer of oils on troubled waters, and I was thrilled to bits when he cast me in his own first film, *Gumshoe*, in which Albert and I played a sort of parody Humphrey Bogart and Lauren Bacall.

With the first efforts of Sellers, Finney and Frears, I felt totally at ease as an actress. They were natural-born directors. I felt I fitted into their world.

The reason I was myself a bit tearful while shooting *Charlie Bubbles* was that I was pregnant with Matthew. The prop boys – who missed nothing – knew this even before I did, because I felt too sick to drink coffee during the morning break. One morning an enormous jar of Bovril turned up. One of the boys said: 'Here you are, Bill, I think you'd better have this for your coffee break.'

About a week later I had my pregnancy confirmed. I made a phone call to Robert, who was playing roulette in Baden-Baden. Still involved in his divorce, he must have been somewhat stunned by the news. He told me he was very happy, then returned to the gaming tables.

I was delighted. My sister had taken a specimen of my urine to the doctor for me. She wasn't at all sure how I would take the fact that I was expecting an 'illegitimate' baby. I didn't give a tuppenny toss whether I was married or not.

Joy Jameson, my agent throughout the Seventies and most of the Eighties, rang up one day in 1973 to say that Alfred Hitchcock had specifically asked for me for a part in his film *Frenzy*.

I was flattered that Alfred Hitchcock knew who I was. Here was yet another notorious monster (to judge by books published after his death) with whom I got on like a house on fire. He sent me a lovely bouquet of flowers, and at the end of the movie gave me a silk négligé. Yet my role was quite insignificant. Apart from Barry Foster and Jon Finch, all the parts in the film were played by well-known English theatre actors. Alec McCowen, Vivien Merchant, Anna Massey and Barbara Leigh-Hunt turned up in this thriller, Hitchcock's first British film in a long time.

Every night, after we'd finished shooting, Hitchcock insisted on inviting me to sit in his caravan. I think he felt the film set to be his home. For hours he regaled me with detailed stories about all the various tricks he had employed in his films, all the secrets of how famous scenes had been shot, and how 'impossible' stunts had been done. It was all wasted on me, as I instantly forgot everything he told me, but I remember that all the details tended to be bloody and told with great relish! (I'm fairly sure he told these same stories to other members of the cast.)

At the stroke of eight thirty each morning, one would find Hitchcock – a very large man indeed – ensconced in his director's chair. He always sat quite some distance away from the camera. I never saw him walking about, never heard him raise his voice to an actor. He just sat there, totally impassive, waiting for the crew to get their act together. The only acting note he ever gave me was when rehearsing one scene he muttered – just loud enough for me to hear: 'I think, Miss Whitelaw, if I thought I was about to be killed, I'd be a little bit more excitable.'

Obviously he prided himself on his experience and knowledge. He had directed films in Britain and America for over fifty years. On the set his direction would consist of a muttered but carefully worded instruction to the cameraman: 'If you would now use lens so-and-so, you will have two inches of the bottom bit of the lampshade fringe sharp on the left edge of the frame. The little girl with the dog will be in focus, and just to the right you will see Miss Whitelaw's left ear and the end of Barry Foster's nose.'

If I remember rightly the cameraman, Norbert Taylor, would respond: 'Yes, I think I've got that, sir.'

I think Hitchcock enjoyed not having to get out of his chair to get exactly what he wanted. He had done his work long before he came on to the set: he had planned everything to the last fraction of an inch on the storyboard.

Another immortal among directors, whom I met briefly when I was hardly twenty, was Orson Welles. He had made a film called *Confidential Report*, and now needed somebody, *anybody*, to dub the voice of his Italian wife Paola Mori, whose voice he didn't think had come through clearly enough. (We had the same agent, so Orson Welles got me.)

I had never been abroad in my life, and had to obtain a passport in a rush before getting myself to Paris.

Mr Welles – no 'Orson' for me – and I worked together for a week. I was of course very much in awe of the maker of *Citizen Kane*. When we went into a bar near the studio at St Cloud where we worked, what he seemed to want, curiously enough just like Hitchcock, was a quiet and ready listener.

He started to talk to me in some detail about the problems he'd had with Rita Hayworth. To me, an absolute beginner, Rita Hayworth was a goddess from another planet, or rather from the Elite Cinema, Duckworth Lane in Bradford. Now here was this man, who had actually been *married* to her. I thought I was dreaming, sitting there, sipping my drink and nodding sagely. I was actually in a state of shock: this great man was going on and on about his troubles – *with Rita Hayworth*!

Even though at a remote distance, I suppose that was my first gentle brush with the world of Hollywood. I came slightly closer to it in the mid-Seventies just after I had done the revival of Beckett's *Not I* at the Royal Court.

A director called Richard Donner (not Clive, who is an old friend of ours, though we have never worked together) asked if I would play the part of a Nanny from Hell in a film he was about to direct. I thumbed my way through the script and thought, this is a bit of old hokum that will probably never see the light of day.

Although I didn't fancy getting up at four thirty in the morning to film all day, then come home and play *Alphabetical Order* in the theatre, I half agreed to do the film. Why not? But on the Friday night before I was supposed to start, I decided I couldn't possibly do it while the play was still on. I tried to ring my agent to get me out of it. Everybody had gone home, and I think Joy by this time had probably got a bit fed up with me and my bouts of panic.

So I was stuck with this thriller, which I had agreed to do, almost against my will.

The film turned out to be *The Omen*, with Gregory Peck and Lee Remick, the only smash hit I've ever been in. Richard Donner was a wonderfully professional director, and an actor's director as well. I am not surprised that a generation later he is thought to be one of the very best in the business.

One of the reasons for the film's enormous commercial success may have been that none of us took it all that seriously. We were all very relaxed on the set. Dick Donner did everything with a leavening of humour. I also found Gregory Peck very laid-back, the perfect gentleman.

Looking back, I remember that we had a lot of fun on this film, a lot of laughs. I even got an award presented to me by Bernard Delfont, and was nominated for an Academy Award, which I didn't get. Dick Donner sent me a cable: 'You were robbed.'

Even now, if people think they recognise me in the street, it's usually because they saw *The Omen* – eighteen years ago!

Dick Donner was a hard worker, yet he never appeared to think his movie was the be-all and end-all of our lives. That attitude served as a useful kind of shorthand to someone like me: 'Don't take yourself too seriously; work hard but try to enjoy it.'

Richard Donner may have had easier actors to work with in *The Omen* than Bud Yorkin, another Hollywood director who gave me a job.

The film was *Start the Revolution without Me*, a sort of cross between *The Corsican Brothers* and *Hellzapoppin*, with Gene Wilder and Donald Sutherland playing double roles. The film was narrated by Orson Welles and I played Marie Antoinette to Hugh Griffith's Louis XVI. Among the many actors in the film was my dear friend Jackie Mac-Gowran, the old Beckettian.

We worked in a studio outside Paris, and Helen, my nanny, and I took an apartment on the Rue de Berri, for the summer of 1968 – during that year's street riots. Our flat was just a few doors away from the Lancaster Hotel, off the Champs-Elysées. In this very elegant French apartment, with the sound of revolution in our ears night and day, Matthew took his first steps.

Bud Yorkin's career hasn't quite taken off into the stratosphere like Richard Donner's, but he too had a wonderfully relaxed sense of humour, and that enviable American way of persuading his actors to enjoy themselves, which I have come to think of as a film director's most important piece of psychological equipment.

Another reason I remember this film with pleasure is that, though I was playing comedy, I looked really good for once. I have the superb French cameraman Jean Tournier to thank for that.

Though the picture became quite a cult movie in America, it was considered ahead of its time, and in England was put out as a second feature. In his *Film and Video Guide*, Derek Winnert describes it as 'lots of British performers doing their daffy turns'. I drink to that!

Shortly afterwards, I was privileged to work with John Boorman. I had seen his film *Hell in the Pacific* and felt flattered to be asked to play an absolute bitch in *Leo the Last*, opposite Marcello Mastroianni.

John's idea was to shoot a colour film with no colour in it at all. Every object was black, white and grey – Beckett-land! All the clothes, even the streets and interiors were painted black and white and grey, so that only the flesh tones of the actors stood out.

Marcello was the most charming man I'd ever met, charm just oozed out of him. I'm sure it was turned on like a tap, but it doesn't matter. It works. Omar Sharif, whom I met at a film festival in Cairo in 1982, has the same quality.

Marcello turned out to be a very sociable animal. Every evening, after we'd finished shooting, he would want to go off to various clubs to enjoy himself. He seemed to think it quite natural to work hard during the day, then go out on the town. I envied him for that. Perhaps it was the inevitable fatigue he suffered the next day, that gave him that unique over-relaxed charm. Far from making me relaxed, fatigue winds me up and makes me feel tense, nervous and high, even if I haven't taken anything to be high on. The only thing that relaxes me is sleep.

The story of *Leo the Last* was set in a mixed black and white community, at that time (1969) a novel idea for a film made in Britain. The last shot in the movie was to show the square where we worked exploding. We were hemmed in by explosives and fireworks like rockets, all of which had to go off at a given moment. I found it all a bit scary. John had told us to hold our ground until the very last explosive had gone off. One of the special effects fellows crept up to me just before shooting started. 'Bill, when the second explosion goes off,' he whispered to me, '*run!*'

John had six cameras trained on us as we waited for the final big bang. It was a case of one shot only. No retakes were possible.

For some reason, the actor Calvin Lockhart wouldn't do the shot.

Time was running out, and it was almost dawn. In another half-hour we wouldn't be able to shoot the scene: it would be too light and there would be no ending to the movie. John was keeping very calm, but Calvin persisted that he could not do the shot. Finally Marcello went up to Calvin, put his arm around him and, speaking quietly in his beautiful Italian accent, said: 'Come on, Calvin, I am so tired. We all want to go home. Please, Calvin.' Calvin finally agreed.

We had two turbo-jet engines blowing at us, actually lifting me off my feet. The big bang came, the building went up in smoke, the engines were turned on, we were swept along the street like dry leaves. But as the cameras rolled, and all the explosives started to fire – no going back now! – Calvin accidentally kicked over a camera that was taking the master shot. Though he had lost his master shot, John could only shrug. Anyway, he had had five other cameras on the scene.

I still don't know how such a quietly sensitive man can manage to create such an atmosphere of melodramatic high tension and violence on the set of his films.

John Boorman's *Leo the Last* gave me another experience I would have been sorry to miss. The film opened the 1970 Cannes Film Festival. From our room at the Carlton, Robert and I watched buses going up and down the Croisette, all with huge blow-ups of Marcello on one side and me on the other. All you could see were these enormous likenesses of Mastroianni and me sailing along the Croisette.

By this time I was well into my middle thirties, and I'd been around a bit. I didn't take ballyhoo very seriously. But it all amused me no end. On the night of the opening, I had the experience of posing in the hall of the Carlton, and later swanning up and down the steps of the Palais de Festival, as it was then, with all the paparazzi in hot pursuit. At the end of the performance, the Croisette was packed with crowds, held back by police. Photographers once again crowded around us, as limousines waited for us to graciously descend the staircase. Publicity men were rushing around whispering into people's ears: 'It's a big success, a big success.'

I was swept off for a big reception at some exotic restaurant in La Napoule. In the process I managed to lose Robert on the pavement, a strange echo of exactly such a scene as he had written as the climax of his first novel, *Cinderella Nightingale*, long before he knew me.

It was a crazy, unforgettable night. I was Queen of the Cannes Festival! I was certainly glad I wasn't twenty-two. I would have been quite confused the following morning.

After breakfast, as Robert and I came down the hotel steps, I was almost knocked down and pushed out of the way by the very same photographers who the night before had been knocking other people sideways for the rare privilege of just a glimpse of me! Clearly it was the turn of the next Queen of the Festival. I had been mercifully forgotten.

A long time was to pass, twenty years in fact, before I was exposed to a similar experience of super-hype. This is when a Hungarian director from Hollywood, Peter Medak, cast me in *The Krays*, in which I was reunited after nearly thirty years with two of my favourite people, Tom Bell and Jimmy Jewell.

Like Jack Garfein, Peter is a man who has had his ups and downs in the business, but I think he quite enjoys an atmosphere of high tension. He knows how to indulge the temperaments of people surrounding him.

Peter and I had met before, when I was in Santa Monica. When he gave me the role of the Krays' mother, he probably didn't think he'd have a problem with me. As the mother of the gangsters, I had to span thirty years, starting off as a young mother giving birth, ending with her death as an old woman: a big, demanding role.

Just after we started shooting, I became ill with pneumonia. I was in hospital for two weeks, but it should have been longer. Shooting continued without me. I didn't noticeably improve. A queue of alarmed doctors kept coming in to see me, wanting to know when I would be back on the set: insurance company doctors, hospital doctors, my own doctors.

Peter Medak rang up every day. In his Bela Lugosi drawl, he enquired: 'My darrling, when do you think you'll be ready to come back to work?'

One day I had a more desperate call: 'They're demanding I re-cast the part,' he said.

Up to now they had shot round all my scenes. Now they had done all they could; it was my turn – or else.

Peter showed incredible loyalty to me. He was in charge of an expensive picture; there was no shortage of actresses waiting to take over from me.

I still felt very weak, but I discharged myself from hospital, though I could barely stand up. I had to ask the second and third assistants to help me climb the three steps into my trailer. I got the giggles because I didn't have enough strength to lift my legs. I was given a nurse and fed spaghetti three times a day, plus Vitamin B shots in my backside each morning. Wherever I worked, I had a camp-bed with a screen round it, where I could collapse between scenes. My long-suffering doctor, Annie Coxon, was by now getting used to keeping me on my feet 'for now', and curing me later.

Poor little me!

Poor little me gave Peter a rough time. One day when he asked me to come in early to do the offstage screams for Susan Fleetwood's lines, I flatly refused. It seems an actress's gratitude is not to be relied on. I was grateful for Peter's patience with me, and I think he made a fine film, and got quite a good performance out of me, although looking back I think I behaved like a first-class cow.

Writing this, I'm reminded of an example of how, in adversity, an actor *should* behave. The time was the summer of 1969. I was in a cast of British actors, working in what was still Yugoslavia, with the director Fielder Cook. The film was *Eagle in a Cage*, in which Kenneth Haigh played Napoleon.

Fielder is not the usual type of American director. He is a tall, lean and elegant Anglophile, modelling his manners on those of the English Gentleman, who hardly exists nowadays.

He coped wonderfully well with very difficult location conditions. We had to work in heavy period clothes, in a temperature of 90 degrees, shooting in a fort that hung high on a mountain which we all had to climb.

The work was most uncomfortable. We were surrounded by locals, whom Fielder used as extras. Kenneth was furious because there wasn't a car to take us up the mountainside. Lee Montague was getting worried because he suffered from vertigo, and was being asked to ride a horse, clutching a vast clock to his chest. (All he could see, as he was riding, was the precipice!)

As for me, I was constantly wanting to go to the loo, which meant running down the mountain to find a hole in the ground. It was the sort of location actresses like to go on and on about, boring the pants off anyone who wishes to listen.

Lunchtime came. Food was carried up to us in little boxes. Ken and I were still busily bitching and complaining, when I happened to look across to another part of the fort. There, having spent the entire morning in the heat of a burning sun, while waiting to play their scene, were Sir John Gielgud and Sir Ralph Richardson. Did *they* grumble? Whinge? The hell they did. They were daintily eating their lunch, looking as though they'd been served cucumber sandwiches in an Oscar Wilde play at the Theatre Royal, Haymarket, or in the gardens of Buckingham Palace. Though in full regalia, and no doubt feeling the discomfort more than the younger folk, they

With Laurence Olivier in *Othello*, 1964, which we played in London, Berlin and Moscow. I thought of him as an old man. He was fifty-seven!

The Dutch Courtesan at the National (Old Vic). A nice photograph but not a successful revival.

Unsuitably cast as the BBC's *Lady of the Camellias* with John le Mesurier. I was lucky to be directed twice on TV by the great Rudolph Cartier. I was a poor replacement for Juliette Greco.

With Michael Gambon in Christopher Hampton's play, *Tales from Hollywood*. Aged fifty-two, I had to do a nude scene. I played opposite Michael again in John Osborne's *The Entertainer* on TV.

(*Below right*) For the Royal Shakespeare Company in Peter Nichols' magnificent *Passion Play*. The part of the wife was divided between two actresses. Eileen Atkins was my *alter ego*.

(*Below left*) *The Greeks*, also for the RSC at the Aldwych – a twelve-hour epic, directed by John Barton. I played Andromache (in photo), Athene, Artemis and Chorus.

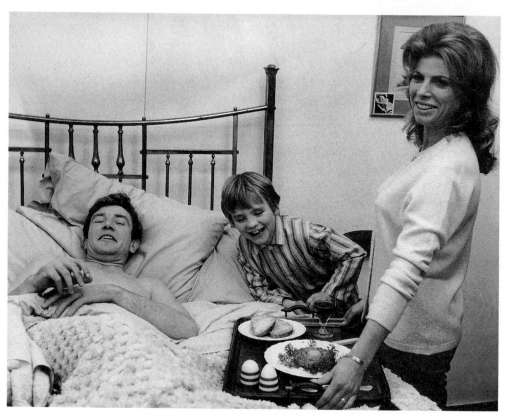

With Albert Finney in *Charlie Bubbles*, the only film he directed. When this picture was taken, I was pregnant but didn't know it.

In *The Krays*, 1990, with Gary Kemp, directed by Peter Medak. During the film I aged thirty years. It was one of the best roles I had in the latter part of my film career.

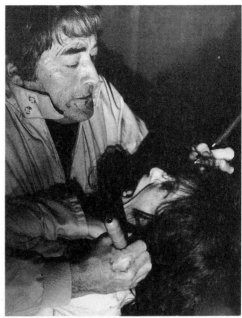

(*Above left*) In *Leo the Last*, with the irresistible Marcello Mastroianni (and here with David de Kayser), directed by John Boorman. For the first and only time I played a first class bitch.

(*Above right*) Gregory Peck stabbing me (as the 'nanny from hell') with a pickle fork in *The Omen*. I almost didn't do it – the most successful film I ever worked in.

On location in Paris, where I played Marie Antoinette in *Start the Revolution Without Me*, 1968. The visitor to the set is my son, Matthew, aged one.

Shortly after his recovery from meningitis, I took Matthew to Upton Park to meet his idol, Bobby Moore, at a practice work-out. 'When you're fifteen, I want to see you here in your football boots,' Bobby said to get Matthew exercising. We're still West Ham fans.

Matthew, long since recovered, at a party with his girl-friend, Nicola. He is stage-manager of the Pavilion Opera Company.

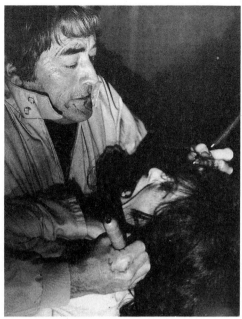

(*Above left*) In *Leo the Last*, with the irresistible Marcello Mastroianni (and here with David de Kayser), directed by John Boorman. For the first and only time I played a first class bitch.

(*Above right*) Gregory Peck stabbing me (as the 'nanny from hell') with a pickle fork in *The Omen*. I almost didn't do it – the most successful film I ever worked in.

On location in Paris, where I played Marie Antoinette in *Start the Revolution Without Me*, 1968. The visitor to the set is my son, Matthew, aged one.

Shortly after his recovery from meningitis, I took Matthew to Upton Park to meet his idol, Bobby Moore, at a practice work-out. 'When you're fifteen, I want to see you here in your football boots,' Bobby said to get Matthew exercising. We're still West Ham fans.

Matthew, long since recovered, at a party with his girl-friend, Nicola. He is stage-manager of the Pavilion Opera Company.

Robert, photographed by his friend, Wolf Rilla. Looking thoughtful, having put up with me for twenty-nine years.

Happy Ending. In our cottage in Suffolk, where Robert writes and I 'potter'. At sixty-two I regard myself as an incredibly lucky woman.

Progress to the Park – my first West End show in 1961 as a leading lady.
Kenneth Tynan, Bernard Levin and Robert Muller (whom I had never met then)
gave me the kind of rave notices I probably didn't deserve.

had spread out their paper napkins to look like tablecloths, and conversed with calm and dignity.

I thought, what an example to all of us of how to behave! They didn't complain or raise their voices. They remained courteous and dignified through all the heat and stink and mess around them. None of it applied to them. *Noblesse oblige.*

But back to *The Krays*. The film turned out to be Peter Medak's biggest success, and despite my volatile behaviour we've remained friends. We had good notices in the States, and I was flown to New York for the première by the Weinstein Brothers, who run Miramax, a firm specialising in distributing foreign films. They decided to push out the boat for me, and I was reminded of my Queen for a Night experience in Cannes two decades previously. I was given a suite at the Plaza, which was three times bigger than any hotel room I've ever known. They put a large white stretch limo about the size of my cottage at my disposal. I was taken around New York in this limo, giving interviews on radio and television.

I must confess – I did enjoy it! By now I was in my mid-fifties and knew the drill: as soon as my usefulness had been exploited, I was shipped home. Quite right, too.

I've made some films for the money, and a few because I liked the script. Beryl Bainbridge's story, *The Dressmaker*, was certainly up my street, a realistic tale set in wartime Liverpool, scripted by John McGrath. I've known Beryl since childhood. Like her, I knew the background to that movie, which brought back to me a lot of my own childhood.

The director, Jim O'Brien, certainly had a feeling for this period. I only have one quibble with his work: I couldn't fathom why all the women in the picture had to look so *ugly*. I can remember Liverpool in wartime, and my sister and aunts always did everything they could to make themselves look attractive. This was the time of Betty Grable and pin-up girls. I did try to persuade Jim to let me look like a poor imitation of Betty Grable, but he just wouldn't have it. He may have felt it would have detracted from the greyness of wartime living. As I remember it, life really was bloody awful, but the grown-ups would do their level best to brighten themselves up, despite all the shortages and deprivations they suffered. A lot of bottles of peroxide were sold during the war years to tart up the front of Liverpool ladies' hair!

Still, I won awards both for *The Krays* and *The Dressmaker*, and I know I have the talent and determination of Peter Medak and Jim O'Brien to thank for that.

Yet the most exacting taskmaster among directors (besides Samuel Beckett) that I've worked with, was probably Frank Oz of the Muppets – the voice of Miss Piggy and Fozzie Bear.

The film was an ambitious animated feature called *The Dark Crystal*. I had to invent the voice of Augra, a creature with one eye in the middle of her forehead, who, when she needed to look round corners simply took out the eye and poked it round.

About half-way through the writing of this book I realised it was taking up more of my time and imagination than I had anticipated. So I rang my agent, Michael Foster, and said: 'I'm only interested in short, sharp, preferably well-paid jobs. I haven't got time for anything else.'

Michael rang just before Christmas: 'I think I've got the perfect job for you. Franco Zeffirelli is directing *Jane Eyre* and there's a small part in it. He would love you to play it.'

Zeffirelli's producer rang up shortly afterwards to say: 'Zeffirelli is going to give you the choice of two parts. Take your pick. Would you like to talk to Franco about this?'

'Well, yes,' I said, 'if he's got time.' He told me that Zeffirelli was on location in the North of England, and gave me his telephone number.

I thought, no big director is going to be interrupted during shooting by an actress he's offered a small part to, when he's just started this massive production of *Jane Eyre*. I knew that William Hurt was playing Rochester, and word had already seeped through that they were not getting on.

I rang, and Zeffirelli picked up the phone himself. In fact, we had met thirty years earlier, when he came to the National to direct a Shakespeare play, but I wasn't in it. We all knew who he was, wandering about the theatre, but I didn't, for one moment, expect him to remember who the hell I was.

To my astonishment the most flamboyant, outrageous flattery came down the phone. I usually run a mile if someone flatters me so openly but this was quite impressive: 'Oh Billie,' he exclaimed, 'I cannot believe that you are considering to be in my movie, I am so thrilled, I am so honoured, this is so fantastic for me that someone of your standing is even going to consider playing one of these parts, because they are not very big. If I can get someone like you, this is so marvellous for me.'

One of the small parts he had offered me was Grace Poole. In the script she is described as a six foot four mulatto from the West Indies, about forty years of age. I thought, perhaps he really doesn't remember me. He may think I'm a man, and perhaps he thinks I'm black. So I said: 'Look, you *do* know I'm not black, don't you?'

He said: 'Yes, of course I know, I know your work, it's marvellous for me.'

So I told him I'd like to play the smaller part of Grace Poole because it was more interesting and fun to do.

'Oh, you are so right,' Zeffirelli said, 'yes, this is a far more interesting part. I am so glad you have made that decision, and I'm looking forward to this. If you want to talk to me any time about any of this, you must ring me.'

I thought this was quite extraordinary, coming from this vastly experienced opera and film director.

Though there were a lot of problems on the picture I would not have missed doing it for the world. Both Franco Zeffirelli and William Hurt I came to like and admire enormously. Yet those two were like oil and water. When they were working together there was, sad to say, a dreadful atmosphere on the set.

One day I saw Franco with his head in his hands after we'd finished working. I heard him say: 'I have now got five pages of hell.'

Next day I told him: 'It was so sad to hear you say, "I've now got five pages of hell."'

He said: 'I was wrong. It wasn't five pages. It was seven.'

When I started playing one of the scenes, Zeffirelli said: 'No, no, no, you are sitting there like an Oracle from Delphi, no, no.' Far from being upset or hurt or losing my confidence, I said: 'OK, what shall we do then?'

We got on very well. At the end of the shoot I said: 'If you've got a drawer that's labelled "Old Bags", will you please put the name of Billie Whitelaw in there.'

When I think about television directors, my memory goes into a blur. I have worked in over two hundred television plays and films, and my work with directors in the medium covers a span of several generations. My producer on the second TV series of *Firm Friends* turned out to be Deirdre, the daughter of Andrew Keir, my co-star in *Anna Christie*, which Rudolph Cartier produced thirty years ago.

I started this chapter recalling Ted Kotcheff, but I remember another Canadian director of this period, another talented lunatic called Hank Kaplan, for whom I did Eugene O'Neill's *Beyond the Horizon*. During rehearsals I told him: 'Good heavens, you're so like Ted Kotcheff.'

He nearly hit the roof: 'Ted Kotcheff is like me!' he barked at me. 'He's always modelled himself on me.'

Yet another Canadian I worked with was Silvio Narizzano, who directed Anthony Hopkins and me in *The Poet Game*, a television play based on the lives of Dylan Thomas and his wife – although no one was supposed to know that, and the author changed the Welsh poet into an Irish writer.

Sometimes we went around with *Dylan in America* under our arms, hoping that Dylan's widow Caitlin wouldn't suddenly turn up. I never felt Tony Hopkins was a happy man. His extraordinary talent was obvious. He was not afraid to dive into the deep end of a part. We worked well together in *The Poet Game*, and that was over twenty years ago.

I was very sad while writing this book to hear that Rudolph Cartier had died. He was a director steeped in the Central European tradition, and his wonderful visual sense was far ahead of its time in British television. He asked me to play Anna Christie in Eugene O'Neill's play, the part Garbo had played in 1930. I hadn't seen her version then, which is perhaps just as well, since I don't think we had much in common as actresses, to put it mildly. Just before I went to the National Theatre, Cartier called me again in an emergency to say that Juliette Greco had dropped out of playing *The Lady of the Camellias* for the BBC. Evidently she had panicked about her English, or lack of it. I had ten days to jump into the breach.

I think on that one Rudy gave up on me half-way through. I felt like a fish out of water. I just didn't know the cultural and historical background that the part required. After a while Rudy just sat in a corner and tried to go to sleep.

I think Rudolph Cartier was probably drawn to Juliette Greco's glamour and air of mystery. I didn't have much of either to offer him, I'm afraid. It had been a bit of a coup for him to land Juliette Greco at this time, and I fear I wasn't a very good swap. (By coincidence, I played the older friend, Flora, in a remake with Greta Scacchi in the title role of *Camille* which Desmond Davis, with whom I have enjoyed working many times, directed in the mid-Eighties.)

In those days, when directors got an early chance to show what they could do in television, the medium itself was thought by the élite to be a very minor craft. Nearly all the television directors I worked with wanted only one thing: to be allowed to direct a *movie*. Many of them turned out to be much better television directors than film directors.

There was a strange snobbishness about television in the late Fifties and early Sixties. One day I went to see a film director who'd seen me on television, and thought I'd given some splendid performances, especially the night before, when I'd played the lead in a real gutsy, down to earth drama. He talked about it at length, and was very flattering.

Then he said: 'But of course, that's television.'

That was that. I walked out without getting a job.

This view of television as a poor relation was shared by most of the people who worked in theatre and films at that time. Having done very many leading roles on television, and won Best Actress Awards, I had the feeling that most theatre critics felt they had to explain to their readers who I was. When they kept writing about this 'interesting new face', I felt like telling them I'd been working my butt off on television for about fifteen years!

If I wrote about all the directors I have worked with in television, this chapter would be endless. I was lucky to work with real masters of the medium, like Alan Bridges, James Ferman, Philip Saville and Herbert Wise, and remember with particular pleasure my work with Tristram Powell.

Tristram directed the Beckett stage productions for BBC Television, and did these unbelievably difficult things superbly. One arts programme he directed in 1976 was a beautiful evocation of the marriage of Thomas and Emma Hardy, called *A Haunted Man*, written by Denis Constanduros. So much that one does on television is here today, gone tomorrow, but I have a feeling that *A Haunted Man*, which has never been repeated (nor, as far as I know, has it ever been shown outside this country), is a very rare piece of television.

After Emma died, the second Mrs Hardy, along with Hardy himself, elected to burn all of Emma's poems. The young boy gardener was told to make a bonfire and burn her papers.

When we came to shoot that scene, I became aware of an old gentleman standing nearby, intently watching the shooting.

Somebody said: 'Do you know who that is? He was the young gardener who burned Emma Hardy's papers.'

That gave me a very odd feeling: here we were dressed in period costume, doing a period piece, and standing opposite was a man who was actually involved in the events of over fifty years ago that we were trying to recreate.

Emma died very painfully. I based the performance of my death on what I had observed of Matthew's pet white rabbit, George, who died in my arms. I recognised the *feeling* of death. It was all around poor George. I could swear the animal knew he was dying. I just copied what I saw: an animal, in this case a human animal, taking leave of this world.

I feel that, as a director, Tristram Powell is terribly under-rated. I would love to work with him again – perhaps because of his link with Samuel Beckett. For when all is said and done, the director I felt most in harmony with was Beckett himself.

In the end we almost became like one unit. I wanted what he wanted, and what he wanted from a play was never in any way in opposition to me. For me, our working relationship has remained unique. We worked in harness and harmony for a quarter of a century.

Robert, more of a film buff than I am, has pointed out how unusual it is for a creative working relationship between director and actress to last that long. One of the most fruitful and famous partnerships in movies, that of Marlene Dietrich and Joseph von Sternberg, which is so often quoted in film histories, in fact only lasted six years.

8

Late Calls

Alan Schneider always glowed with health. When he came over to London to direct a play called *The War at Home* by James Duff at the Hampstead Theatre in the spring of 1984, he was sixty-seven, but still looked a vigorous man in his fifties.

We discussed working together again. Like Jack Garfein, Alan felt that the *Rockaby*/*Footfalls* bill still had a lot of life in it.

One day, while I was sitting in my agent's office, a call from Clare, the wife of Alan's friend David Deutsch, was put through to me. Clare told me that Alan was lying unconscious in an Intensive Care Unit in the Royal Free Hospital in Hampstead.

I rushed over to the hospital. I couldn't believe what I saw: Alan lay there, attached to a machine, with a cloth across his groin. Curiously enough, there wasn't a mark on him.

What had apparently happened was that just before starting rehearsal in Swiss Cottage, Alan had excitedly nipped across the road to post a letter to Sam. He always had a child's enthusiasm and energy; he wanted to impart this energy to other people. Crossing the road, he was hit by a young motor-cyclist. Had he fallen on his hand or his arm, he might just have twisted his wrist or perhaps broken a little finger, but he fell backwards. His skull hit the kerb and he suffered a brain haemorrhage.

I rang Robert to tell him what had happened and stayed overnight at the hospital with Alan, until his wife arrived from New York. I was given a little bed at the side of the Intensive Care Unit, and there I waited. Alan never regained consciousness. Jeannie Schneider arrived with their son David and a close friend, Sheila Weber.

I found Jeannie's behaviour incredibly calm, brave and dignified. Alan was on a life support system; there was nothing more the doctors could do. Jeannie had to make a terrible decision.

Next day, while Jeannie, Sheila and David sat in the ante-room, I went to try and make some tea in the nurses' room. While I was boiling the kettle, I looked up at the doctor's rota, written on a blackboard. There, in large chalky letters at the side of Alan's name, I read: BECKETT. The hair stood up on the back of my neck.

For one moment I thought Jeannie, in her distress, had scribbled Sam's name at the side of Alan's. But of course she hadn't. I've always had a feeling that Sam himself believed that when extraordinary things like that happened, they weren't really 'coincidences'. A nurse later confirmed that Beckett was the name of the consultant on duty.

That night Jeannie took on the awful decision of cutting Alan off the life support. The neurologist had told her that Alan couldn't get better; he was already brain-dead.

It wasn't unlike attending an execution. Jeannie and David went in to say goodbye to Alan. When they came out of the Intensive Care Unit, we walked slowly and silently to the lift. While waiting there, we saw the neurologist coming up to us.

'I'm so very sorry,' he said.

It had been done. We went down in the lift and got a black cab to go back to my home. I'd rung Robert to tell him we were all coming back.

In the taxi, I shared an extraordinary experience. I was watching Alan's son, in his early twenties at the time. In the hospital he had seemed to me like a young puppy, a bit frightened, casting nervous little glances at his mother to see what he could do at this dreadful time.

In the seven minutes it took to get to Camden Square, I watched David metamorphose from a boy to a man. He stared with some disbelief at the space in front of him, but he was actually looking inward. Every now and again he shook his head. Jeannie just sat back in silence. When we got home, Robert was making tea for us. The phone rang. It was Donald Davis, a close friend of Alan's. The previous day, I would have handed the receiver over to Jeannie without hesitation. But now I handed it to David. Within a matter of minutes he had become the head of the family. He was in charge. He took up the receiver and said simply: 'David Schneider speaking.'

I called Paris to let Sam know what had happened. A couple of days later he rang back, still evidently in some distress. He said he'd just received a letter from Alan. It was the one he'd rushed out excitedly that morning to post.

*   *   *

Some time after Alan's death, I was asked to go to the Adelaide Festival in Australia with Beckett's *Rockaby* and *Footfalls*.

As Sam would say: 'Problem here.' Sam, who had directed *Footfalls* in the past, no longer felt up to directing. Alan was dead. I did not then feel capable of re-directing the play. Robbie Hendry, who'd been in on all the Royal Court productions of Sam's plays, felt he could get Beckett's production of *Footfalls* going again. I also had enormous faith in Rocky Greenberg, who had lit the plays in New York so effectively, and was a director in his own right. I felt that with Rocky and Robbie's help, I'd be able to make the trip to Australia.

Christine Collins, who was to play the mother in *Footfalls*, had a friend John Frost, a leading entrepreneur in Australia, who agreed to get Rocky over from New York.

It was decided to try this revival out at the Riverside Studios in Hammersmith. During rehearsals, I had long conversations both with Jeannie and Sam. I didn't want to do anything that would upset either of them.

We had a most successful try-out at Riverside. Jocelyn Herbert managed to get one of her students to re-make the masterpiece of a dress created for the original production of *Footfalls* at the Royal Court. It had been thrown out by mistake, because it looked just like a jumble of rags.

In Alan's absence, there were many problems to solve. We had endless trouble with the rocking chair in *Rockaby*, which has to rock backwards and forwards on its own. I wanted to stay close to all of Sam's precise ideas of how he wanted the chair to look. It had to be a specific colour, typically enough a *non-colour*. Jocelyn came up with the phrase 'the colour of bleached wood that had been thrown up on the beach and was lying in the sun'.

The chair that had been specifically made in America was too warm in colour for Sam's taste, so we had another chair made, which turned out to be too small. In Sam's absence, some people must have thought I was mad. I felt the chair should have arms that almost embraced me, because there's a line in *Rockaby* where the woman says: 'Those arms at last . . .'

We didn't get the colour of the chair right until we got to Australia, but eventually we managed to get the *Rockaby* engine running once more. Yet again the run at Riverside was sold out: people queued up for returns every night. These short, sad little plays always found an audience. Many people wanted to see them. Some wanted to come and see them again and again.

Alan would have been very pleased to see the queues round the theatre in Hammersmith. I regarded performing *Rockaby* in London, and then Australia, as some sort of homage to Alan Schneider. Wherever we went, I always took a turquoise blue folder that he'd given me to enfold the story of *Enough*. At rehearsal in New York I had kept scattering the pages all over the place. Just before the first night, Alan rushed in with this folder. I just looked at him.

'Alan, a turquoise blue folder in a Beckett play?'

We both laughed, but the turquoise folder has stayed with me.

Off we went to Adelaide. Christine Collins and I became good friends. One couldn't believe that the disembodied deep voice that came out from behind the curtain could possibly belong to this attractive, slight young woman.

In the text of *Footfalls* there is a sentence: 'Slip out at nightfall and into the little church by the south door, always locked at that hour.' At one point during rehearsals Sam had said: 'I think south sounds too warm. Make that the *north* door, it sounds colder.' He obviously didn't give a damn whether it was north, south, east or west. He simply wanted the word to convey a certain feeling. I latched on to that. Strangely enough, in Australia this now caused a bit of a problem. Here, north is warm and south is cold!

I rang up Avigdor Arikha all the way from the other end of the world to ask him: 'Please try to find Sam. Ask him whether in Australia I have to say north or south.'

Soon the answer came back: it didn't matter one way or another, it was up to me. 'I trust you.' So I changed the line back to south.

Our production worked well in Adelaide, but when we went on tour to Sydney and Melbourne, we found ourselves performing cheek by jowl with a war play performed by a company of actors who were all Vietnam veterans, an emotional piece about their experiences. Bruce Springsteen had let them use his music, and waived his royalties. For the length and breadth of Australia, our hushed little Beckett dramas were played to the accompaniment of the Vietnam war and Springsteen at full throttle.

In Sydney we managed quite well, but in Melbourne there was only a thin wall between the two theatres. *Footfalls*, with lines such as: 'But, let us watch her move, in silence,' was almost entirely done in delicate whispers. No dying old lady in *Rockaby* could compete with a re-creation of modern war.

I had to send Beckett another cry for help. I wanted to know whether, if conditions didn't improve, I had his permission to walk off the stage or withdraw the play altogether.

Métiers de la rue - N° 19

Paris   28.3.86
Dear Billie
Thanks for your letters from Sydney
and great news of your progress.
Confirm my card to you via Robert.
If you walk out in Melbourne we'll be
arm in arm.
                    Greetings to Robbie
                         Much love
                              Sam

Sam wrote back immediately: 'If you walk out in Melbourne we'll be arm in arm.'

At the end of our first night in Melbourne, I rose from my rocking chair like a ghost and told the audience: 'If I were you I'd go to the box office and ask for my money back.'

Then I bowed and walked off the stage.

Fortunately the actors in the two companies had become theatrical mates. On most nights, we all met after the show. We managed to play the week out. The Vietnam company even tried to act their war story *sotto voce* – an effort doomed to failure. But I was moved by their attempt.

Now the local papers had something to write about. Their angle was that the two 'competing' companies were at each other's throats. Nothing could have been further from the truth.

Meanwhile, Matthew was in his first job as student stage manager in California, Robert was doing his Albert Schweitzer television series in Germany, and I was touring Australia. We tried to call one another at least every other day, and it became something of an art to work out each other's time zones. (Robert called me in Melbourne from a payphone in a moving train in Germany. Something went wrong with the phone's mechanism and we spoke for half an hour for nothing.)

In Sydney, incidentally, quite a few people turned up to see *Rockaby* and *Footfalls* for quite the wrong reason. The Jack Gold and Jack Rosenthal movie *The Chain* (with a big cast including Warren Mitchell, a great favourite in Australia, and myself) was currently playing; quite a few people must have thought they would see the same merry widow I played in the movie on the stage 'in person'. Instead, what they got were a couple of old hags, one pacing up and down with a broken back, the other rocking herself to death in a chair.

I received quite a lot of hate mail; they just couldn't understand why I had come all the way to Australia to play in such incomprehensible rubbish.

One night, as we were about to go on, there was a bomb alert. We were all convinced that an outraged member of the audience had found a way to get his own back. We had to leave the theatre and sit outside for an hour or so. Then we were permitted to troop back. By this time our houses were getting a bit sparse.

Shortly after the Australian tour was finished, I went for a holiday to Penang with Robert, and then returned to America for a last shot at *Rockaby* and *Footfalls* at the Purchase Theater Festival in New York State.

But I don't want to leave my memories of Australia on a downbeat note. Sydney was one of the most exciting cities I ever visited. If I were ever asked to go back, I'd go like a shot.

Something else happened in Sydney which was to have quite an important effect on my future: the head of the local university's English Literature department asked if I would talk to his students about Beckett. I had to tell him that I wasn't an academic. I had barely been to school. I had never studied Beckett's work as a whole.

When he persisted, I found myself one morning in a hall full of people, having to talk about Samuel Beckett, without a script, or even notes.

Curiosity seekers and students kept on arriving, so we had to keep the doors open because they spilled out into the corridors. I chattered away to them quite happily for two hours. No one stopped me. I expected the hook at any moment, but I didn't get it. What this experience brought home to me was that people of all kinds seemed to want to be informed about Sam, both as a writer and as a person. It hadn't occurred to me that I had anything to say about him. The professor came up to me afterwards and said: 'Why don't you do this more often? For their work on Beckett, students need a personal link. What you can pass on is something much more direct than textbook theory.'

Evidently young people were battling with dry academic books about an author whose work they had never seen come alive.

It made me think.

The nearest thing I'd come to 'lecturing' was some years previously when Homer Swander (Murph to his friends) from the Arts Faculty at Santa Barbara University, California, had asked me if I'd talk to his students. At the time I was doing a play for the Royal Shakespeare Company. I assured him it would be a hopeless waste of time for all concerned. We discussed my reluctance until four o'clock in the morning. Then Murph said: 'Look, do what you've been doing half the night. That's all I want.'

I told him: 'OK, but I'm just a chatterbox, so on your head be it.'

I went out to Santa Barbara, still full of doubts. I know I wasn't very good, I still hadn't got my act together at all. I had little idea of what the young people expected of me; I felt that, lecturing at a university, I was sailing under false colours.

Much later, I was asked by Len Berkman to talk about Beckett at Smith College for a five-week semester. I was about to turn it down, but Robert dissuaded me. He worked out a structure of talks for me, giving me a set of cards on which he had written summaries of my various encounters with Sam's work. That sent me hopping in the right direction.

I still wouldn't allow the word 'lecturer' to be applied to me. But I agreed to come and 'chatterbox'. To my surprise, I found that I took to this new work like a duck to water. I was spontaneously bursting into renderings of Beckett's work, and I sensed that the students were warming to this unorthodox approach to Sam's work.

If I had not overcome my reluctance, the final chapters of my professional life might have worked out very differently.

*   *   *

Though after *Rockaby*, Samuel Beckett no longer wrote stage plays for me, or for anyone else for that matter, I still felt part of his own creative work-in-progress. We were still working partners. Some time before *Rockaby*, in the late Seventies, Sam had started to write short plays for television, which the BBC produced. The director was his old friend Donald McWhinnie, and Sam came over to London to help with the production. The two new plays were called *Ghost Trio* and . . . *but the clouds* . . . and they were presented with *Not I*, in a treble bill called *Shades*.

In *Ghost Trio* there is only one character, played by Ronald Pickup, while I am an off-camera voice; in . . . *but the clouds* . . . I am just a close-up face which moves in and out of the action.

Sam was at all the rehearsals, and seemed to be happy and in good form. During the production, we both enjoyed ourselves.

When we came to record my voice for *Ghost Trio*, I asked Sam to come to the recording booth with me. We sat opposite each other, with a mike standing on a table between us. As in *Footfalls*, we worked by conducting each other, and I could always tell by the expressions on his face when he was satisfied.

This time it was Donald who sometimes said: 'No, I'm sorry, that won't do at all.'

I saw a look of sheer horror come over Sam's face. It was the only time someone in my presence had told him that what we had rehearsed together was not good enough. But Donald was invariably right; we had to try all over again.

For the television plays, we began with Donald and me working together; then, while Donald worked with Ron Pickup, Donald would say: 'Well, Billie, you and Sam can now go off together and do your conducting in the corner.'

I realised that this conducting of ours, which must have looked very odd to other people, had become routine for us, a necessary rehearsal exercise.

It was while rehearsing *Ghost Trio* that I found myself able to observe closely the way Sam worked on his plays with other people. I had time to watch. As in *Happy Days* and *Footfalls*, he was deeply concerned with body movement, with the almost lyrical shapes a body can make. I loved watching Sam working in meticulous detail with Ronald Pickup. Sam sat on a stool, patiently showing Ron exactly what he wanted. Whenever Sam did it, the 'shape' pulsated with life. It was never a dead thing. Every part of the body exuded intense concentration. Sam worked with Ron for hours, just to get sitting on a stool right. Ron had to be absolutely still, bent over his cassette recorder. I recognised the process from *Footfalls*.

During *Footfalls* I had felt very strongly that we were on to something new, that he wanted to create shapes – to paint with light and to work like a sculptor to create movement. In *Ghost Trio*, I found it most exciting to observe Ron's figure starting to take on a new life, sensitive, vibrant and unique. There was certainly far more in all this than the stage directions had indicated. I found it not unlike watching a sculptor or painter at work. It was during this time that it hit me how unbelievably fortunate I had been to work with a genius.

Beckett liked working with Ron. I could see that he wanted to get at Ron's centre, the way I'd felt him getting at mine.

When the character he played in *Ghost Trio* moves to the door, Ron looked like something out of a silent expressionist German movie. When Sam did it, it also had an extraordinary humanity and pathos, although Ron always got there in the end. In *Footfalls* I had always known when my shape was right. It had a harmony – a oneness. Now I was able to watch another actor go through this metamorphosis. I found the images were unforgettable. I still can't begin to understand how Sam arrived at them. When we were working together, they seemed to grow quite naturally – from nothing.

Beckett was clearly beginning to involve himself with something more than just composing words for actors to speak. Writing this in 1994, over five years after his death, I fear this 'something' – the precisely planned visual aspect of his work in production – may be something to go out of the window in the future.

Ghost Trio is set in the 'familiar chamber' which, later on, I recognised when I did *Eh Joe* – a bleak room with a little camp-bed, a 'pallet' as he called it, with one window, a rectangular door – all composed in shades of grey. The male character walks somnambulently, as if under instruction from the off-screen voice. Ronald Pickup became this grey and dusty man of indeterminate age, bent over a tape recorder (shades of *Krapp's Last Tape*?) Even the old-fashioned little tape recorder is painted in shades of grey.

Beckett had become quite fascinated with the possibilities of television and often talked about the technicalities of television-writing to Robert.

I had already seen another television play he had directed: *Quad*, where (as in *Breath* for the stage) he had written – if that's the right word – a *drama* without the use of words. *Quad* was a mesmerising exercise, almost mathematical in concept – a short piece for four male actors who moved about with great precision to a beat. When they got to the central point on the set, it was as if an electric shock passed through them and they ricocheted back to where they'd come from. To me this seemed like the work of a choreographer, not a writer.

In *Ghost Trio* my voice speaks directly to the viewer, beginning with: 'Good evening, mine is a faint voice, kindly tune accordingly.' Then, after a pause, the next line goes: 'Good evening. Mine is a faint voice. Kindly tune accordingly. It will not be raised nor lowered, whatever happens.'

The voice then takes the viewer with her to the 'familiar chamber', a variation of the *Eh Joe* room, describing it as a director would describe the set to his cast at first rehearsal: 'The colour is grey, if you wish, shades of the colour grey.'

I must admit this made me laugh – a Beckett play is rarely anything other than shades of grey!

The voice then vocally seems to lead the figure of a man dressed in a long, shabby, dusty grey coat around the room. To begin with the man is listening to his tape, playing a specific excerpt from Beethoven's 'Ghost' Trio, music that, like a character, keeps fading in and out as the man moves to and fro. Sometimes the music grows faint, sometimes it gets louder. To my knowledge this was the only Beckett drama in which a piece of existing music is prominently used – apart from the end of *Happy Days*, where Winnie sings the waltz from *The Merry Widow*.

. . . *but the clouds* . . . had a patch of central light. A little man, who reminded me of one of the salt and pepper containers in the Mother's Pride flour ad, is first seen in a bowler hat and long black coat, and then in nightshirt, nightcap and shawl. The man shuffles into the central area of light, his head slightly bent. Then he shuffles off to disappear into areas of darkness, always waiting for the romantic face to fill the image; then to return to the light; then to disappear into another section of darkness.

My own contribution to this surrealist piece was minimal – a static close-up, with my eyes left wide open, and a bright light shining on me, sometimes to whisper words, but mostly remaining silent.

Sam insisted: 'I don't want you to blink at all. Just keep your eyes open.'

I remember laughing, asking him: 'Is there anything you ever write for an actor that isn't physically painful?'

When I spoke, I mouthed one line from Yeats, but apart from that there was just the still image of my face, lips moving sometimes, while the little salt and pepper man comes and goes.

Once during rehearsal Beckett asked his actors if we knew this particular Yeats piece. We didn't, and Sam spoke it from memory. He stood quite still for a few seconds, head down, looking inward, then, deep from his centre, the Yeats poem came out of his mouth. Ron and I were mesmerised. I asked Sam if I could put it on my own cassette recorder. I might have been asking him to drink arsenic. He physically recoiled, saying: 'Oh no, no, no.' But as I've written before, Beckett could read not only Yeats, but also his own work, better than anyone I've ever heard.

I remember this working period with Sam with pleasure. By this time, Donald McWhinnie, Ronald Pickup and I knew each other well. We all enjoyed each other's company.

Sam looked so much better then than when I'd first met him for *Play* in 1964, a dozen years previously. He was at ease, we were all at ease with each other. Sam knew that this time he wasn't going to be asked to leave, as happened so frequently in the theatre.

Though I inevitably found my work with Beckett the greatest challenge in that medium, it would be absurd to give the impression that my work in television over forty years was mainly concerned with Beckett's plays.

I'm very honoured to have worked for the small screen with writers like Dennis Potter, Peter Terson, Hugh Whitemore, Jack Pulman, Peter Ramsley, Philip Mackie, Peter Tinniswood, Frederic Raphael and many more. And over the years I have worked five times (in the UK and in Germany) with my husband, whose work dropped through my letterbox without me having read a word of it before. I wouldn't have anything to do with his plays unless they came from the production office, even though they were sitting in Robert's study, waiting to be read by me.

I was excited to be part of the plays that Beckett wrote for TV, but the BBC also filmed the stage productions of *Not I* and *Happy Days* in the Seventies. (I hope they haven't wiped them.)

It was ten years later that the German producer Rainer Moritz asked Walter Asmus, who had worked with Sam in Germany, to direct me in a triple TV bill of *Eh Joe*, *Footfalls* and *Rockaby*.

It was in preparation for this work that Sam and I were to work together for the last time.

We met in Paris and rehearsed *Eh Joe* at the huge PLM Hotel, which had been built just opposite his flat: an ultra-modern building, crowded with Japanese businessmen. Inside the hotel, there was a coffee bar which Sam liked, where we sometimes met in those late days. I noticed he had become very frail. He wore a mustard coloured beret and a great-coat, and was no longer steady on his feet. It never occurred to me that, after this meeting, I would never see Samuel Beckett again.

Sam started to read bits of *Eh Joe* to me. The visible figure, played originally by Jackie MacGowran, and now by Klaus Hern, was silent. The only sound was the female voice in his head. When Sam had finished, I read the play back to him. Sam would interrupt occasionally to say: 'Slower, much slower.' It was as though he wanted it to be taken at an even slower pace than *Footfalls*.

A man, once again sitting in the 'familiar chamber', dressed in an old worn dressing-gown and carpet slippers, hears in his head the voice of a woman. This voice speaks of another woman who seems to have committed suicide. Sam drew a diagram on a scrap of paper to show exactly how she walked between the rocks, and how she put her face at the side of the water – to drown herself, I suppose. I had a sneaking suspicion that he knew this place. I also felt he had known this woman: 'The green one . . . The narrow one . . . Always pale . . . The pale eyes . . . Spirit made light . . .'

His close friends, the painter Avigdor Arikha and his poet wife Anne, lived round the corner. Later that day I joined Anne and read some of *Eh Joe* to her. It made her cry.

For an actor appearing in a Beckett play, it is wise not to count his or her lines to see how big their role is. I've found over and over again that, after watching a Beckett play, a small, sometimes silent part, is the image that lingers for ever in the mind. There is no such thing as a small part in Beckett.

In the TV version of *Eh Joe*, it is the silent character of Joe one remembers, not necessarily the voice of the woman. And in *Catastrophe*, in which I never appeared myself, but which I regard as one of Beckett's most moving and most accessible works, there is a figure which has haunted me ever since I saw it in London. David Warrilow played the part of a man who is all humanity. He just stands on a plinth in silence, while two other characters move around him and pummel him about, and instruct the non-speaking character as if he were not there. I find this to be a deeply political piece about man's casual enslavement of man. Sam wrote it for the playwright Vaclav Havel, who is now the Czech President.

A group who performed *Catastrophe* on London's fringe some time later may have missed the point somewhat (or perhaps they needed to save money) by constructing *all humanity* out of wire!

Poor Sam.

Intermission Four:
Radio Days

When I was sixteen years old, Trevor Hill, who had taken over from Nan MacDonald at the BBC in Manchester, said to me: 'Billie, I'm not going to let you play any more little boys.'

Then he cast somebody else to play Bunkle, which left me heartbroken, but Trevor insisted the time had come for me to start playing girls' roles.

I didn't know where to start. From the beginning, when I was speaking dialogue, I had instinctively pushed my voice down my throat. This did my voice and throat no good whatsoever. But I suppose I did learn to twist my voice to make the sounds that were required of it.

When I first came to London, imagining myself to be a veteran radio actress, with a couple of hundred programmes under my belt, I rang up Broadcasting House, expecting the big 'hello'. I was told to fill out an audition form.

I went and auditioned. I failed. That was the end of that. I didn't do radio work again until I'd made a name for myself on television. From failing my audition I went straight to play the leading role in Caryl Brahms' *Trottie True*. It was a *Saturday Night Theatre* production. (It had also been a movie with Jean Kent.)

Over the years I have done a lot of radio, playing leading parts, far removed from the little boys I started with: *Vassa Sheleshova* by Gorky, Madame Ranevskaya in Chekhov's *The Cherry Orchard*, Hilda Wangel in Ibsen's *The Master Builder*, the wife in A.E. Whitehead's *Alpha Beta*, and *Filumena Maturano*, a radio version of the Edoardo de Filippo play Joan Plowright had done in the West End.

Several times I went back to do radio in the North, one time to play Amy Johnson, the famous flyer. Believing that anyone from the North never quite loses their accent, no matter how rich or successful they become, I played Amy Johnson with a rich round Yorkshire accent. I knew almost nothing about her, and was too lazy to do the necessary research. I'm afraid we made a dog's dinner of poor Amy Johnson, and that goes for the young director whose name was Alan Ayckbourn too.

It turned out that Amy Johnson had gone to elocution teachers. As a result, she spoke with a frightfully 'refained' Thirties accent. Her original voice had been elocutionised out of all recognition. Incidentally, I thought it was rather cheeky of this Alan Ayckbourn to use the same name as Alan Ayckbourn, the playwright. I had no idea they were one and the same person!

Early on in my relationship with Beckett, Martin Esslin, for many years head of BBC Radio Drama, asked me to play in a radio production of *Rough for Radio 2*. I imagine Sam called it that because he didn't regard it as a completed piece. He had written *Rough for Radio 1* and *Rough for Radio 2*.

In *Rough for Radio 2*, Harold Pinter played the writer; I was a stenographer who keeps mouthing secretarial platitudes. Patrick Magee played a man, locked in a cupboard, who is thrashed every now and again with a bull's pizzle, which Sam explained was a bull's penis. Patrick was brilliant in this part. I wouldn't have minded playing that role; I could understand being locked in a cupboard and being beaten into activity by a bull's penis; it was a Beckett touch I recognised. (In *Play* we had been beaten into activity by a lacerating light.)

In the late Eighties, Everett Frost of New York University, and his partner Faith Wilding, decided to record Samuel Beckett's radio plays for American public broadcasting and on cassette. He asked me to play in *Embers* and *All That Fall*. The latter, which we recorded in New York, is an early Beckett work from the Fifties, which Donald McWhinnie had already directed for the BBC. David Warrilow played Mr Rooney; I played a colourful character called Maddie Rooney. The play describes the journey poor Maddie makes to the station to meet her husband.

Before I went to America, Sam read bits of the play down the telephone to me. Though he no longer had the energy to get involved in production, the two of us would discuss the piece. Sam gave me guidelines. I wouldn't have wanted to do the work without his help while he was able to give it. Even in his last years, when I did *Rockaby* in America, and later at the National, we spent hours working together down the telephone.

Apart from letting me hear a certain *tone* that he required, which from long practice I was able to pick up very quickly from him, he invariably said one particular thing, usually in passing, that gave me the key to the part. This time he said that Maddie Rooney was 'bursting with abortive explosiveness'. Suddenly I saw this image of a Michelin tyre of a creature blowing up in front of me. That's how I played her – huffing and puffing, dragging her feet, shod with ill-fitting shoes, walking and weaving her way to the station, before she exploded out of her stays.

Everett Frost came to London to direct *Embers*, which gave me a chance to work with Barry McGovern, the Irish actor, who must be tired of hearing people say that he seems to be a reincarnation of Jackie MacGowran.

Though Barry does look and sound like Jackie, he's a much bigger and stronger man, and certainly a fine, original actor in his own right.

Ada in *Embers* was a voice I felt I'd come across before in Sam's work – a voice which somehow had to be fetched up *from beyond the grave*. I don't think Ada ever existed, except as a creature imagined in somebody's head. She seems to come out of the ether, which is what I used in the performance I gave.

The longer Beckett and I worked together, the more I came to recognise certain recurring ideas in his work. In *Footfalls* he had told me: 'Don't be too earthbound,' as though the character's voice was not quite of this world. In *Rockaby*, he had told me right away to make the voice monotonous, like a lullaby: 'No colour,' he advised again, 'no colour'.

It was during one of our last conversations, when we discussed *All That Fall*, that I suddenly realised that Beckett, who hated to have his voice recorded, didn't know that he had an Irish accent.

'She should have a bit of an Irish accent,' he told me.

I said: 'A bit like yours?'

He said: 'No, no, a bit of an Irish accent.'

So I used a slightly stronger version of his own accent for Maddie Rooney.

I realised then that when Sam wrote dialogue, the music he heard in his head was Irish. Whenever I'm reading his work through for the first time, I either read it in my own North Country voice, or I use the voice in Sam's head, which he may never have realised was his own.

Epilogue

9

A New Start

O n Boxing Day 1989 I had a phone call from Sam's nephew Edward. As soon as Edward said the words: 'Hello, Billie, this is Edward Beckett speaking,' I knew what had happened. Sam had died just before Christmas, at the age of eighty-three. The funeral was very private. When it was over, Edward wanted to call me from Avigdor and Anne's house.

My deep regret and sadness is that after he had gone into a nursing home, when his health had begun to deteriorate seriously, though we often spoke on the telephone, and he told me how nice it would be if I could come and visit him, and I said: 'Yes, I will,' I left it too late.

It took a long time for it to sink in that Samuel Beckett was dead. It was Christmas; one got on with the usual festivities and visits. I tried to get on with my life.

In the New Year I often woke up in the middle of the night, not knowing why I was crying.

I had to go off to do some television in Scotland, and would be sitting in the hotel restaurant with my script on the table, not thinking about Sam at all. Suddenly I would find myself crying uncontrollably. I would have to leave.

For a long time I carried a heavy weight around in my diaphragm. Even now, when I see a photograph of Sam unexpectedly, I get something akin to an electric shock. Sam's death was for me like an amputation. For twenty-five years, he had been a major part of my professional and personal life. I wasn't prepared for the hole his going would leave, a hole that can never be filled.

His death had a more lasting effect on me than I would have thought possible. All desire to work ceased, certainly work I would need to take seriously.

If important parts were now offered, I often turned them down out of hand (though this may have been partly due to the *Who's Afraid of Virginia Woolf?* experience). Peter Hall wanted me to work with him; more than once Richard Eyre asked me to work at the National. I said no to all these offers. I felt I had lost the heart to work. A light had gone out of my life.

More than anything I wanted to potter around in the countryside, and not have to think too deeply. The irony of turning down so much serious work was that, in the end, I often accepted lighter, less demanding parts, work I enjoyed, but that didn't involve my centre. I was not happy with many of my performances at this time; I think I was bringing guns to them that were too heavy, not really needed.

Robert and I had just moved to an idyllic spot in the Stour Valley in Suffolk. In 1974 we had bought a small labourer's cottage there, and for fifteen years used it for weekends and holidays. When the young writer Craig Brown, who lived in enjoyable chaos in the adjoining cottage, decided to move, he kept his promise to give us first refusal. We knocked the two cottages together and left London to live permanently in Suffolk, keeping a small flat in Hampstead for when I was working.

After our nearly thirty years together, this was one of the biggest decisions Robert and I made. For neither of us was there any question of retirement. Robert wouldn't know what to do with his mornings if he had no writing to do. We simply decided to alter the emphasis in our lives. I became consumed with the beauty and variety of Nature that now surrounded us. We got to know all the birds in our garden; some of them were incredibly tame. The cheeky robins walk through the kitchen door, peck at the dogs' food bowl and walk out again. And the pheasants bang on the window if they want food.

My idea of a garden is possibly quite different from other people's. I like to plant what other people want to pull up. I collect seeds from the hedgerows. I love wild hedgerows and it grieves me when I see them manicured in the image of a suburban garden. It also destroys wildlife cover.

I have always wanted a secret garden. The strip of land at the bottom of the garden, next to a field, had been a piggery. I had it dug up, churned, and re-set with tons of earth. I also wanted the sound of running water, not a fountain or a pond, but a sort of babbling puddle. In Cambridge I found Marney (a niece of an old friend, the writer and director R.D. Smith), who specialises in just the sort of wildlife garden I wanted. She helped me to have this little idyll built. I told myself that it was no good someone saying to me:

'This will look great in fifteen years' time.' I wanted us to enjoy all this here and now. We made an instant garden which looks as if it had been here for donkey's years – full of wild flowers and roses and old Victorian plants.

The Beckett memorials in London, Paris and New York, to which I contributed, were very important to me. I found them not only moving but exhilarating. The one in Paris, held at the Pompidou Centre, was packed out. We needed radio link-up for the people waiting outside. I noticed that most of the Beckett enthusiasts were young. When the ceremonies were over, they came flooding in from outside. I found it unbearably moving to stand on the same stage as Madeleine Renaud while her husband Jean-Louis Barrault, not well enough to take part, sat in the front row. Both were to die quite soon afterwards, while I was writing this book.

In Paris I enjoyed exchanging memories with Delphine Seyrig, who had played *Footfalls* there. Sitting in a restaurant, we spoke the lines of the play together, Delphine speaking in French, while I spoke in English. We both realised that the play was more difficult to perform in French. Perhaps this was why Delphine had not been totally happy with her performance. At the time I didn't know that Delphine was fighting cancer. I mistakenly took her turban to be a fashion accessory.

Sam wrote in three different languages: French, German and English. He could hear the music of those languages, and often told me that some plays lent themselves better to the music of one language than another. *Footfalls* worked better in German than in French, *Not I* better in English and German than in French. (He was reluctant to translate *Not I* into French, but eventually did so out of respect for Madeleine Renaud, who wanted to do it.) The ideal language for *Happy Days* was probably the original French version.

The memorial in London was held at the National Theatre. Peggy Ashcroft and Harold Pinter gave readings at the Olivier. As with the Barraults, it was probably Dame Peggy's last public appearance. A whole era in theatre seemed suddenly to have ended. I performed the last two stanzas of *Rockaby*, the last stage play of Sam's I had done.

Christopher Morahan directed the memorial, and Jocelyn Herbert, Beckett's closest collaborator and friend in England, set the stage, which she did simply and beautifully. I shall never forget the concentrated look on Jocelyn's face, as she silently went about her business.

I remember asking Christopher for a microphone on this occasion. I wanted my voice to sound like *thought*. Christopher was shocked. He said he'd never known an actress ask for a microphone at the National Theatre! I explained to him that I had worked at the Olivier before, and was quite capable of filling the theatre with my voice. I wanted to produce a tone that seemed to be coming from beyond the grave. I knew I could only achieve this effect with a personal microphone. I got what I asked for. Once he heard me, Christopher told me he realised why I'd asked for the microphone. Dame Peg asked for one as well.

I was then asked to go to New York to read the end of *Rockaby* at the Lincoln Center: '*Time she went down, down the steep stair, time she went right down . . . ,*' gently rocking towards death.

Barry McGovern was there and so was Rick Cluchy, whom I called Rick from Sam Quentin. He had been a prisoner there, a lifer without parole. A theatrical company had come to San Quentin to perform *Waiting for Godot*. Rick told me later he had no idea what the play was about, but had felt at the time that a character with a length of rope tied round his neck, weighed down with bags, barely able to speak, *who was called Lucky*, was something he had to investigate. He went to the prison library, and began to read everything Sam had ever written. He became obsessed with it. He formed a company of his own within the prison, called the San Quentin Players, and from time to time they allowed Rick out to perform Beckett. When, after many years, Rick was finally released, he began touring Beckett's plays round the world. He has done so ever since. I know Sam was deeply moved by Rick's story; he sensed his work had actually changed somebody's life.

At the end of the New York memorial, I locked myself in my dressing-room and howled. Then I told myself: 'Well, that's it. I'm never going to perform Beckett again.'

Around this time, I was also asked to take part in a big Beckett festival in Dublin. I didn't really want to do it, but finally allowed myself to be persuaded to give two lunchtime performances of *Footfalls* and *Rockaby*. The time approached; I was dreading it. At virtually the last minute I backed out. I fear I shall not be forgiven in Dublin.

Before Sam died, we had often spoken about requests I was getting from universities in the States to talk about our work together. This had come out of my chatterboxing sessions at Santa Barbara, and something similar I'd done at Balliol College, Oxford, where

Anthony Branch and Earl Gister from Harvard University ran summer courses for their British-American Drama Academy.

At Balliol I worked among students. I didn't do it well. I was still self-conscious about my lack of education. I hadn't even attended a lecture, let alone given one! Yet in some way I was now getting through to young people. More and more, I began to realise this was something I would like to do.

Sam had encouraged me while he was alive, but I knew I couldn't go on fumbling my way through my subject as I had been doing. The turning point, briefly referred to before, came when Professor Leonard Berkman from Smith College, Northampton in Massachussetts, a very eminent ladies' college, came to see me in England, to ask me if I'd lecture for a whole semester. I found his enthusiasm infectious and inspiring. Len wore a long ponytail and sneakers. His informality put me at ease.

I explained to him that I could only talk about the works Beckett and I had done together. I had nothing whatsoever to say about plays in which I hadn't appeared. I agreed to 'teach' at Smith's for five weeks, fearful that I had not enough material to last me that time. To my astonishment, I found I could have gone on for double that time. I think it was Jeannie Schneider, Alan's former director colleage, and Joan Thorne, who fixed me up with Smith's behind my back. I shall be for ever grateful to them for that.

Gradually I was made to see that I had something to offer. I began to feel a sense of mission. I found I was putting as much effort into this work as into performing. I took the students on 'a journey I've made with a man called Samuel Beckett, a journey that was to last twenty-five years'. I went on to tell them: 'I want to take you over this journey step by step, and try and re-live it with you.'

I felt the students and I were metaphorically holding hands, and off we went. With Len's encouragement, I felt myself becoming a conduit between Sam and these young people. They responded well, the classes grew bigger, mature students came in from outside. Actors were coming in from Boston; professors arrived from other colleges. When there was a holiday, and the University was closed for twenty-four hours, the students told me: 'If you're prepared to come in, we'll come in.'

I thought, I can't be doing this all wrong.

I went on to Dartmouth College in New Hampshire, where I made another good friend, Louis Crickard, whom I had previously met at Denver University, when I went there in the late Eighties to work with Martin Jenkins, head of BBC Radio Drama. Louis has a very good film school at Dartmouth, where he went to great trouble to put on a retrospective of some of my film work.

On my last evening at this college, I put together what I called 'An informal evening with Samuel Beckett', made up of a selection of work Sam and I had done together, linked with anecdotes and stories of our preparations and rehearsals.

I had to make the point that what the students were seeing wasn't a genuine *Beckett production*, which requires precise lighting and stage management, but an attempt to recreate the atmosphere of our work over the years.

Without being conscious of it, this informal evening gradually grew to become a self-made One-Woman Show, that I have been able to do for charity and at colleges all over the world.

Sometimes, as I sit writing in a cosy study in this funny little cottage, looking out over mile after mile of the unspoiled Stour Valley, I am reminded of the Marschallin's confessional monologue in *Der Rosenkavalier*, the first opera Robert took me to see, and the first record he bought me.

If I have to write about myself, *my self*, how can I do this with honesty? Who is this *self*, when I still tend to think of myself as an eleven-year-old stuttering girl, who can hardly string a sentence together, who lives on bread and scrape, who once a week, at ten minutes to five, has to clutch the lavatory pan at the BBC North Region in Manchester, vomiting into the bowl before doing a *Children's Hour* that goes out live, telling herself: 'Oh please God, please God, get me through this, and I promise I'll never be naughty again.'

How can *this* self be the same person who is supposed to be a 'Commander of the British Empire', who was appointed the first Annenberg Fellow at Reading University, who has scholastic awards and academic citations on her shelf, and who, thanks to Bradford University, can even call herself a Doctor of Literature . . .

How very absurd. How unlikely.

The worst piece of direction I think that any director has ever given me was to tell me: *'Just be yourself.'*

It stopped me in my tracks. I still have no idea who 'myself' really is. Like most people, particularly actors, I am made up of many selves. Some of them aren't very nice. As a toddler, I was supposed to be a happy and chirpy little thing with blonde ringlets. Yet this three-year-old had quite another 'self' to her. Whenever thwarted, this little girl would, without any emotion at all, present an ultimatum: 'If you don't let me do this, or if you don't stop doing that, I'm going to stamp my foot and scream.'

I never got bad-tempered. I just made my intention quite clear to anybody who wanted to listen. Then I found a bit of hard floor and calmly carried out my threat. When I was even younger, in Coventry, I apparently charged up and down along the garden fence, having imaginary rows with the little girl next door. I think the very first words I learned, after 'Mummy' and 'Daddy', were a somewhat threatening: 'I tell you . . . ,' spoken with great force and determination. I was a bossy-boots at two, and I still am. I screamed and stamped my feet: nobody took the slightest notice. That was before I had learned to be sneaky. Today, I'm still apt to announce what I will do in a certain situation, not as a threat, but as a statement of fact.

Yet I know there to be another side to me. In a real crisis, I will put other people's needs first. When Robert was ill, when Matthew needed something, I was never in a quandary as to what to do. My actions were automatic, as natural to me as breathing. On any list of priorities, before either Robert's wishes or my own, my son always comes first – possibly a mixed blessing for Matthew.

I don't blame anyone or any circumstance for anything I have done. The most positive influence on my character was the knowledge that I was loved at home. My father loved me until he died, my mother loved me all her life. There were a lot of things we didn't have when I was young, but the one thing I never lacked was love. I think my mother probably loved my sister more than she loved me, but that seemed quite normal. She was the first-born. I also know I wasn't really wanted when she became pregnant with me. My parents were no longer on the best of terms, to put it mildly.

All these bits that make up 'myself' seem to be a jumble of contradictions. I am not socially generous, I don't give many presents, yet I have always tended to want to *give things away*. Mum had to rush down the street and tell neighbours: 'I'm sorry, Billie's given that away by mistake. It's her birthday present. Can we have it back, please?' She might have been saving up all year for a three-wheeler bike, yet I would run it up and down the road, and end up giving it to a little friend.

In the same way, Robert often gets impatient with me when, in the street, I empty my pockets and purse of all my change, putting it into the hands of beggars. I feel I don't need the change (and if I do, I can always ask Robert!).

Getting on with my life on my own has always been high on my list of priorities. I can remember this being a conscious decision in early adolescence, having been evacuated at the age of seven, my father having died when I was nine, my sister being away in the Forces, and Mum out at Sharpes' factory till all hours – I started training myself to be *by myself*.

Like most people, I have a half-belief in the superstition of astrology. I'm a Gemini, Robert is a Virgo. Without a Virgo at my side I don't think I would have much left of anything. Yet I am aware of a blind faith that somehow I will always be given everything I need. From the age of eleven, it has never entered my head that I can't earn the money I need to keep myself. I may not have the conventional Christian beliefs, but I certainly believe in a Good Fairy on my shoulder – a sort of guardian angel who protects me, if necessary even from myself.

I've always felt I am living in a place which isn't good enough. It's a feeling I recognise to this day: a sense of inadequacy that where I live is not good enough to ask other people round. Even twenty years or more after leaving bad times behind, when I was living in a large house in Camden Square, I had a feeling that it was not good enough, not as good as other people's homes.

People like Peter Hall, Peggy Ashcroft and her mother, and Harold Pinter did come round to Camden Square, but that was only, I felt, because I had asked them to come after a Samuel Beckett first night. I would offer my home to Sam so that he could meet all the people he felt he had to, and get it over in one fell swoop. I would have done the same thing if I'd lived in a garden shed. For some reason I felt that if all these people had just come to see me, I would have to offer them something special. As a hostess I have always felt more than a little inadequate.

I feel that every part I've ever played has always been about me, certainly in the plays by Samuel Beckett. I seem to have within me not only the seeds of the characters I play, but in real life the seeds of being both failure and winner, depressive and optimist. Like most people, I am a Jekyll and Hyde, often frightened and nervous, yet, when I feel strongly about something, capable of being a leader, of walking through brick walls without feeling pain.

Viewing my various selves, I must confess to several negative characteristics: I can be extremely intolerant and arrogant, and have a tendency to write people off. I am judgemental, and in that, often quite wrong. I have an elastic view of my 'duties' in life, of doing things that, to other people, would be a matter of course. My husband has written work for me, which has been successfully produced, yet I've only read a fraction of what he has written. Interviewers have often found this rather strange, but Robert writes in both English and German. I wouldn't dream of acting as his critic or adviser. To me, it seems natural to let him get on with his work, while I get on with mine.

On the positive side, I honestly believe I am not possessive with members of my family, with people I love. I need my own space around me, and don't like people to enter it. I respect other people's space and don't enter theirs. This is sometimes misunderstood.

Although I try to get my own way and usually manage to do this, my love for Robert and Matthew has never, I hope, been possessive. I like to think I love with an open hand. When Matthew had his eighteenth birthday, and had just left school, he went to California to do his first job, which was to last eighteen months.

A friend asked me: 'How can you bear to let him go off like that?'

I told her that I wanted to see him flap his wings, I wanted him to take off, fly on his own. Metaphorically, I put a pair of scissors into his suitcase so that he could cut the umbilical cord. I'm a bit of a mother hen. I knew he had to free himself from me.

I think I'm quite good to have around in a crisis. I don't make social demands on other people, in return for which I won't let them make social demands on me. Everyone can do what they like and when they like – provided it is not assumed that I will join in.

Solitude never depresses me. I am quite often alone. I don't need people buzzing around me in order to function. Yet I certainly need to live inside a nucleus. That nucleus is Robert and Matthew and this cottage.

I am not a good member or joiner of things, neither in my profession nor in village life. Reclusive by nature I may be, but I do enjoy a good gossip at the shops, or with fellow dog-walkers.

Living in Suffolk is like being in the middle of a constantly changing painting. One becomes aware of the different seasons, the beautiful, altering light. No wonder Constable was always painting this landscape and Gainsborough was content to live up the road. Surrounded by Nature, by birds and rabbits, I feel at one with the earth. I don't mind if the rabbits eat the carrots or the deer nibble at the roses.

That part of me, the part that identifies with the earth (and will probably land me in *Private Eye*'s Pseuds' Corner), is also the part that stops me from being frightened of death. I have always lived close to death – a bit too close sometimes. I lost my father, and nearly lost the other two most important men in my life – husband and son. By a whisker, Robert and Matthew are still here, but had they gone, I would have taken my own leave without regret.

I promised my mother I would never let her die as painfully as my father had died. Had it come to that, I would gladly have given her the means to die without pain. I would willingly go to jail to stop Robert or Matthew from being assailed by unbearable pain. And when I have had enough of my own life, I want to go with a jar of Valium and a magnum of champagne. I don't consider it a sin to commit suicide.

Though brought up to believe in God, I have no time for religious institutions. I've never been able to understand why the churches all over the world are so rich, apart from worker priests and certain rogue elements, which seem to be frowned upon. Nor have I understood why in so many countries the churches have always supported right-wing dictatorships. I can't believe that is what Jesus Christ had in mind. Nor can I remember as a child ever being told that we worshipped a Jew. I don't think Jesus Christ would have got very far had he been around in the Thirties, or in our own day, come to that.

As for politics, I seem to be for ever going leftwards. Perhaps that's because I was never able to admire Mrs Thatcher, as she was then. She brought some energy to public life in Britain when she came to power, but, in my view, spent most of her years in office encouraging all those things that I have spent my life trying to hack out of myself. I think she encouraged greed, she made people worship 'success' and the accumulation of money. Those who have followed her lead often seem to believe that if you can get away with something, it must be moral. It is only my opinion, but Lady Thatcher (and that dreadful son of hers) stand for everything that from the age of fourteen have made me so often feel ashamed to be a member of the human race.

I can't understand why it's OK to make millions out of arms deals with dictators, or from exporting death in the form of tobacco to the Third World, where people are mostly ignorant of the consequences of smoking.

Why are these dealers in death not hounded with the same rage as some politician, whose extra-marital affair may have produced life?

Today I am not attracted to any particular political party, but like so many members of my generation, who experienced the Depression and war, emotionally I feel myself to be of the Left. When I was very young, Socialism seemed the nearest thing to Christianity.

Yet I have lived to see Christianity going hand in hand with Fascism. And in many countries where Socialism has succeeded, the results seem to be dire.

Now, at sixty-two, I often feel that, despite the guilt feelings that never go away, I may have earned the right, within reason, to do my own thing in my own way. I am still working on removing the words 'should' or 'ought' from my vocabulary. Although I cannot let go of a fifty-year-old feeling that I should be 'earning a living', I feel I don't have to apologise (which of course means that I *do* apologise) if I spend some days doing nothing – just clutching a mug of tea and pottering around the garden. That is certainly what I like to do first thing in the morning and last thing at night.

I'm unbelievably lazy. Robert gallantly calls my laziness being a 'minimalist'. No wonder, he says, that I was so much at one with Beckett. The fact is, when not working I'm bone idle. It's no great problem for me to spend the day in house and garden, doing a bit of domestic stage-managing and décor here and there, listening to birds, looking at the various bits of weeds I may well have planted.

I no longer feel driven, no longer feel the need to prove myself. There are certain things I feel I have to repay emotionally, but in that way I am quite unlike Robert, whose over-developed sense of duty requires him to tick off a hundred (possibly imaginary) duties he feels he must complete, before he has the right to draw breath or enjoy himself. I suppose that's what's known as survival guilt.

Lorin Maazel, the conductor, once said to me: 'You've paid your dues, you should now feel free to live your life the way you want to live it, not the way *other people think you should.*'

I drink to that.

I live in my own time-warp – and have never felt that love and friendship have anything to do with the amount of time one spends with people, or with the number of miles one is apart. I feel I can transcend that, if needs be. I also like to think that if I admire people, it's not because of their position, talent or 'success'. I admire women like our district nurse in Camden Town, now retired, a saint of a woman who, on her days off, would go to King's Cross and Euston stations to find girls who were pregnant and homeless. She would take them in and somehow looked after them on her wretched nurse's salary. I admire men like Dr Freudenberg in Kentish Town, who saved my son's life. I admire Helen Bamber, and all the people who work with her at the Medical Foundation for the Care of Victims of Torture, and Steve Dayman, who founded Meningitis Research and who works tirelessly to help eradicate this dreadful disease.

Such people do not worship at the shrine of success, which has long, long ago ceased to have any real meaning to me. My idea of 'making it' has nothing to do with its twentieth-century interpretation. Alas, I am far too self-centred ever to be a Helen Bamber.

I have had a long career which spans nearly six decades. I couldn't have started younger. I have gone from playing children as a child, teenagers as a teenager, young women as a young wife, middle-aged women as a mistress, and I am now being asked to play witches and grandmothers, which is as it should be – though it does surprise me sometimes.

When I look in the mirror at the external manifestation of what I am and have become, illogically I still expect to see someone around the middle thirties – which is how I think about myself. I may well continue to do so until the day I die.

I shall be only too happy to be a real grandmother. The process of ageing concerns me no more deeply than the thought of dying. Getting old is in some way liberating. Luckily in my career I've never been given work that is based on looking glamorous.

I have no desire to look, or be taken for being, younger than I am. I have considerable vanity, but that makes me want to look good for the age I am.

I remember walking down a country lane one day, and Robert saying to me: 'Aren't we lucky? We can't die young any more.'

That meant a lot to me. It gave me a marvellous feeling of freedom. I feel if Robert or I were to die tomorrow it wouldn't really matter all that much. I have no frustrated ambitions left in me. I have lived my life.

In my younger days, I became aware of something in my character which just blew where the wind took me. I think that is how I first got into radio, and then into the theatre. That's how I fell into marriage to Peter Vaughan. That's why I moved with Robert to a big house in Camden Square in 1970, when what I really wanted to do was to stay in my little house by the river in Datchet. That's why I accepted the part in Beckett's *Not I*, which, at the time I read it, I would have given anything *not* to do. For the first forty years of my life I bobbed along like a piece of driftwood.

In the second half of my life I feel I have been incredibly lucky. To me, these precious final years have been the happiest times of my life. It still astonishes me when I remind myself that I can do this and don't have to do that. It's a heady feeling like having drunk iced champagne.

When I wake up at dawn, and that grey cloud of work anxiety is

there, I only have to get up and open the window to feel so free and happy that I think I'm going to go off pop. It's taken quite a long time to arrive at that feeling.

In writing this book, I have chosen to leave out quite a lot of what I have experienced in over sixty years of living. I haven't wanted to confess all my many sins, or give away secrets. I haven't told tales that are nobody's business but my own. Some mysteries of the self, or selves, must remain unsolved riddles to the end – even to me.

SUFFOLK
January 1995

Selective List of Principal Performances in Theatre, Film, Television, Radio and Lectures

Theatre

EASY MONEY, Harry Hanson's Company, Leeds   1948
PEG O' MY HEART (Hartley Manners) dir. John de
    la Noye (Theatre Royal, Leicester)   1950
WHERE THERE'S A WILL (Delderfield) dir. Chloe
    Gibson (pre-London tour)   1951–2
HOTEL PARADISO (Feydeau) dir. Peter Glenville
    (Winter Garden, London)   1954
PROGRESS TO THE PARK (Owen) dir. Harry H.
    Corbett (Theatre Workshop) and dir. Ted
    Kotcheff (Saville Theatre, London)   1961
ENGLAND, OUR ENGLAND (Waterhouse and Hall)
    dir. John Dexter (Princes Theatre)   1962
THE DUTCH COURTESAN (Marston) dir. Bill Gaskill
    (NT)   1963–5
OTHELLO (Shakespeare) dir. John Dexter (NT)   1963–5
HOBSON'S CHOICE (Brighouse) dir. John Dexter and
    Piers Haggard (NT)   1963–5
TRELAWNEY OF THE 'WELLS' (Pinero) dir. John
    Dexter and Desmond Donovan (NT)   1963–5
PLAY (Beckett) dir. George Devine (NT)   1963–5
A TOUCH OF THE POET (O'Neill) dir. Toby Robertson
    (Venice, Dublin and Golders Green)   1966
AFTER HAGGERTY (Mercer) dir. David Jones (RSC/
    Criterion)   1970
NOT I (Beckett) dir. Anthony Page (Royal Court)   1973 & 1975
ALPHABETICAL ORDER (Frayn) dir. Michael Rudman
    (Hampstead and Mayfair Theatre)   1975
FOOTFALLS (Beckett) dir. Samuel Beckett (Royal
    Court)   1976
MOLLY (Gray) dir. Stephen Hollis (Comedy
    Theatre)   1978

HAPPY DAYS (Beckett) dir. Samuel Beckett (Royal Court)	1979
THE GREEKS (Aeschylus) dir. John Barton (RSC, Aldwych)	1979
PASSION PLAY (Nichols) dir. Mike Ockrent (RSC, Aldwych)	1981
ROCKABY (Beckett) dir. Alan Schneider (Buffalo and La Mama, NY, USA)	1981
ROCKABY (Beckett) dir. Alan Schneider (NT)	1982
ROCKABY and FOOTFALLS (Beckett) restaged: Robbie Hendry (Riverside Studios)	1984
TALES FROM HOLLYWOOD (Hampton) dir. Peter Gill (NT)	1984
ROCKABY and FOOTFALLS (Beckett) dir. Alan Schneider (Samuel Beckett Theater, NY, USA)	1984
ROCKABY and FOOTFALLS (Beckett) restaged: Rocky Greenberg and Robbie Hendry (touring Adelaide, Sydney and Melbourne, Australia, and Purchase Theater Festival, New York State)	1986
WHO'S AFRAID OF VIRGINIA WOOLF? (Albee) dir. David Thacker (Young Vic)	1987

Films (a selection)

THE FAKE, dir. Godfrey Grayson, with Dennis O'Keefe	1953
THE SLEEPING TIGER, dir. Joseph Losey, with Dirk Bogarde, Hugh Griffith	1954
MIRACLE IN SOHO, dir. Julian Amyes, with John Gregson, Cyril Cusack	1956
SMALL HOTEL, dir. David Macdonald, with Gordon Harker	1957
GIDEON'S DAY, dir. John Ford, with Jack Hawkins, Anna Massey	1958
CARVE HER NAME WITH PRIDE, dir. Lewis Gilbert, with Virginia McKenna, Paul Scofield	1958
DANGER WITHIN, dir. Don Chaffey, with Richard Todd, Bernard Lee, Richard Attenborough	1958
BOBBIKINS, dir. Robert Day, with Max Bygraves and Shirley Jones	1959
THE FLESH AND THE FIENDS, dir. John Gilling, with Peter Cushing	1959

HELL IS A CITY, dir. Val Guest, with Stanley Baker,
Donald Pleasence   1959

MAKE MINE MINK, dir. Robert Asher, with
Terry-Thomas, Athene Seyler   1960

NO LOVE FOR JOHNNIE, dir. Ralph Thomas, with
Peter Finch, Stanley Holloway   1960

MR TOPAZE, dir. Peter Sellers, with Herbert Lom,
Leo McKern   1961

PAYROLL, dir. Sidney Hayers, with Michael Craig   1961

THE DEVIL'S AGENT, dir. John Paddy Carstairs, with
Peter van Eyck, Christopher Lee   1962

THE COMEDY MAN, dir. Alvin Rakoff, with Kenneth
More, Cecil Parker, Dennis Price   1964

CHARLIE BUBBLES, dir. Albert Finney, with Albert
Finney, Liza Minnelli   1967

TWISTED NERVE, dir. Roy Boulting, with Hayley
Mills, Hywel Bennett   1968

THE ADDING MACHINE, dir. Jerome Epstein, with
Phyllis Diller, Milo O'Shea   1968

START THE REVOLUTION WITHOUT ME, dir. Bud
Yorkin, with Donald Sutherland, Gene Wilder   1968

LEO THE LAST, dir. John Boorman, with Marcello
Mastroianni, Calvin Lockhart   1969

EAGLE IN A CAGE, dir. Fielder Cook, with John
Gielgud, Ralph Richardson, Kenneth Haigh   1970

GUMSHOE, dir. Stephen Frears, with Albert Finney   1970

NIGHT WATCH, dir. Brian Hutton, with Elizabeth
Taylor, Laurence Harvey   1972

FRENZY, dir. Alfred Hitchcock, with Jon Finch, Alec
McCowen, Barry Foster, Vivien Merchant   1973

THE OMEN, dir. Richard Donner, with Gregory
Peck, Lee Remick, David Warner   1976

LEOPARD IN THE SNOW, dir. Gerry O'Hara, with
Keir Dullea, Kenneth More   1977

THE WATER BABIES, dir. Lionel Jeffries, with James
Mason, Bernard Cribbins   1978

AN UNSUITABLE JOB FOR A WOMAN, dir.
Christopher Petit, with Paul Freeman   1981

THE DARK CRYSTAL (voice only), dir. Jim Henson
and Frank Oz   1982

TANGIER, dir. Michael E Briant, with Ronny
Cox   1982

SLAYGROUND, dir. Terry Bedford, with Peter
  Coyote, Mel Smith   1983
THE CHAIN, dir. Jack Gold, with Warren Mitchell,
  Bernard Hill, Nigel Hawthorne   1984
MURDER ELITE, dir. Claude Whatham, with Ali
  MacGraw   1984
SHADEY, dir. Philip Saville, with Anthony Sher,
  Patrick Macnee   1984
MAURICE, dir. James Ivory, with James Wilby,
  Hugh Grant, Denholm Elliott   1987
THE DRESSMAKER, dir. Jim O'Brien, with Joan
  Plowright, Jane Horrocks   1987
JOYRIDERS, dir. Aisling Walsh, with Patricia
  Kerrigan   1988
THE KRAYS, dir. Peter Medak, with Gary Kemp,
  Martin Kemp, Susan Fleetwood   1990
FREDDIE AS F.R.0.7 (voice only), dir. Jon Acevski,
  with Ben Kingsley   1992
DEADLY ADVICE, dir. Mandie Fletcher, with
  Edward Woodward, Jane Horrocks   1993
JANE EYRE, dir. Franco Zeffirelli, with William
  Hurt   1995

Television (selection)

THE SECRET GARDEN (Burnett) dir. Dorothea
  Brooking (BBC)   1950
PATTERNS OF MARRIAGE (Willis) dir. Caryl
  Doncaster (BBC)   1952–3
NO TRAMS TO LIME STREET (Owen) dir. Ted
  Kotcheff (ABC)   1959
LENA, O MY LENA (Owen) dir. Ted Kotcheff
  (ABC)   1960
ANNA CHRISTIE (O'Neill) dir. Rudolph Cartier
  (BBC)   1960
BEYOND THE HORIZON (O'Neill) dir. Hank Kaplan
  (Granada)   1961
RESURRECTION (Tolstoy)   1963
LADY OF THE CAMELLIAS (Dumas) dir. Rudolph
  Cartier (BBC)   1964
THE PITY OF IT ALL (Barstow) dir. Hugh Burnett
  (BBC)   1966

THE BALLAD OF QUEENIE SWAN (Willis) dir. Dennis
    Vance (ATV)   1966
A WORLD OF TIME (Muller) dir. Don Leaver (ABC)   1966
YOU AND ME (Muller) dir. Kim Mills (ABC)   1967
DR JEKYLL AND MR HYDE (Stevenson) dir. Charles
    Jarrott (Canada)   1968
THE POET GAME (Terpiloff) dir. Silvio Narizzano
    (BBC)   1970
NOT I (Beckett) dir. Tristram Powell (BBC)   1973
WESSEX TALES: 'The Withered Arm' (Hardy) dir.
    Desmond Davis (BBC)   1973
NAPOLEON AND LOVE (nine plays) (Mackie) various
    directors (Thames)   1974
THE SEXTET (eight plays) various directors (BBC)   1974
EUSTACE AND HILDA (two plays) dir. Desmond
    Davis (BBC)   1976
THE FIFTY POUND NOTE (Muller) dir. Mark
    Cullingham (BBC)   1976
COUNTESS ILONA (Muller) dir. Simon Langton
    (BBC)   1977
THE WEREWOLF REUNION (Muller) dir. Simon
    Langton (BBC)   1977
GHOST TRIO, NOT I and . . . BUT THE CLOUDS . . .
    (Beckett) dir. Donald McWhinnie   1977
A HAUNTED MAN (Constanduros) dir. Tristram
    Powell (BBC)   1978
HAPPY DAYS (Beckett) dir. Tristram Powell (BBC)   1979
THE SERPENT SON (Raphael and McLeish) dir. Bill
    Hays (BBC)   1979
A TALE OF TWO CITIES (Dickens) dir. Jim Goddard
    (Hallmark, USA)   1980
PRIVATE SCHULZ (Pulman) dir. Robert Chetwyn
    (BBC)   1981
JAMAICA INN (du Maurier) dir. Lawrence Gordon
    Clarke (HTV)   1983
CAMILLE (Dumas) dir. Desmond Davis (TVM &
    CBS)   1984
OLD GIRLFRIENDS (Muller) dir. D. Haugk (WDR,
    Germany)   1986
THE PICNIC (Bruce) dir. Paul Seed (BBC)   1987
THE SECRET GARDEN (Burnett) dir. Alan Grint
    (Hallmark, USA)   1987

IMAGINARY FRIENDS (Lurie) dir. Peter Sasdy (Thames)	1988
ROCKABY, FOOTFALLS and EH JOE (Beckett) dir. Walter Asmus (RM Productions)	1988
LORNA DOONE (Blackmore) dir. Andrew Grieve (Thames)	1989
THE FIFTEEN STREETS (Cookson) dir. David Wheatley (Tyne-Tees)	1989
HOMMAGE À SAMUEL BECKETT (documentary)	1990
A MURDER OF QUALITY (le Carré) dir. Gavin Millar (BBC)	1991
DUEL OF HEARTS (Cartland) dir. John Hough (ITC)	1991
THE CLONING OF JOANNA MAY (Weldon) dir. Philip Saville (Granada)	1992
FIRM FRIENDS (four episodes) (Wakefield) dir. David Hayman (Tyne-Tees)	1992
SKALLAGRIG (Nigel Williams) dir. Richard Spence (BBC)	1993
THE ENTERTAINER (Osborne) dir. Nick Renton (BBC)	1993
FIRM FRIENDS II (four episodes) (Wakefield) dir. Sara Harding (Yorkshire TV)	1994

Radio (selection)

ROUGH FOR RADIO 2 (Beckett), dir. Martin Esslin
THE MASTER BUILDER (Ibsen)
HINDLE WAKES (Houghton)
JANE EYRE (Brontë)
THE FEMALE MESSIAH (Roose-Evans)
ALPHA BETA (Whitehead)
THE CHERRY ORCHARD (Chekhov)
VASSA SHELESNOVA (Gorky)
FILUMENA MATURANO (de Filippo)
ALL THAT FALL and EMBERS (Beckett), dir. Everett Frost

Lecturer at US Colleges and Universities

Smith College, Northampton, Massachusetts
Dartmouth College, New Hampshire
Washington College, Maryland

Franklyn and Marshall, Pennsylvania
Wellesley College, Massachusetts
Barnard University, New York
Boulder University, Colorado
Northern Illinois University, de Kalb Illinois
Boston College, Mass.
Knox College, Illinois
Santa Barbara University, California
Knoxville University, Tennessee
Madison University, Wisconsin
ATHE, Pennsylvania (educational conference)

Index

Index

Works by Samuel Beckett appear under their titles; works by
others appear under authors' names